DENNIS & GNASHER

Biggest Joke Book EVER!

THE BEANO books
geddes & grosset

Published 2005 by BEANObooks geddes&grosset
an imprint of Geddes & Grosset,
David Dale House, New Lanark ML11 9DJ, Scotland.
First published 2000, reprinted 2001, 2002, 2003, 2005

© D. C. Thomson & Co., Ltd, 2000

ISBN 1 84205 011 7

Printed and bound in the UK.

Why did the sailor grab a piece of soap when he was sinking?
So he could wash himself ashore.

What are the best kind of letters to read in hot weather?
Fan mail!

What is out of bounds?
An exhausted kangaroo!

Wife – Doctor, doctor, my husband's broken his leg.
Doctor – But madam, I'm a doctor of music.
Wife – That's all right, it was the piano that fell on him!

What do you call a toffee train?
A chew chew!

What do you give a deaf fisherman?
A herring aid?

What birds are cowboys afraid of?
Toma-hawks.

Why is Cinderella such a rotten footballer?
Because her coach is a pumpkin!

What did the Mona Lisa say to the gallery attendant?
I've been framed!

What is short, green and goes camping?
A boy sprout!

Eck – Why wouldn't they let the butterfly into the dance?
Bob – Because it was a moth ball!

How should you dress on a cold day?
Quickly!

Doctor, my husband thinks he's a clothes line.
Bring him round to the surgery.
What, and have all my washing fall on the ground?

Ticket collector – Are you first class?
Second-class passenger – Oh, yes, I'm fine, thank you. How's yourself?

Knock! Knock!
Who's there?
Senor.
Senor who?
Senor father out and let me in!

Why is a fish shop always crowded?
Because the fish fillet!

Boastful angler – I once had a three-hour fight with a salmon.
Bored friend – Yes, tin openers can be a nuisance at times.

Landlady – I don't allow cats, dogs, radios or record players in my house!
New lodger – Er … do you mind if my shoes squeak a little?

Teacher – What happens to gold when it is exposed to the air?
Smiffy – It's stolen!

Mrs McDougall – I want a pair of fur gloves!
Assistant – Yes, madam. What fur?
Mrs McDougall – What fur? To keep my hands warm, of course!

Father – Sidney, are you tall enough to reach that package on the mantelpiece?
Sidney – Not if it's my cough mixture!

Diner – I find that I have just enough money to pay the dinner, but I have nothing left to give you a tip.
Waiter – Let me add up that bill again, sir.

Farmer to man – If you can guess how many chickens I have, I'll give you both of them!

What do you get when you cross a sparrow with a haddock?
Cheep fish.

Why did Smiffy stand in front of the mirror with his eyes closed?
To see what he looked like when he was sleeping.

What do you get if you cross a football team with an ice cream?
Aston Vanilla!

Smiffy couldn't tell the difference between toothpaste and putty.
All his windows fell out.

Why is a football pitch always wet?
Because of all the dribbling during matches.

Danny – Why do you call your new dog Ginger?
Sidney – Because he snaps!

Brring! Brring!
Who's there?
Hurd.
Hurd who?
Hurd my hand, so couldn't Knock! Knock!

Smiffy – I went to the dentist yesterday.
Toots – Does your tooth still hurt?
Smiffy – I don't know – the dentist kept it.

First tramp – I have heard of a millionaire who wears a suit of clothes only once.
Second tramp – So do we, but it's a longer once.

Teacher – What is the name of the pine with the longest and sharpest needles?
Danny – The porcupine.

Fisherman – Do the fish in this river bite?
Gamekeeper – Bite? They're so fierce that you have to hide behind a tree while you are baiting your hook.

Minnie – There's something without any legs running across the yard.
Dad – What is it?
Minnie – Water. You left the tap on.

Smith – Did I leave an umbrella here yesterday?
Restaurant manager – What kind of umbrella?
Smith – Oh, any kind. I'm not particular.

Wilfrid – Why does it rain, Dad?
Dad – To make the grass grow.
Wilfrid – Then why does it rain on the streets?

Who became a space hero by mistake?
Fluke Skywalker.

Teacher – If you use this text book, you will get your homework done in half the time.
Danny – Great! Can I have two?

Teacher – Brian, how old were you on your last birthday?
Brian – Seven, Miss.
Teacher – Very good! That means you'll be eight on your next birthday.
Brian – No, Miss. I'll be nine!
Teacher – But that's impossible!
Brian – No it isn't. I'm eight today, Miss!

Danny – What has ten legs, a yellow back, a green eye and a long, horned tail?
Cuthbert – I don't know.

Danny – Neither do I, but I've just seen one swimming in your soup!

Plug – What is black and white and red all over?
Teacher – I know that one, Plug, a newspaper!
Plug – No sir, a zebra with a sun tan!

Boss – So you can do anything? Can you wheel a barrow full of smoke?
Workman – Yes, if you fill it for me.

Lazy Larry – Well, here I am to see about the job you advertised.
Contractor – Oh, do you think you are fit to work?
Lazy Larry – Work? I thought you wanted a foreman!

Why are you running?
There's a lion loose.
Which way did it go?
Do you think I'm following it?

Speaker – How long have I been speaking? I haven't got a watch with me.
Danny – There's a calendar behind you.

Teacher – What is meant by extravagance?
Sidney – Wearing a tie below a beard.

Waiter – Are you the filleted kipper, sir?
Diner – No. I'm the lonely sole with an empty plaice waiting for someone to fil-let

Old lady – I suppose sailors are very careful when you are at sea?
Old sailor – No, not at all, ma'am. In fact, we try to be as wreckless as possible.

Doctor – Do your teeth chatter when you are in bed?
Patient – I dunno. I put them on the dressing-table at night.

Teacher – If I stand on my head, the blood rushes into it. Now tell me, when I stand on my feet why doesn't the blood rush into them?
Danny – Because your feet aren't empty, sir!

Headmaster (to boy who has been fighting) – You should be ashamed of yourself. You shouldn't hurt a hair of your friend's head.
Boy – I didn't. I punched him on the nose.

Airman (after crashing into a tree) – I was trying to make a record.
Farmer – You did. You're the first man to climb down that tree before climbing up it.

Jones – What do you think of my dia-mond tie-pin?
Smith – It's quite nice, but, of course, it's not a real diamond.
Jones – Isn't it? Then, by jove, I've been swindled out of £2.

'Erbert – I can hear a pin drop twenty yards away.
Wilfrid – Really?
'Erbert – Yes, a rolling pin.

Where does a monkey cook its toast?
Under a gorilla!

Smith – I hear your car goes like a top.
Brown – Yes, I've just been out for a spin.

Mr McTavish – Don't run up any more bills. I can't face them.
Mrs McTavish – I don't want you to face them, dear. I want you to "foot" them.

Office boy – The cashier kicked me, sir.
Boss – Well, what about it? I can't do everything myself.

Lawyer – So you want me to defend you? Have you any money?
The accused – No, but I have a sports car.
Lawyer – Well, you can raise some money on that. Now, what are you accused of stealing?
The accused – A sports car.

Spotty – Why did the disco dancer put a stone to her left ear, and a bun to her right ear?
Fatty – I don't know.
Spotty – Because she wanted to hear rock and roll!

What do you buy only to throw out?
Streamers!

First salesman – How's the trampoline selling business going?
Second salesman – Oh, up and down!

Patient – So the x-rays show I'm perfectly normal?
Doctor – Yes, both your heads are all right.

What is the fastest part of a car?
The dashboard!

Old man – Here's £1. It makes me happy to think I'm helping you to get a bit of food.
Tramp – Make it a fiver guv'nor, and thoroughly enjoy yourself!

WHAT DO YOU GET IF YOU CROSS A DOG WITH A PHONE?
A Golden Receiver!

WHY DON'T THEY HAVE TELEPHONES IN CHINA?
You might wing the wong number!

WHAT AWARD DID THE INVENTOR OF THE DOOR KNOCKER WIN?
The No Bell Prize.

Why did the burglar take a bath before breaking out of jail?
He wanted to make a clean getaway!

What does a frog with no money say?
Broke! Broke!

Toots – Is the Headmaster really mean?
Sidney – Mean? Why, if he were a ghost he wouldn't even give you a fright!

Smiffy – What is the date?
Toots – I dunno. Why don't you look at that newspaper that's on the table.
Smiffy – Oh, that's no use – it's yesterday's.

Teacher (after a lesson about a rhinoceros) – Now, tell me something that has a big horn and is very dangerous?
Smiffy – A motor car.

Mac – Can I see that new device of yours for preventing the theft of a watch?
Jock – I can't show you it, it was stolen from me yesterday by a pickpocket.

Teacher – What is hail?
Smiffy – Please, sir, it's hard-boiled rain.

Where does Dracula live when he's in New York?
The Vampire State Building!

Why do witches fly about on broomsticks?
Because vacuum cleaners don't have a long enough cord?

Teacher – What's the shape of the world?
Toots – Round.
Teacher – How do you know it's round?
Toots – All right, it's square, then. I don't want to start an argument about it.

Captain – Wash the prisoner and put him in irons.
Stowaway – First I was collared and now I'm being washed and ironed. Is this a ship or a laundry?

What's worse than a snake with sore ribs?
A centipede with athlete's foot!

If you get referees in football, and umpires in cricket, what do you get in bowls?
Goldfish!

Teacher – Now, Smiffy, what does the word "asset" mean?
Smiffy – A young donkey, sir

Knock! Knock!
Who's there?
Doris.
Doris who?
Door isn't locked, just come in.

What rides at the amusement park do ghosts like best?
The scary-go-round and the roller ghoster!

Headmaster (to visitor) – By the way, what was the first thing that struck you about the school chemistry lab?
Visitor – A pea from a pea-shooter.

Mother – What? You've been fighting with Billy Biggs? I thought he was a peaceable child. He had such a nice face, too.
Freddie – Well, he hasn't now.

Tourist – Hey! One of your bees stung me. What are you going to do about it?
Beekeeper – Sorry. Just tell me which one did it, and I'll punish him.

King – You shall die, but you may choose to die any way you wish.
Slave – Then, Your Majesty, I choose to die of old age.

Librarian – Please be quiet, Tim. Those people beside you can't read!
Tim – They should be ashamed of themselves! I've been able to read since I was six!

Smiffy went to the dentist to get wisdom teeth put in.

When Smiffy went hitch-hiking, he left early to avoid the traffic.

Smiffy was listening to the match last night and burnt his ear.

WHAT'S ROUND, WHITE AND GIGGLES?
A tickled onion.

WHAT DO YOU GET WHEN YOU CROSS A HYENA WITH A BEEF CUBE?
A laughing stock.

Little Willie – Gran, was Dad a very bad boy when he was small?
Gran – Why?
Little Willie – Because he knows exactly what questions to ask when he wants to know what I've been doing.

Mother – Dennis, what are you reading?
Dennis – I don't know, Mum.
Mother – But you were reading aloud.
Dennis – I know, but I wasn't listening.

What did the rocket's door say?
Gone to launch!

Teacher – Sidney, what is that swelling on your nose?
Sidney – I bent down to smell a brose, sir.
Teacher – There's no "B" in rose, Sidney.
Sidney – There was in this one.

What is the fastest liquid in the world?
Milk, because it is pasteurised before you see it.

Paperboy – Special! Read all about it. Forty-nine people swindled!
McSporran – I don't see anything here about a swindle.
Paperboy- Special! Read all about it! Fifty people swindled.

'Erbert – How do you spell blind pig?
Wilfrid – Easy – B.L.I.N.D. P.I.G.
'Erbert – Wrong! B.L.N.D. P.G.
Wilfrid – Why is that?
'Erbert – Because if it had two "I"s it wouldn't be a blind pig.

McGraw – How old is old Archie?
McGill – I dunno, but everybody was overcome by the heat from his candles at his last birthday party.

Doctor – Now take a deep breath and say nine three times.
Smart Alec (after inhaling) – Twenty-seven!

Frankie – Please, Mrs Smart, is Bobby coming out to play?
Mrs Smart – No, Frankie, it's too wet.
Frankie – Well, is his football coming out, then?

Bob – With patience, you can do anything.
Bill – Can I fill this sieve with water?
Bob – Yes, if you wait till it freezes.

Teacher – Now, Billy, what letter in the alphabet comes before "J"?
Billy – I dunno.
Teacher – What have I on both sides of my nose?
Billy – Freckles.

Judge – You are sentenced to ten years' imprisonment. Have you anything to add?
Prisoner – No, but I'd like to subtract.

Doctor – Have you taken the box of pills I gave you?
Oswald – Yes, but I feel worse. Perhaps the cardboard disagreed with me.

Mrs Perkins – Have you eaten these sandwiches?
Mr Perkins – Yes.
Mrs Perkins – Well, you'll have to clean your shoes with meat paste, for I put the boot polish on the sandwiches by mistake.

Policeman – I arrested a man for stealing a calendar yesterday!
Joe – What did he get?
Policeman – Twelve months!

If "L" on a car means learner, what does "GB" mean?
Getting better.

Why is a baby like a diamond?
Because it's such a dear little thing.

What sort of fish sings songs?
Tuna fish.

Gnock! Gnock!

Who's there?
Lettuce.
Lettuce who?
Lettuce out, it's cold in here!

What vegetable is green and strong?
A muscle sprout.

Plug – I saw something last night that I'll never get over.
Danny – What was that?
Plug – The moon!

Diner – I say, waiter, bring my hat.
Waiter – It's on your head, sir.
Diner -Then don't bother. I'll look for it myself.

Smiffy – I wish I'd lived at the very beginning of the world.
Toots – Why?
Smiffy – Because I wouldn't have had to learn history.

It was my wife's birthday yesterday, so I bought her a rocket.
Was she delighted?
Yes, over the moon.

What was awarded to the inventor of door knockers?
The No-bell prize!

Mum – What are you doing, Tommy?
Tommy – I'm writing a letter to my sister.
Mum – Don't be silly, you can't write.
Tommy – That doesn't matter, she can't read.

Patient – Doctor, my family think I'm a little odd.
Doctor – Why?
Patient – Because I like sausages.
Doctor – Nonsense. I like sausages too.
Patient – You do? You must come round to see my collection. I have hundreds.

Danny – I have a great memory. I can recite all the names on five pages of the telephone directory.
Wifrid – I don't believe you!
Danny – Right then – Smith, Smith, Smith, Smith, Smith …

Why did you give up singing in the choir?
I was ill last week and didn't go, and after the service someone asked if the organ had been mended.

Angler (telling tall story) – Yes, the fish I caught was so big that I simple couldn't pull it out of the water.
Sarcastic listener – It was a whale, I suppose?
Angler – A whale? Goodness, no! I was baiting with whales.

Diner – Waiter, this bread has got sand on it.
Waiter – Yes, sir, it helps to keep the butter from sliding off.

What is white and goes up?
A stupid snowflake!

Grandpa – How long have you been going to school, Angus?
Angus – Too . . .
Grandpa – Two years?
Angus – No, too long.

Auntie – Do you ever help your little brother, Andrew?

Andrew – Yes, Auntie, I helped him to spend the five pounds you gave him yesterday!

What do you get if you cross a chip shop with a famous train?
The Frying Scotsman!

The new bank clerk's hobby is climbing trees.
He must want to be a branch manager!

Knock, knock!
Who's there?
The Invisible Man.
Tell him I can't see him at the moment!

What are the two fastest fish in the sea?
A motor pike and a side carp!

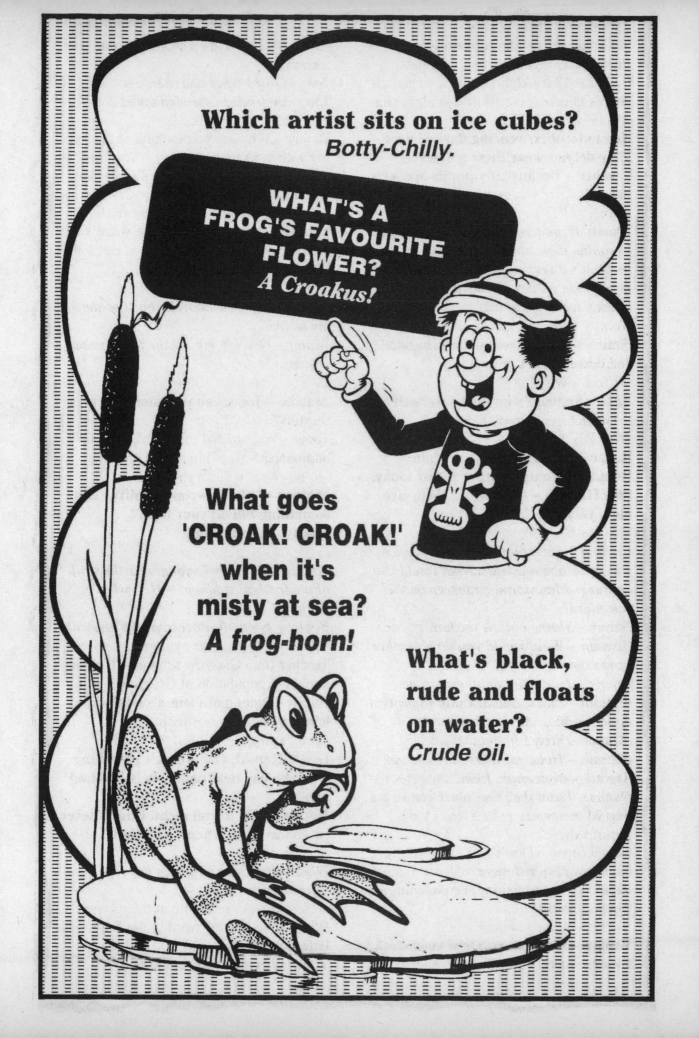

Fat Fred – What? Four pounds for a shave? Your sign says two pounds!
Barber – That's right, but you've got a double chin!

Boy to teacher wearing dark glasses – Why do you wear these glasses?
Teacher – Because my pupils are very bright!

Tourist at the edge of high cliff – Don't you think there should be a warning sign here? It's a very dangerous cliff!
Tour guide – They did have one, but nobody fell over so they took it down!

Fatty – I'm going to grow a moustache and beard when I grow up.
Wilfrid – Why?
Fatty – So that I won't have so much face to wash.

Baker – Good morning, madam. Bread's gone up another penny today.
Mrs Hardup – Oh, has it? Well, give me a yesterday's loaf.

Captain – Let's find out just how much you know about a boat. What would you do if a sudden storm sprang up on the starboard?
Danny – Throw out the anchor.
Captain – What would you do if another storm sprang up aft?
Danny – Throw out another anchor.
Captain – And if another storm sprang up forward, what would you do?
Danny – Throw out another anchor.
Captain – Hold on. Where are you getting all your anchors from?
Danny – From the same place you're getting your storms.

Gamekeeper – Don't you know you're not allowed to fish here?
Sandy – I'm not fishing. I'm teaching a worm to swim!

Waiter – How did you find your steak?
Diner – Easy. I'm a detective!

Tim – My Dad's got a leading position in a circus!
Tom – Gosh! What does he do?
Tim – He leads in the elephants!

Danny – Why are you looking at the mirror with your eyes shut?
'Erbert – I want to see what I look like when I'm asleep.

How did the witch know she wasn't well?
She had a dizzy spell.

Diner – Waiter, waiter, there's a spider in my soup.
Waiter – Oh, yes, sir. All the flies are on holiday.

Teacher – Toots, can you name the four seasons?
Toots – Yes, sir! Salt, mustard, vinegar and pepper!

Mother – What's wrong, Smiffy? Did something fall on your head?
Smiffy – Y-yes. I did!

Policeman (to boy looking over the wall of the football stadium) – Hey, what's the game?
Bobby – Football. Rovers versus United!

Teacher (in a Glasgow school) – Do you know the population of Glasgow?
Jimmy – Not all of them. I've only been here a week!

Dad – Harold, you mustn't go fishing with the boy next door – he's just had measles.
Harold – Oh, it's all right, Dad. I never catch anything when I go fishing.

What's the longest night of the year?
A fortnight!

What is the longest word in the English language?
Smile – because there's a mile in it.

Weary Willie – Why don't you look for work?
Lazy Len – I'm afraid.
Weary Willie – Of what?
Lazy Len – Finding it!

Bill – Have you heard that they're not making lampposts any longer?
David – Why?
Bill – They're long enough already.

Freddie – My brother has taken up French, Italian, Spanish and Greek.
Old man – Goodness! What does he do?
Freddie – He's a lift boy.

Headmaster – I don't see why you're grumbling. This is splendid tea.
Teacher – Yes, sir, but Olive, the dinner lady, says it's soup!

Young girl – Please, Mother says will you give me the broom you borrowed last Thursday?
Neighbour – Yes, but don't forget to bring it back.

Sidney – How many pieces of that toffee do I get for fifty pence?
Shop assistant – Oh, two or three.
Sidney – I'll take three, please.

Danny – What do you think you're talking about?
Cuthbert – I don't think – I know.
Danny – I don't think you know either.

How's business?
I manage to keep my head above water.
Well, wood floats, you know.

'Erbert – Mother Nature is wonderful! A million years ago she didn't know we were going to wear spectacles, yet look at the way she placed our ears.

What lives under the sea and carries sixty-four people?
An octobus!

Teacher – Dennis, what do we call a person who is very talkative, yet uninteresting?
Dennis – A teacher.

An absent-minded professor went into a shop to buy a jar. Seeing one upside down, he said, "How stupid, this jar has no mouth!" Turning it over, he was more astonished. "Why, there's no bottom in it, either!"

Patient – Doctor, doctor, I think I'm shrinking!
Doctor – Well, you'll just have to be a little patient.

When did the Scottish potato change its nationality?
When it became a French fry!

Two flies were on Robinson Crusoe's head. "Goodbye for now," said one. "I'll see you on Friday!"

What do you call a man who breaks into a meat factory?
A hamburglar!

Teacher – Why have you got cotton wool in your ear? Is it infected?
Smiffy – No, sir, but you said yesterday that everything you told me went in one ear and out the other, so I'm trying to stop it.

Where do pigs play?
In a play-pork!

What kind of monkeys make the best wine?
Grey apes.

Why is a game of cricket like a pancake?
Because they both depend on a good batter.

Who tells chicken jokes?
Comedihens!

Knock! Knock!.
Who's there?
Midas.
Midas, who?
Midas well open the door!

What was the first smoke signal sent by an Indian?
HELP! My blanket's on fire!

Black – Have you ever seen wrinkles on the brow of a hill?
Brown – No, but I've seen a field furrowed with care!

Painter – Why are you hurrying?
Apprentice – I haven't much paint left and I want to finish the door before it's all gone!

Cuthbert's father (as Cuthbert entertains guests) – He will go far with his violin, don't you think?
Guest – I hope so.

Tailor – That suit fits you like a glove, sir.
Customer – So I see. The sleeves cover my hands.

Angler – Is this stream private?
Passer-by – No, sir.
Angler – Then it won't be a crime if I land any fish?
Passer-by – No, it'll be a miracle.

Visitor to jail – It must be terrible to be shut up all the time in a small room like this. What were you before you came here?
Prisoner – A lift attendant.

Teacher – Why does the earth turn round the sun?
Smiffy – Because it doesn't want to get toasted on one side.

Farmer – I haven't ploughed that field yet, but I'm thinking of doing so.
Squire – Oh, I see, you've only turned it over in your mind.

Ron – Is there any truth in the report that Mean McTavish has bought Wilson's garage?
Don – Well, I don't know for sure, but it looks like it. The free air sign has been taken down.

How do you play truant from a correspondence school?
Send them an empty envelope.

Customer – You said this parrot was worth its weight in gold and yet it won't talk!
Pet shop owner – Well, silence is golden, isn't it?

Bobby – I found a horseshoe this morning.
Mother – Do you know what that means?
Bobby – Yes, it means that some horse is running around in his bare feet.

Cuthbert – Teacher, Danny hit me with a ruler.
Teacher – Why did you hit Cuthbert with a ruler, Danny?
Danny – Because I couldn't find a stick.

Why is a banana like a pullover?
They're both easy to slip on!

Teacher – How many days of the week begin with the letter T?
Sidney – Four – Tuesday, Thursday, Today and Tomorrow.

Teacher – How many seconds in a year?
Pupil – Twelve, sir. Second of January, February, March, etc.!

What's the biggest potato in the world?
A hippopotatomus.

Man – How much do I owe you for my new hearing aid?
Shopkeeper – Forty pounds.
Man – Did you say fifty pounds?
Shopkeeper – No, sixty pounds.

Mum – Now don't eat those sweets all at once, Alistair, or you'll be ill.
Alistair – All right, Mum. I'll eat them one by one.

Terry – So your brother lost his job with the fire brigade?
Jerry – Yes. It was because of his near-sightedness.
Terry – What happened?
Jerry – He squirted water on a red-headed woman before he discovered she wasn't the fire.

Smith – So Binky told you I was a musician?
Smythe – Well, he said you blew your own trumpet a lot.

Doctor – You will only have to wear these glasses at your work.
Patient – That's impossible.
Doctor – Why?
Patient – I'm a boxer.

Owner of an old car – Someone has stolen my car.
Friend – These antique collectors will stop at nothing.

Shopper – Can I stick this wallpaper on myself?
Shopkeeper – Yes, but it would look better on the wall.

What's white when it's dirty, and black when it's clean?
A blackboard.

What biscuit flies?
A plain biscuit.

What is the chiropodists' theme song?
There's no business like toe-business …

Little boy – Would you mind moving along a bit, mister?
Fat man – Why?
Little boy – To give the wind a chance to get at my kite.

What do you get if you cross an elephant with a kangaroo?
Big holes in Australia!

What do you give a pony with a cold?
Cough stirrup!

Why did King Arthur want a round table?
He was fed up with square meals.

What's big and hairy and flies at two hundred m.p.h.?
King Kongcord!

Harry – What would you get if you crossed your teacher with a crab?
Larry – I don't know!
Harry – Snappy answers!

Housewife (seeing man pretending to eat grass in her garden) – Whatever is wrong, my man?
Man – I'm so hungry, I'm having to eat grass.
Housewife – Well, come round to the back. The grass is longer there.

Spotty – Is my back tyre completely flat, Smiffy?
Smiffy – No – only a little bit at the bottom.

Absent-minded Alfred – I seem to recollect seeing you somewhere.
Forgetful Frank – Yes, I've often been there!

Jones – What sort of fellow is Brown?
Smith – Well, if ever you see two men speaking and one looks bored to death, the other is Brown.

Guide – … and this stone is where the great General fell in the battle.
Tourist – No wonder! I almost tripped over it myself.

What key is the hardest to turn?
A donkey.

Angry customer – I've just sent my boy for eight pounds of plums and you've only sent seven pounds. I know I'm right, because I've weighed them.
Shopkeeper – What about weighing your son?

There were three mice in an airing cupboard. Which one was in the army?
The one on the tank!

What do robots eat for dinner and tea?
Micro chips!

Teacher – Anyone here quick at picking up music?
Tim – I am, sir!
Teacher – Right, boy, move that drum kit!

Bill – Can I share your sledge?
Ben – Sure, we'll go halves.
Bill – Golly, thanks!
Ben – I'll have it for downhill, and you can have it for uphill.

Knock! Knock!
Who's there?
Four eggs.
Four eggs, who?
For example!

Landlady – Why have you put your tea on a chair, Mr McTaggart?

Boarder – It's so weak that I thought it had better have a rest.

Butcher – Have you tried our sausages, madam?
Customer – Yes, and found them guilty!

Teacher – Find the lowest common denominator.
Smiffy – Is that thing lost again?!

What is the best thing to do when the brakes of one's bike give way?
Aim for something cheap.

Recruit – What's that noise, sergeant?
Sergeant – That's the Last Post.
Recruit – I'll go and see if there are any letters for me.

Visitor – You're a very small man to be a lion-tamer.
Lion-tamer – Yes, but that's the secret of my success. The lions are waiting for me to grow bigger.

Golfer (far out in rough) – Say, caddie, what are you always looking at your watch for?
Caddie – It's not a watch, it's a compass.

What is the difference between a gardener, a billiard player and a church caretaker?
The first minds his peas, the second his cues, and the third his keys and pews.

Fortune-teller (reading palm) – Your future looks very indistinct.
Customer – What do you recommend?
Fortune-teller – Soap!

Diner – Waiter, what on earth is this in my bowl?
Waiter – It's bean soup.
Diner – I don't care what it's been, what is it now?

A parachute firm advertised – No one has ever complained of one of our parachutes not opening!

Clerk – My salary is so small, sir, that I can't afford lunch.
Boss – Then from tomorrow we will cut out your lunch break.

How did Noah find his way in the flood?
He used the radars (Raiders) of the Lost Ark.

How do you raise a baby elephant?
With a crane!

Which footballers wear matches in their hair?
Strikers!

What do snake charmers feed their snakes on?
Self-raising flour!

Angler – You've been watching me for three hours. Why don't you try fishing yourself?
Smiffy – No, I don't have the patience.

Actor – Did Jones get his new play used?
Producer – Yes, the stage manager tore up the manuscript and used it in a snow-storm scene.

Simon – Did you hear the joke about the rope?
May – No.
Simon – Oh, skip it!

What did the north wind say to the south wind?
Let's play draughts.

What's a pig's favourite football team?
Queen's Pork Rangers.

Jill – Did you hear about the man who said he was listening to the match?
Jack – No, tell me.
Jill – He burned his ear!

Mum – You can't come in the house unless your feet are clean!
Minnie – They are clean, Mum. It's only my shoes that are dirty!

What did Dracula say when the dentist wanted to pull out his teeth?
No fangs!

BARMY BOOKS
The Unwelcome Visitor by Gladys Gone.
Gone Shopping by Carrie R. Bag.
Who's to Blame? by E.Z.E. Diddit.
The Invitation by Willie B. Cumming.

What did the bald man say when he got a comb?
I'll never part with you!

Knock! Knock!
Who's there?
A little old lady.
A little old lady who?
I didn't know you could yodel!

What did the orange squash say to the water?
I'm diluted to meet you!

Smith – Why are you talking to yourself?
Jones – First, because I want to talk to a sensible man and second, because I like to hear a sensible man talking to me.

Tom – I'm thinking of going to America. What will it cost me?
Travel agent – Nothing.
Tom – What do you mean?
Travel agent – Well, it doesn't cost anything to think.

Boxer – You're a poor publicity man. I win a fight and all you get me in the paper is four columns.
Publicity agent – What are you grumbling for? Look at the big fights Nelson won and he only got one column.

Interviewer – Are you quick?
Job applicant – Quick? Why, I blew out the candle last night and was in bed and asleep before the room was dark.

Minnie – I want to ask you a question, Mum.
Mother – Well, go ahead.
Minnie – When a hole appears in a pair of tights, what becomes of the piece of material that was there before the hole appeared?

Tim – Don't be afraid of my dog. If he thinks you're afraid, he'll bite off your hand.
Tom – That's what I'm afraid of.

What do you call a cow eating grass in your front garden?
A lawn mooer!

What do you call a person who rolls in the mud then crosses the road twice?
A dirty double crosser.

Why did six planks stand in a circle?
They were having a board meeting.

Why is a red headed idiot like a biscuit?
He's a ginger nut!

What's an alien's favourite sweet?
Martian Mallows.

Tom – Ouch! I've scalded my hand in the hot water.
Tim – Why didn't you feel the water before you put your hand in it?

What do you get when you cross a rabbit with a spider?
A harenet!

Minnie – I woke up last night with the feeling that my watch was gone. So I got out of bed and looked everywhere for it.
Dad – And was the watch gone?
Minnie -No, but it was going!

What falls but never gets hurt?
Snow!

Knock! Knock!
Who's there?
Noah.
Noah who?
Noah good place to eat?

Patient – I keep seeing double, doctor.
Doctor – Lie down on the couch then.
Patient – Which one?

What do you get if you cross an elephant with a fish?
A pair of swimming trunks!

Fred – Did you know that Columbus was crooked?
Jack – No, he wasn't.
Fred – He was. He double-crossed the ocean.

Commanding officer (to raw recruit) – Now, my man, I want you to regard the regiment as a big band of brothers and me as the father of the regiment. Do you understand?
Recruit – Yes, Dad.

What did the pencil say to the rubber?
Take me to your ruler!

When is an artist dangerous?
When he draws a gun!

Driving instructor – Now, young man, this is the gear lever; down there is the brake; yonder is the accelerator, and over here is the clutch.
Pupil – Let's take one thing at a time – teach me to drive first.

Visitor – What's wrong with that dog of yours? Every time I take a drink of water he growls.
Tommy – Oh, he won't bother you. He's just annoyed because you're drinking out of his cup.

Prison visitor – And what brought you here?

Prisoner – Competition.
Prison visitor – Competition?
Prisoner – Yes, I made the same kind of banknotes as the Government.

Why did Smiffy take a ladder to school?
Because he wanted to go to High School!

Patient – Doctor, doctor, I feel like a pencil.
Doctor – Can we get to the point?

Why did the Gingerbread Man wear trousers?
Because he had crummy legs!

How do fish call their friends?
By tele-fin.

Which three letters of the alphabet do all the work?
N.R.G.!

Doctor – What you need is a change of occupation. Your present job seems to be making you unhappy. What do you do?
Patient – I'm a joke writer.

Comedian – The last time I was on the stage, the people were heard laughing a mile away.
Producer – Really? What was going on there?

Father – Tommy tells me you said he was a very promising pupil. Is that right?
Music teacher – Yes, that's right. He always promises to practise, but never does.

Diner – Is this a first-class restaurant?
Waiter – Yes, but we don't mind serving you!

Tourist – Is this part of the country good for rheumatism?
Old man – Yes! I got mine here.

Sandy – Jock, what can I send my brother for his birthday that'll not cost much?
Jock – Why not send him a pair of homing pigeons?

Danny – What position did your cousin play in the football team?
Wilfrid – He was a back.
Danny – Left-back?
Wilfrid – No, a drawback.

Hairdresser – Sharon, why are your hands so dirty?
Apprentice – Nobody's been in for a shampoo yet today.

Patient – Doctor, I feel like a glove.
Doctor – I think you need a hand here.

Why do witches fly on brooms?
Because they like to sweep across the sky!

What's yellow and has no brains?
Thick custard!

What do you get if you cross a jelly with a sheepdog?
The collie wobbles!

What illness do you get in China?
Kung-flu!

What do you get if you cross a baby with a U.F.O.?
An unidentified crying object!

What does a ghoul take for a bad cold?
Coffin drops.

Johnny – How did you break your arm?
Tommy – Do you see those cellar steps?
Johnny – Yes.
Tommy – Well, I didn't!

What do porcupines eat with cheese?
Prickled onions!

MacTavish – Did you hear about Sandy MacMeanie finding a box of corn plasters?
MacCulloch – No, did he?
MacTavish – Yes, so he went home and looked out his oldest, tightest shoes.

Unsuccessful actor – You know, when I'm acting, I'm carried away by my feelings. I forget everything but the part. The very audience seems to vanish.
Manager – You can't blame them.

Foreman – Look at that man carrying two loads of bricks at once, and you only carry one.
Labourer – Huh, he's just too lazy to go up the ladder twice.

Aunt – Hello, Jimmy, we don't see as much of you as we used to.
Jimmy – Well, I wear long trousers now!

Patient – Doctor, I think I'm a hi-fi system!
Doctor – Well, you certainly are a loud speaker.

What's the difference between a piano and a fish?
Anyone knows that you can't tuna fish!

Teacher – Now, Harry, tell us what you know about the Iron Age.
Harry – Er . . . I'm afraid I'm a bit rusty on that subject, sir.

What do cats use to freshen their breath?

Mousewash!

Twenty sets of snooker balls were stolen yesterday. Police say they still haven't had a good break!

Customer – What kind of bird is this, waiter?
Waiter – It's a wood pigeon, sir.
Customer – I thought so – would you bring me a saw?

What keeps the moon in place? Its beam!

Where do farmers go when they have caught a cold?
A farmacy!

Miss Screecher – I'm going away to study singing.
Neighbour – Good! How far away?

Visitor – Yes, I can see you one day stepping into your father's shoes.
Sammy – I suppose you're right. I'm wearing all his other old clothes now.

Teacher – Weight put on by overeating can be taken off by a simple reducing exercise.
Fatty – How?
Teacher – Move the head firmly from side to side when somebody suggests another helping.

Defeated boxer – I weighed in all right before the fight.
Manager – Yes, but the trouble is that you didn't wade in during the fight.

Park attendant – Excuse me, sir, but could you lend me a pencil and a piece of paper?
Visitor – Certainly. Here you are.
Park attendant – Now, give me your name and address. I saw you walking on the grass a moment ago.

Why did the egg go into the jungle?
Because it wanted to do some eggsploring!

What has three wings, three eyes and two beaks?
A canary with spare parts!

Hotel guest – Boy, dash up to room six and see if my raincoat is hanging behind the door. Hurry, because I have a train to catch.
(A few minutes later.)
Bellboy – Yes, sir. It's there as you said.

What do jelly babies wear on their feet?
Gum boots!

Teacher – First came the Ice Age, then the Stone Age. What came next?
Minnie – The sausage!

What do you call a judge with no thumbs?
Justice Fingers!

What did the mother ghost say to her child when they got into the car?
Put on your sheet belt!

What does an electric rabbit say?
Watts up, Doc!

How do you catch a squirrel up a tree? Climb up, and act like a nut!

Sheriff – Have you seen the Brown Bag Kid?
Cowboy – Nope, what does he look like?
Sheriff – He has a brown paper bag for a saddle on his horse, wears a brown paper bag hat, and a brown paper bag shirt.
Cowboy – What do you want him for?
Sheriff – Rustling!

How do you get rid of a white elephant?
Put him in a jumbo sale!

What's the easiest way to double your money?
Fold it!

Teacher – If your mum gave you nine hundred pounds, and your dad gave you eight hundred pounds, what would you have?
Janey – Rich parents!

A girl in a sweet shop is one metre and fifty centimetres tall, and wears size four shoes. What does she weigh?
Sweets!

What is yellow and flickers?
A lemon with a loose connection.

Judge – Do you mean to say that a broken-down wreck such as the prisoner gave you that black eye?
Witness – He wasn't a wreck till he gave me the black eye.

MacTavish – How did MacAndrew come to be an elephant trainer?
MacLaren – Well, he used to have a set of performing fleas then his eyesight got bad!

Dave – So, you're a golfer? What's your favourite course?
Harry – Soup!

Old lady (at concert) – Is that a popular song he's singing?
Old man – It was before he sang it!

Boastful artist – I once painted a picture of Santa Claus and it was so natural they had to take it down off the wall every month to trim his beard.

Auntie – If your mother gave you a large apple and a small apple and told you to give one to your brother, which would you give him?
Nephew – Do you mean my big brother or my small brother?

Patient – Doctor, doctor, I swallowed a fairy-tale book yesterday.
Doctor – Sit down and tell me the whole story.

Trainer – Did you find your horse well behaved?
Jockey – Yes, beautifully mannered. Every time we came to a fence he let me go first.

What would you do if you saw three skeletons walking down the road?
Jump out of my skin and join them!

Who was the world's greatest thief?
Atlas, because he held up the whole world!

What do you call a baby whale?
A little squirt!

When is it bad luck to have a black cat following you?
When you're a mouse!

What did Dracula say to his wife when they were going out?
You look fangtastic!

Diner – Waiter, look at the ends of this sausage.
Waiter – Why, there's nothing the matter with them, is there, sir?
Diner – Rather close together, aren't they?

Burglar Bill – I am deeply indebted to you, sir. What should I have done without you?
Lawyer – Seven years' hard labour.

Foreman – What's all the row for?
Workman – The steamroller driver is threatening to go on strike unless they call him a chauffeur.

Miles – The people in the flat above are very annoying. They were jumping about and banging on the floor till after midnight last night. It was very distracting for me.
Giles – You were working late, I suppose?
Miles – No, I was practising on my saxophone.

Teacher – Name four members of the dog family, Joe.
Joe – There's Mummy dog, Daddy dog, Sister dog and Brother dog!

What do you get if you cross a parrot with a woodpecker?
A bird that tells knock-knock jokes.

What do you get if you cross a dog with a stick insect?
An animal that fetches itself.

What do you get if you cross a skunk with a homing pigeon?
A bad smell that won't go away.

Uncle – What are you looking so worried about, Jack?
Young Nephew – Well, yesterday my teacher said two and two are four, and today Dad said one and three are four, and I don't know which to believe.

Which driver never commits a traffic offence?
A screwdriver!

What can you hold without touching it?
A conversation.

Hotel manager – Rooms overlooking the sea cost £5 extra.
Miser – How much does it cost if I promise not to look?

David – If you call somebody who lives in Scotland Scottish, what do you call somebody who lives in the North Pole?
Tom – I don't know!
David – Daft!

Bill – How do you confuse a boomerang?
Ben – I don't know!
Bill – Throw it down a one-way street!

Officer – Have you cleaned your boots this morning?
Private – No.
Officer – No, what?
Private – No polish.

Dad – What's the time?
Dennis – Half past.
Dad – Half past what?
Dennis – I dunno. I've lost the hour hand of my watch!

Alec – What was your mother so angry about?
Jim – She sent me for some cold cream and I got ice-cream. It was the coldest they had.

Teacher – If you had twelve sweets, and Johnny took half, what would he have?
Tommy – A black eye!

Fireman – Hey! Come on! Can't you see your house is on fire?
Patient – Can't help it. The doctor told me not to leave my bed for two days.

Diner – There's a funny kind of film on this soup, waiter.
Waiter – Well, what do you expect for two pounds – a full-scale thriller?

Youth – Shall I have a chance of an early rise in this job?
Boss – Most certainly! Six o'clock every morning.

Boss – I want a man who is clever, hard-working and punctual.
Lazy Larry – You don't want one man, you want three.

Teacher – If you had two pounds and you asked your dad for another two pounds, how much money would you have?
Johnny – Er … two pounds, sir.

Where do old Volkswagens go?
The Old Volks' Home!

When a fly from one side of the room and a flea from the other side meet, what is the time when they pass?
Fly-past-flea!

Doctor, doctor, I keep on getting a sore throat every time I take a cup of tea.
Doctor – Have you tried taking the spoon out.

Which land do kittens like best?
Lapland!

What do you call a map-reading back-seat driver?
A nag-ivator!

Boss – What do you mean by arguing with that customer? Don't you know our rule? The customer is always right.
Assistant – I know. But he was insisting that he was wrong.

Flying instructor – If anything goes wrong, leap out of the plane and pull the cord of the parachute.
Cadet – Supposing the parachute doesn't open?
Flying instructor – Bring it back and I'll give you another.

Mother – Johnny, you ought not to eat so fast.
Johnny – But, Mum, I'm only trying to get it down before the price of food goes up again.

Smiffy – Dad, why is a sponge full of holes?
Smiffy's Dad – Er . . . well, if it wasn't for the holes, people wouldn't know it was a sponge.

Old lady – Little boy, don't pull faces at that poor bulldog!
Little boy – Well, he started it!

Knock! Knock!
Who's there?
Euripedes!
Euripedes who?
Euripedes, and you'll pay for a new pair!

Doctor – How long have you been thinking you're a ghost?
Patient – Ever since I've been walking through walls.

What is green inside and yellow outside?
A cucumber dressed up as a banana!

What would you call a Scottish cloak-room attendant?
Angus Coatup!

Doctor, doctor, I feel like a bucket!
Yes, you do look a bit pail!

Doctor – How are you coming along with your reducing diet?
Patient – Not very well. I must be one of those poor losers.

What kind of running means walking?
Running out of petrol!

Teacher – Really, Fatty, why don't you wash your face? I can see what you had for breakfast this morning.
Fatty – What was it?
Teacher – Egg.
Fatty – You're wrong. That was yesterday morning!

Spotty- My uncle was the weather fore-caster in our town and he predicted sunny weather for last summer. He had to leave the town.
'Erbert – Why?
Spotty – Because the climate didn't agree with him.

Old lady – And how did those enor-mous rocks get there?
Guide – The glaciers brought them, madam.
Old lady – And where are the glaciers now?
Guide (fed up) – They've gone for more rocks.

'Erbert – I used to have trouble with my eyes – I saw spots in front of them.
Toots – Do your glasses help?
'Erbert – Yes. Now I can see the spots much better.

Percy – My mum hung my socks up last Christmas – and oh, did I have a headache!
Horace – How could hanging up your socks give you a headache?
Percy – She forgot to take me out of them!

Old lady (in animal shop) – What would you recommend for a flying fish – a bowl or a birdcage?

Father (enraged) – This new saw I bought is useless. It wouldn't cut butter.
Dennis – Oh, yes, it would, Dad. I cut a brick in half with it this morning.

Busy greengrocer (who has gone into next-door shop, which is a beauty parlour) – Will you massage those prunes for me, please, miss? We've run out of plums.

Tim – Do you know that boy Jones?
Jim – Oh, yes, he sleeps beside me in history.

Little brother – What's etiquette?
Slightly bigger brother – It's saying "No, thank you!" at a birthday party when you want to say "Yes, please!"

Dennis – What's the time, Walter?
Walter – Twenty-five minutes to ten.
Dennis – I'll never remember that. You'd better give me your watch.

Optician (holding up a dinner plate) – What is this?
'Erbert (getting his eyes tested) – Bring it a little nearer. I don't know whether it's a five pence or a ten pence.

Teacher (after looking at Smiffy's homework) – I didn't think it was possible for one person to make so many mistakes.
Smiffy – It wasn't only one person, Teacher. Dad helped me.

Gentleman – Are you still looking for your lost pound coin, little boy?
Boy – No, my little brother found it.
Gentleman – Then what are you looking for?
Boy – My little brother.

Mother – Why didn't you take the medicine the doctor gave you for your cold?
Minnie – Because it says on the bottle, "Keep tightly corked."

Poet – This poem of mine will make everybody's heart miss a beat.
Editor – Then it won't do. We never print anything that interferes with the circulation.

Pupil – I can't read this correction of yours, sir.
Teacher – It says, "You must write more clearly."

First weightlifter – I am stronger than Hercules.
Second weightlifter – That's nothing. I knew a man who could pick himself up by the scruff of the neck and swing himself out at arm's length.

Bill – How long did you work last week?
Ben – One day.
Bill – Gosh! I wish I could find a steady job like that.

Teacher – The people of Poland are Poles; the people of Sweden, Swedes. Can you tell me what the people of Germany are called?
Minnie – Yes, Germs.

Foreman – Look how that man's doing twice the work you are.
Workman – That's what I've been telling him, but he won't stop.

Teacher – Why are you late this morning?
Jock – Please, sir, I stopped a fight.
Teacher – That's right, always be a peacemaker. How did you stop them?
Jock – I punched them both.

Novice (hiring boat) – I've no watch so I hope I shall know when my hour is up.
Boatman – Oh, yes, you'll know by the water. The boat fills up to the seat in about an hour and a half.

Diner – I ordered a dozen oysters, and you've only given me eleven.
Waiter – I thought you wouldn't like to sit thirteen at the table, sir.

Confused judge (to noisy prisoner in court) – Quiet please! We want nothing but silence, and very little of that.

Visitor (to little boy) – If you had twelve apples, and I gave you two, how many would you have?

Little boy – I don't know. We do our sums in oranges.

Guide – Beneath that slab lies King Richard's heart; over there lies good Sir Frances Drake; and who do you think is lying here?

Tourist – Well, I don't know for sure, but I have my suspicions.

Baldheaded circus performer – Ladies and gentlemen, I offer £100 to anyone who can name anything I can't do.

Voice (from the audience) – Part your hair, in the middle!

Manager – Come here at once, John. Look at the dust on this desk. Why can't you keep it polished like the banister rails?

Office junior – Well, sir, I can't slide down your desk.

Farmer -Did you count the pigs this morning, Paddy?

Paddy – I counted nineteen, but one ran so fast that I couldn't count him at all.

Customer – You said the tortoise I bought from you would live three hundred years, and it died the day after I bought it.

Dealer – Now, isn't that too bad! The three hundred years must have been up.

Patient – How much is it to have a tooth extracted?

Dentist – Thirty pounds.

Patient – What! For three seconds' work?

Dentist – All right, I'll take it out in slow motion.

Mother – Why are you jumping up and down, Minnie?

Minnie – It's all right, Mother. I forgot to shake my medicine before I took it, so I'm doing it now.

Patient (in asylum yard, to new superintendent) – Who are you?

Superintendent – I'm the new superintendent.

Patient – Oh, it won't take them long to knock that out of you. I was Napoleon when I came here.

First gardener – What was the last card I dealt you?

Second gardener – A spade.

First gardener – I knew it.

Second gardener – How?

First gardener – You spat on your hands before you picked it up.

Teacher – Tommy, what is one-fifth of three-seventeenths?

Tommy – I don't know exactly, but it isn't enough to worry about.

Boss – What do you mean by taking the whole day off yesterday, when I gave you a half day?

Clerk – Well, you always told me never to do things by halves.

Willie – I lost a pound coin this morning, Tim.

Tim – Hole in your pocket?

Willie -No, the man who dropped it heard it fall.

Chief – We must dismiss that salesman who tells all our clients that I am an ass.

Partner – I'll speak to him, and tell him not to discuss company secrets.

Steward (to seasick passenger) – Can I fetch you anything, sir?

Seasick passenger – Yes, a small island – quick!

Angry customer – These eggs aren't fresh.

Grocer (indignantly) – Not fresh? Well, sir, the boy only brought them in from the country this morning.

Customer – Which country?

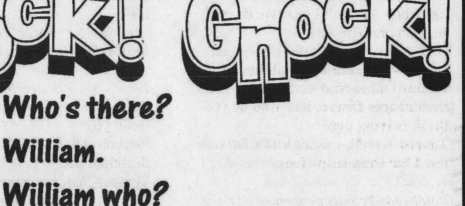

Gnock! Gnock!

Who's there?

William.

William who?

William mind your own business?

Gnock! Gnock!

Who's there?

Boo.

Boo who?

Don't cry!

Fat man – Are you laughing at my expense?
Little boy – No, sir; I'm laughing at your expanse.

Waiter -Your coffee, sir: it's special from South America.
Diner – Oh, so that's where you've been all this time, is it?

Old man (entering office) – There is a boy, John McNab, working here. May I see him? I'm his grandfather.
Clerk – You're just too late, sir. He's gone to your funeral.

Bore – Yes, I'm very fond of birds. Yesterday one actually settled on my head.
Fed-up listener – It must have been a woodpecker.

Prospective purchaser – Is this aeroplane safe?
Manufacturer – Safest on earth.

Bailiff – Can't you read that notice, "No fishing here"?
Angler – Yes, but the man who put that up didn't know what he was talking about. I've caught twenty in ten minutes.

Mountain guide – Be careful not to fall here. It is dangerous. But if you do fall, remember to look to the left, as you get a most wonderful view.

Mother – Didn't I tell you not to jump over that tar barrel again!
Jimmy (now in the barrel of tar) – Well, I didn't.

Bill – They say there's two feet of ice on the duck pond.
Ben – Why, I had the same in bed last night.

Teacher – Henry, are you learning anything?
Henry – No, sir, I'm listening to you.

Husband – I've just swallowed a cuf-flink!
Wife – Well, at least you're sure where it is.

Boss – Peter, are you sweeping out the shop?
Peter – No, I'm sweeping out the dirt and leaving the shop.

Farmer – Do you see that pig over there? I call him Ink.
Visitor – Why?
Farmer – He keeps running out of the pen.

Builder – How is the new chap you took on this morning? Is he steady?
Foreman – If he was much steadier he'd be motionless.

Sergeant (addressing platoon) – Does any man here know anything about music?
Recruit (swiftly) – Yes, Sergeant.
Sergeant – Then go and shift the piano in the sergeants' mess room.

Gentleman – Now, what ought you to say to a gentleman who gives you fifty pence for carrying his bag?
Tim – It isn't enough these days.

Minnie – Sing for us, Dad.
Dad (pleased) – Why?
Minnie – Because we're playing at ships and we want to have a foghorn.

Diner – Waiter, what sort of pie is this?
Waiter – Cottage pie, sir.
Diner – Then this must be the foundation-stone.

A teacher caught a boy scribbling on a piece of paper which contained these words – Blow, blow, suck, blow, suck, blow, blow, suck, blow.
Teacher – What is the meaning of this?
Boy – Please, sir, it's the music for my mouth-organ.

Why are medieval
times called the
dark ages?
*Because there were
so many knights.*

What do you
call a very fast fungus?
A mush Vroom!

Why did the
skeleton go to
the restaurant?
He wanted spare ribs.

How did the baker get
an electric shock?
*He stood on a bun
and the currant ran
up his leg!*

Footballer (in black and white jersey) – How do you like our new colours?
Supporter – What's the idea – half mourning for the matches you've lost?

Boxing instructor – That was a half-hook.
Pupil (dreamily) – Well, just keep the other half for yourself.

Mother – Where are your manners, Dennis? You shouldn't eat your jelly with your fingers.
Dennis – I've tried a spoon but the jelly's so excited it won't stay on.

Defeated jockey – Well, anyhow, I wasn't last. There were two horses behind me.
Disgusted owner – Rats! Those were the first two in the next race.

Fireman – At one fire, I saved ten lives.
Smith – And who were they?
Fireman -A child and her pet cat.

Sergeant – Is the man seriously wound-ed?
Policeman – Well, two of the wounds are fatal, but the third doesn't amount to much.

Policeman (to motorist) – Why didn't you slow down? Didn't you see the notice – "Slow down here"?
Motorist -Yes, but I thought it was describing your village.

Burglar – Have you paid your dog license?
Brown – I haven't got a dog.
Burglar – Have you paid your tele-phone bill?
Brown – I haven't got a telephone.
Burglar – Good! I'm safe. Now open that safe for me.

Fat man (to boy in railway carriage) – Why are you looking at me?
Small boy -Because there's nowhere else to look.

Tourist – Why is there no fence at this precipice?
Guide – Well, the more people that fall over the more famous the place becomes.

Perkins – Who's that chap? His face seems familiar.
Jenkins – I'm not surprised. He's a retired jailer.

Diner – There's only one sandwich on that plate. I asked for a choice.
Waiter – Well, you've got a choice: take it or leave it.

Roger – Dad, give me a pound coin.
Dad – Don't you think that you're too big to be always begging for coins?
Roger – I expect you're right, Dad. You'd better give me a fiver.

Teacher – Now, Smiffy, whose emblem is the leek?
Smiffy – Er . . . the plumber's?

Jinks – Did the cyclone damage your house very much?
Binks – I don't know. I haven't found it yet.

Plug – I suppose this horrible-looking thing is what you call modern art?
Art dealer – I beg your pardon, sir, that is a mirror!

Auntie – Why are you eating those cakes so quickly, Smiffy?
Smiffy – I'm afraid that I will lose my appetite before I'm finished.

Teacher (during test) – I hope I didn't see you look at your book, Sidney?
Sidney – I hope you didn't, either.

Small footballer – Are you the fellow who kicked me a few minutes ago?
Burly footballer – Yes. What are you going to do about it?
Small footballer – Er . . . I just wanted to tell you that I'm feeling all right now.

WHAT DOES A TEN FOOT TALL PARROT SAY?
Anything it likes!

WHAT HAPPENED WHEN TWO T.V. AERIALS GOT MARRIED?
They had a really great reception.

Hasn't the doctor sent that sleeping pill yet, nurse?

Not yet, sir.

Well, it'll be too late if it doesn't come soon. I can hardly keep awake.

Jim – I suppose you find skating hard to learn?

Tim – Oh, no, you soon tumble to it!

Uncle – Well, Dennis, what did you see at the museum?

Dennis – Well, nearly all the things were called "Do not touch."

Teacher – Give me a sentence with the word "gladiator".

Pupil – The lion pounced on the woman and was glad he ate her.

Inspector – Have you caught that burglar yet?

P.C. 94 – No, but I've got him so scared he won't show his face while I'm about.

Teacher – Can anyone tell me what goldfish are?

Danny – Sardines that have grown rich.

Teacher – Now, if you had five marbles and Danny said he'd give you five, how many would you have?

Sidney – Just five, miss. Danny would only be kidding. I know him.

Employer – Did you put that note where it would attract Mr Smith's attention?

Office boy – Yes, I stuck a pin through it and put it on his chair.

John (to his brother) – Where shall I put my sweets?

Brother – Put them in my mouth.

Policeman (to boy watching football match from the top of the fence) – Hi, what's the game?

Boy – No score yet.

Bus conductor (to passenger) -Why did you ring the bell at both ends of the car?

Stupid passenger – Well, don't I want both ends to stop?

Bobby – I dropped my watch in the river yesterday, and it's still running.

Billy – Your watch?

Bobby – No, the river.

Passer-by – Why are you fishing under here?

Small boy – Well, the fish will all come under the pier to shelter from the rain!

Card player (ominously) – Somebody's cheating here. Bill Jones isn't playing the hand I dealt him.

Mother – Now, Bobby you've been good all day. As a special treat you may choose something you want to do tomorrow.

Bobby – Then, may I be naughty all tomorrow?

Angus -If I gave you £100, what would you do?

Sandy – Count it!

Dentist – Don't cry. The tooth is out.

Harold – I know. I'll have to go back to school now.

Dick – Dad, would you like to save money?

Dad – Yes, of course.

Dick – Then buy me a bike, and I'll not wear out so many pairs of shoes.

Jimmy (watching tasty treats being taken into his brother's sick-room) – Please, Mummy, can I have the measles when Jack is done with them?

Plumber – Well, here we are, and we haven't forgotten a single tool.

Householder – No, but you've come to the wrong house.

Smith – Is that new watchdog of yours any good?

Brown – Very! If you hear a suspicious noise at night, you've only got to wake him, and he barks.

Prison visitor – What brought you here?

Prisoner – A mistake on my part.

Prison visitor – Really?

Prisoner – Yes, I thought I could run faster than the policeman – and I couldn't.

Railway manager – Another farmer is suing us on account of his cows.

Lawyer – Killed by trains, I suppose?

Railway manager – No. He says that the passengers have got into the habit of leaning out of the windows and milking the cows as the train goes by!

Customer – You told me that this suit will wear like iron.

Tailor – Well, it has, hasn't it?

Customer – I've had it two months and it has begun to look rusty!

Tom – If you had a wish, what would you wish?

John – If I had a wish, I'd wish that I'd get every wish I wished!

Bobby – I've been an awful good boy since I started going to Sunday school, haven't I?

Mother – Yes, dear, you've been very good indeed.

Bobby – And you don't distrust me any more, do you?

Mother – No, dear.

Bobby – Then, why do you hide the chocolate biscuits?

Teacher – Give me a sentence with the word frequent in it.

Toots – The living skeleton escaped from the circus, and nobody knew where the freak went.

Jock – Do you know how to get a hot meal without cooking or using a fire in any way?

Sandy – No, it's impossible.

Jock – Not at all. Eat bread and mustard.

Fat lady (to train attendant) – Do you mind helping me out? I cannot get out the proper way? I have already gone two stations past my town. You see, I am too stout and I have got to go out backwards and the porters, thinking I am getting in, push me back in again.

Dennis – How much is it for an empty bottle?

Pharmacist – Well, if you want the empty bottle it'll be seventy pence, but, if you have something put into it, we won't charge you anything for the bottle.

Dennis – Sure, that's fair enough. Put in a cork.

Jack (showing a photograph of himself on a donkey) – I had this taken at Margate. Isn't it like me?

Pat – Very. But who is that on your back?

Jimmy – You can take your finger off that leak now, Dad!

Dad – Why? Has the plumber come?

Jimmy – No, the house is on fire!

Uncle (telling story of the princes in the Tower) – And so they hid the two princes under the staircase, and they weren't found for a long time.

Nephew – But didn't the gasman find them when he came to look at the meter?

Gent – Hey, boy! What's the quickest way to get to the station?

Boy – Run.

Old gent (to boy fishing) – How many have you caught?

Boy – Well, when I get another, I'll have caught one.

Why did the boa constrictors get married?

They had a crush on each other.

Why did the dog have its puppies in a dustbin? *It said "PLACE YOUR LITTER HERE"!*

Old lady (in a greengrocer's) – What have you in the shape of cucumbers? Nervous shop assistantEr . . . bananas?

Boy (entering police station) – Where is the cashier, please?
Inspector – We don't have one at a police station.
Boy – Well, who counts the coppers, then?

Cavalry sergeant – Hey, you've only got one spur on! You can't ride a horse with only one spur. Where's the other?
Recruit – Well, sir, it's broken, but I thought that if I could get one side of the horse to go the other would follow.

Diner – Waiter, would you close that window?
Waiter – Is there a draught, sir?
Diner – Well, not exactly, but this is the third time my steak has blown off my plate.

Tim – Jim, do you know what I've just seen? A duck swimming on a pond and a cat sitting on its tail.
Jim – What nonsense! Why, I don't believe it.
Tim – It's a fact, honestly. Er . . . the cat was sitting on its own tail, of course!

Man – Can you tell me the nearest way to the hospital?
Little boy – I don't know, sir, but if you step in front of that car you'll get there soon enough.

Cannibal chief – What was that you served me with just now?
Cook – Motor cyclist, your majesty.
Chief – He tasted very burnt.
Cook – Yes, he was scorching when we caught him.

Mother – Hurry up, Smiffy. Have you got your shoes on yet?
Smiffy – Yes, all but one.

Jones – Your dog bit me.
Neighbour – He did not.
Jones – Then prove it.
Neighbour – First, my dog has no teeth. Second, he is not ferocious. Third, he is particular about whom he bites. Fourth, I haven't got a dog.

Smith – That's a ripping little dog of yours.
Jones – He is. He ripped up my best overcoat and slippers yesterday.

Toots – Is 'Erbert really short-sighted?
Plug – I should say so. I saw him once at the zoo, and he was looking at an elephant through a magnifying glass.

Minnie – How do you make a currant roll?
Dad (fed up answering questions, sarcastically) – Blow it up with a bicycle pump, and shove it down a hill.

Jack – When people's teeth ache they have them filled, don't they?
Mother – Yes.
Jack – Well, my stomach aches. Could I go along to the sweet shop and get it filled?

Smith – It's always dangerous to jump to conclusions. You're liable to make yourself look ridiculous.
Brown – Yes, you're right. I jumped at the conclusion of a ferryboat once, and missed!

Policeman – Can't you see that notice, "No Fishing Allowed"?
Boy – Sure, but I was fishing quietly.

Inspector – What is nothing?
Pupil – Nothing is a footless stocking without a leg.

Motorist – My tyre punctuated today.
Friend – Punctured, you mean.
Motorist – I dunno, but it came to a full stop.

Gnock! Gnock!

Who's there?

Water.

Water who?

Water you, a gorilla?

Gnock! Gnock!

Who's there?

Wednesday.

Wednesday who?

Wednesday saints go marching in!

Teacher – If I gave you sixteen nuts to share equally with your little brother, how many would he get?
Jimmy – Six.
Teacher – Nonsense! You can't count.
Jimmy – Oh, yes, I can, but my little brother can't.

Jimmy – Oh, Dad, there's a big black cat in the kitchen.
Dad – Oh, never mind. Black cats are lucky.
Jimmy – Yes, this one was. It's just eaten the fish for your supper.

Smith – Hello, old chap. How are you?
Jones – Not so bad. Had an accident on my bike the other day, though.
Smith – Oh, was it bad?
Jones – Fairly. I was knocked speechless, and my wheel was knocked spokeless.

Sergeant (drilling a recruit squad) – Fire at will.
New recruit (pointing his rifle among the ranks) – Which one is Will?

Angry Dad – Didn't I tell you not to have another fight with Jimmy Brown?
Son – It wasn't another fight, Dad. We were just finishing the last one.

Teacher – Now, if I gave you two apples, Bobby gave you three oranges, Tommy gave you five grapes, and Willie gave you two pears, what would you have?
Pupil – I think I'd have a pain, sir.

Billy (doing crossword puzzle) – Give me the name of a motor car that starts with "T".
Friend – Don't be an ass. You know they all start with petrol.

Lady (to weary salesman) – Can't you see the notice on the gate, "No Salesmen"? Didn't you go to school?
Salesman (sarcastic) – No, lady. I went to night school, and I can't read in the daytime.

Customer (to fishmonger) – I don't like the look of that haddock.
Fishmonger – Well, if it's looks you're after, why don't you buy a goldfish?

Where did Brown get all his money?
In the hold-up business.
Never!
Yes. He manufactures suspenders.

First Boy – My dad is so strong he can tear up a pack of cards.
Second Boy – That's nothing. My dad was late this morning, so he tore up the road.

Page – Didst thou call me, my liege?
Enraged knight – Aye, varlet. Go thou quickly and procure a tin-opener. There's a wasp in my armour.

Jim – I had a terrible fight with Bill Smasher, the boxer.
Jack – Really, did he hurt you?
Jim – Oh, no! It was a long-distance telephone call.

Dennis – Say, Billy, can you sprint very fast?
Billy – Can I? Why, yesterday I ran around a half-mile track so fast that my shadow was just starting out when I got back.

Mother – You were a tidy boy not to throw your orange peel on the floor of the bus. Where did you put it?
Dennis – In the pocket of the man sitting next to me.

Artist – Would you stand there a few moments? I want to get some local colour.
Local – You've already got it, mister. I've just painted that bench you're sitting on.

Mechanics instructor (to class) – Are there any questions?
Pupil – Yes, sir. What is the horse-power of a donkey-engine?

WHAT DO YOU GET IF YOU CROSS AN ELEPHANT WITH A SPARROW?
Broken telephone wires.

DID YOU HEAR ABOUT THE TWO DEER WHO RAN AWAY TO GET MARRIED?
They antELOPED!

WHAT'S AS BIG AS AN ELEPHANT AND WEIGHS NOTHING?
An elephant's shadow.

Shipwrecked sailor (playing noughts and crosses with his companion) – I guess we'll have to turn the raft over now, Bill!

First passenger – Pardon me, does this train stop at Paddington?
Second passenger – Yes, watch me, and get off two stations before I do.

Theatre attendant – Only stalls and boxes left, sir.
Farmer – What do you take me for – a horse?

First fireman – Where's the fire?
Second fireman – There isn't one.
First fireman – But you said the fire bell had gone.
Second fireman – So it has. Someone's pinched it.

Tommy – My father has one of Drake's flags.
Willie – That's nothing. My father has one of Adam's apples.

Cuddles – I think my drum annoys the man next door.
Dimples – How do you know?
Cuddles – Well, he gave me a penknife this morning, and asked me if I knew what was inside my drum

Jones – Honestly speaking, would you think I'd bought the car second-hand?
Smith – No, I though you'd made it yourself.

Flying instructor – And if the parachute doesn't open – well, gentlemen, that is what is known as jumping to a conclusion.

Landlady – Good morning! How do you find yourself?
Lodger – I didn't know I was lost.

Hiker – I look upon hiking as a tonic.
Tourist – Yes, and on a passing lorry as a pick-me-up, I suppose!

Tradesman (loftily) – In twenty years of business, no customer has ever complained of my work.
Neighbour – Wonderful! What are you?
Tradesman – An undertaker.

Little boy – I've asked for money, I've begged for money, and I've cried for money.
Auntie – Have you ever tried working for it?
Little boy – No, Auntie. I'm going through the alphabet and I haven't got to "W" yet.

Gent – Now, I want a really high-bred dog.
Salesman – Yes, sir. What about a Skye terrier?

Teacher – There is no difficulty in the world that we cannot overcome.
Pupil – Have you ever tried squeezing the toothpaste back into the tube, sir?

Old lady (at the zoo) – Mr Keeper, if one of the lions escaped what steps would you take?
Keeper – The biggest I could!

Smiffy's Grandad – I remember when I could walk right round the square, but now I can only walk halfway round and back.

Photographer – Do you want a large or a small photograph?
Sitter – A small one, please.
Photographer – Then close your mouth, please.

Prison visitor (to prisoner) – And why are you here, my poor man?
Prisoner -Because they've got all the doors locked.

Johnny – Pa, it's raining.
Pa (vexed at being interrupted) – Well, let it rain!
Johnny – I was going to.

Bully – Why run away? I thought you said you could fight me with one hand tied behind your back?
Small boy – So I could. I'm just running home for the string.

Actor (in the Wild West) – I'll be hanged if I act here again!
Manager – Yes, or shot!

Manager – You should have been here at nine o'clock.
Office junior – Why, what happened then?

Lady – The watch I told you about wasn't stolen. I've just found it.
Detective – Too late! We've arrested the thief.

Bailiff – Oh, most excellent majesty, this man hath stolen our sacred white elephant.
Rajah – Search him!

Bill – You've enough brass in your neck to make a kettle.
Harry – Yes, and you've enough water in your brain to fill the kettle.

Smiffy – What's the matter?
Plug – I can't get my new boots on at all.
Smiffy – Don't worry. You never can get new boots on till you've worn them once or twice.

Grocer – What are you doing here? I thought I sacked you last night.
Jimmy – I know. And don't do it again. I got an awful row when I went home.

Teacher – Has anyone a question to ask?
Wilfrid – Yes, sir. Can a short-sighted man have a faraway look in his eyes?

Victim – Wow! I thought you extracted teeth without pain?
Dentist – Correct! I assure you I felt no pain whatever.

Arctic explorer – It was so cold where we were that the candle froze and we couldn't blow it out.
Second explorer – That's nothing! Where we were the words came out of our mouths in pieces of ice, and we had to fry them to see what we were talking about.

Mike – Have you seen my boots, Pat?
Pat – Are you sure you had them on when you took them off?

Teacher – Can any lad tell me what a bison is?
Jimmy – Please, sir, a bison is what my mother cooks her puddings in.

Employer – If anyone asks for me, I'll be back in half an hour.
New office junior – Yes, sir, and how soon will you be back if no one asks for you?

Film producer – Your story is too highly coloured.
Writer – In what way?
Film producer – Why, in the very first act you make the old man turn purple with rage, the villain green with envy, the hero white with anger and the coachman blue with cold.

Man (on the telephone) – Hello, gasman, come at once! There's an awful leak in our gas-pipe!
Gasman – Have you done anything to it?
Man – Yes, I put a bucket under it.

Teacher – To what family does the whale belong?
Smiffy – Don't know, sir. No family in our neighbourhood owns a whale.

Customer – How much are these chickens?
Farmer – Three pounds.
Customer – Did you raise them yourself?
Farmer – Yes; they were two pounds fifty pence yesterday.

Toots – Smiffy is very absent-minded. The other evening he sat up till midnight trying to remember what it was he wanted to do.
Sidney – Did he remember?
Toots – Yes, he wanted to go to bed early.

Stout man – Can you tell me how to get out of this park, lad?
Jimmy – Have you tried sideways, mister?

Director – Did you have a good reception last night?
Actor – The audience pelted me with flowers.
Director – How'd you get the old black eye?
Actor – Well, they didn't take the flowers out of the pots.

Diner – Oh, goodness, waiter, I've swallowed a fly. What shall I do?
Waiter – Swallow some fly-paper, sir.

Teacher – Sidney, you were not at school yesterday afternoon. Have you any explanation to offer?
Sidney – Please, Teacher, I was going to school, and I saw a steamroller and a policeman says to me, "Mind that steamroller", and I stayed minding it all the afternoon.

Teacher – Johnny, make a sentence using the word "indisposition".
Johnny – When a boxer fights, he stands in disposition.

Dad – What is the matter now?
Small boy – I dropped the towel in the bath, and it has dried me wetter than I was before.

Policeman – What are you standing there for?
Loafer – Nothin'.
Policeman – Well, if everybody was to stand in the same place, how would the rest get past?

Road hog (recognising man he has just run over) – Why, fancy running across you, Smith! I was saying just this morning that I hadn't bumped into you for ages.

Artist (showing a blank canvas) – Look at that picture of a cow eating grass.
Friend – Where's the grass?
Artist -The cow's eaten it.
Friend – Well, where's the cow?
Artist – Oh, it went away when it saw there wasn't any more grass to eat.

Teacher – Now, Bobby, if six eggs cost sixty pence, how many would you get for twenty pence?
Bobby – None.
Teacher – What? Why would you get none?
Bobby – Because I'd buy marbles, miss.

Father – Now, Tommy, what did I say I would do if I caught you stealing the biscuits again?
Tommy – That's funny, Dad. I've forgotten, too.

Doctor (meeting patient on street) – I told you not to come out of doors.
Patient – I didn't. I came out the window.

Customer – I want to take home a small chicken.
Butcher – Do you want a pullet?
Customer – Good gracious, no! I'll carry it with me.

Charlie (to his young brother) – Mrs Dubbs sent you four apples for cutting her grass. I ate two and lost one, and Johnny pinched the other. Mind you thank her when you see her.

Old man – Ah, my poor man, you've fallen down a manhole, haven't you?
Victim (sarcastically) – Oh, no, I happened to be here when the road was being made, and they built it round me.

George – Which is farther away – America or the moon?
Harry – America, of course. You can see the moon, but you can't see America.

Small boy (to very fat uncle) – I say, uncle, what a feed someone could have if he was as roomy as you and as hungry as me.

Diner – Is there any tomato sauce on the menu, waiter?
Waiter – No, sir. I have wiped it off.

First angler – Caught anything yet, Bill?
Second angler – Well, I've caught a salmon tin, but I think the salmon must have got away.

Teacher – What are raised in damp climates?
Schoolboy – Umbrellas, sir.

Dud comedian – I'm thinking of touring South Africa next season.
Friend – Take my advice and don't. An ostrich egg weighs from two to three pounds!

Jack – Say, Dad, what is the ship's hold?
Dad – The ship's hold? Why the anchor, of course.

Absent-minded professor – You see, my dear, I've not forgotten to bring my umbrella home this time.
Wife – But you never took one with you!

First jeweller – I have had it proved to me that advertising brings results.
Second jeweller – How?
First Jeweller – Yesterday, I advertised for a night watchman, and during the night my shop was burgled.

Listener – Did you keep cool when confronted by the bear?
Explorer – Rather. I was so cool that my teeth chattered.

Smiffy – Were you a good pupil at school?
Dad – Yes! I used to say my lessons so well that the teacher made me stay behind and repeat them to her after class.

Auntie – Why don't you eat your sweets, Jimmy?
Jimmy – I'm waiting for Jack Smith to come along. Sweets taste much better if there's another boy looking on.

Terry – What does your brother work at?
Jerry – He's got a very high position in the shipping world.
Terry – A naval captain?
Jerry – No, a lighthouse-keeper.

Airman – I . . . er . . . say, you've heard that saying, "See Naples and die"?
Passenger – Yes, why?
Airman – Well, I'm sorry to say that something's gone wrong with the engine, and we're over Naples now.

Teacher – Jimmy, correct this sentence, "Our teacher am in sight."
Jimmy – Our teacher am a sight.

Zoo keeper – Have you seen my antelope?
Confused man – No, whom did your aunt elope with?

Tourist – I say, do you ever have rain here?
Texan – Say, stranger, we have ducks here that are eight years old and haven't learned to swim yet.

Uncle – You would like me to give you five pounds?
Jock – Yes.
Uncle – Yes, if you . . . what?
Jock – If you can't afford any more.

Jack – I'm head over heels in work.
Jim – What's your job?
Jack – I'm an acrobat in the circus.

Judge – You say the constable arrested you while your were minding your own business?
Prisoner – Yes. He caught me by the collar, and threatened to strike me unless I accompanied him to the station.
Judge – You were attending to your own business then?
Prisoner – I was.
Judge – What is your business?
Prisoner – I'm a burglar.

Angler – Have you any salmon?
Village storekeeper – No, but I have some excellent pork pies.
Angler – Don't be an ass! How could a fellow go home and say he's caught a couple of pork pies?

Householder (to policeman investigating burglary) – I think it must have been a cat burglar.
Policeman – Why?
Householder- Because the milk was stolen.

Mother – Dennis, have you washed your face?
Dennis – Yes, Mum. Just look at the towel, it's filthy.

Teacher – When is the best time to gather fruit?
Roger – Please, sir, when the dog is tied up.

Motorist – I had the right of way when this man ran into me and yet you say I was to blame.
Constable – You certainly were.
Motorist – Why?
Constable – Because his brother is the Lord Mayor, his father is chief of police, and I'm engaged to his sister.

Mike – Hi, Pat, what have you got your fingers in Flynn's ears for?
Pat – Well, I can't find my glasses, and Flynn's reading a letter for me, and I don't want him to hear what it's about.

Teacher (to new boy) – What's your name, my little fellow?
New boy – Jimmy Brown.
Teacher – Always say "sir" when you are speaking to a teacher. Now, what's your name?
New boy – Sir Jimmy Brown.

Flight commander – What's making the airship go so slow?
Engineer – Well, sir, we are passing along the Milky Way, and the propeller is clogged with butter.

Teacher (after a class about how a cat can see in the dark) – What can the cat do that I can't?
Danny – Please, sir, wag its tail!

Terry – My brother ran thirty miles then cleared a five-barred gate at the finish.
Jerry – That's nothing to shout about. Look at the run he took.

Aunt (as wee Jock gets third slice of cake) – I wonder if there is any kind of cake you don't like?
Wee Jock – Yes, stomachache!

Artist -What a pretty cottage. May I paint it?
Farmer – No thanks. It's just been whitewashed.

Sergeant – I wonder why everybody calls me "Zebra"?
P.C. 222 – Because you're a donkey with stripes, I suppose.

Man -What are you crying for?
Boy – I've lost a pound coin.
Man – Here's another. Oh, what are you still crying for?
Boy – Well, if I hadn't lost that pound I'd have had two pounds now.

History teacher – Where did King William die?
Pupil – On page 121, sir.

What do you get if you cross Gnasher with a rose?
Something you wouldn't want to sniff!

What happened to the man who made his dog walk in the gutter?
They both fell off the roof!

That dog bit my leg!
Did you put anything on it?
No, he liked it just the way it was!

What do you get if you cross a dog with a giraffe?
An animal that barks at low flying aircraft.

Fortune-teller – Your prospects are not good, and a man stands in your way.
Client – Heaven help him. I drive a steamroller.

Tailor (to fat man) – Will you hold on to the end of this measuring tape, sir, while I run round with the other end?

Once there was a man named Berry, who owned a shop. One day a dissatisfied customer came in and said,
"You need not look blue, Berry, because I don't care a straw, Berry. Your father, the elder Berry, should not have been such a goose, Berry, so in future I will buy my goods from Logan, Berry."

Stranger – Why are you running that steam roller over the field, farmer?
Farmer – I'm trying to raise mashed potatoes.

Applicant – I came to see if you had an opening for me?
Manager – Yes, there's one behind you. Close it when you go out.

Boy (with pal at dentist's) – Please, I want a tooth out, and I don't want an anaesthetic, because I'm in a hurry.
Dentist – That's a brave boy. Which tooth is it?
Boy – Show him your tooth, Albert.

Binks – I am sorry my hen got out and scraped up your garden.
Jinks – That's all right. My dog ate your hen.
Binks -That's all right, too. I've just run over your dog.

Notice in the window of a suburban house – Piano for Sale.
Notice in the house next door – Hurrah!

Dog breeder (to man with ten children) – Why not buy a nice dachshund and let all the kids play with it at one time?

Guide – These are the ruins of one of the castles of the earliest Norman invaders.
Tourist – Yes, but I can never understand why they built them so far from the railway station.

Mother – Don't forget to pack your toothbrush, Willie.
Willie – But Mother, I thought I was going for a holiday?

Teacher – Now Johnny, what is lukewarm water?
Johnny (after a long pause) – Please, sir, it's water that looks warm but isn't.

Barber – How would you like your hair cut, my boy?
Small customer – Like Dad's, with a hole in the middle.

Customer – What's the charge for this battery?
Electrician – One and a half volts.
Customer – What's that in British money?

Jones – I see they're erecting a statue to the man who invented pneumatic tyres.
Smith – Wouldn't a bust be more appropriate?

Small boy (giving shopkeeper a five pound note for a 50p chocolate bar) – Would you give me 2 pound coins, four fifty pences, a twenty pence, two tens, and two fives as change?
Shopkeeper (sarcastically) – Are there any particular dates you want?

Uncle – Were you pleased with the drum I sent you for your birthday?
Nephew – Yes, very much, Uncle. Mother gives me five pounds every week not to use it.

Grey – If you're going to borrow money, borrow it from a pessimist.
Greene – Why?
Grey – He never expects to get it back.

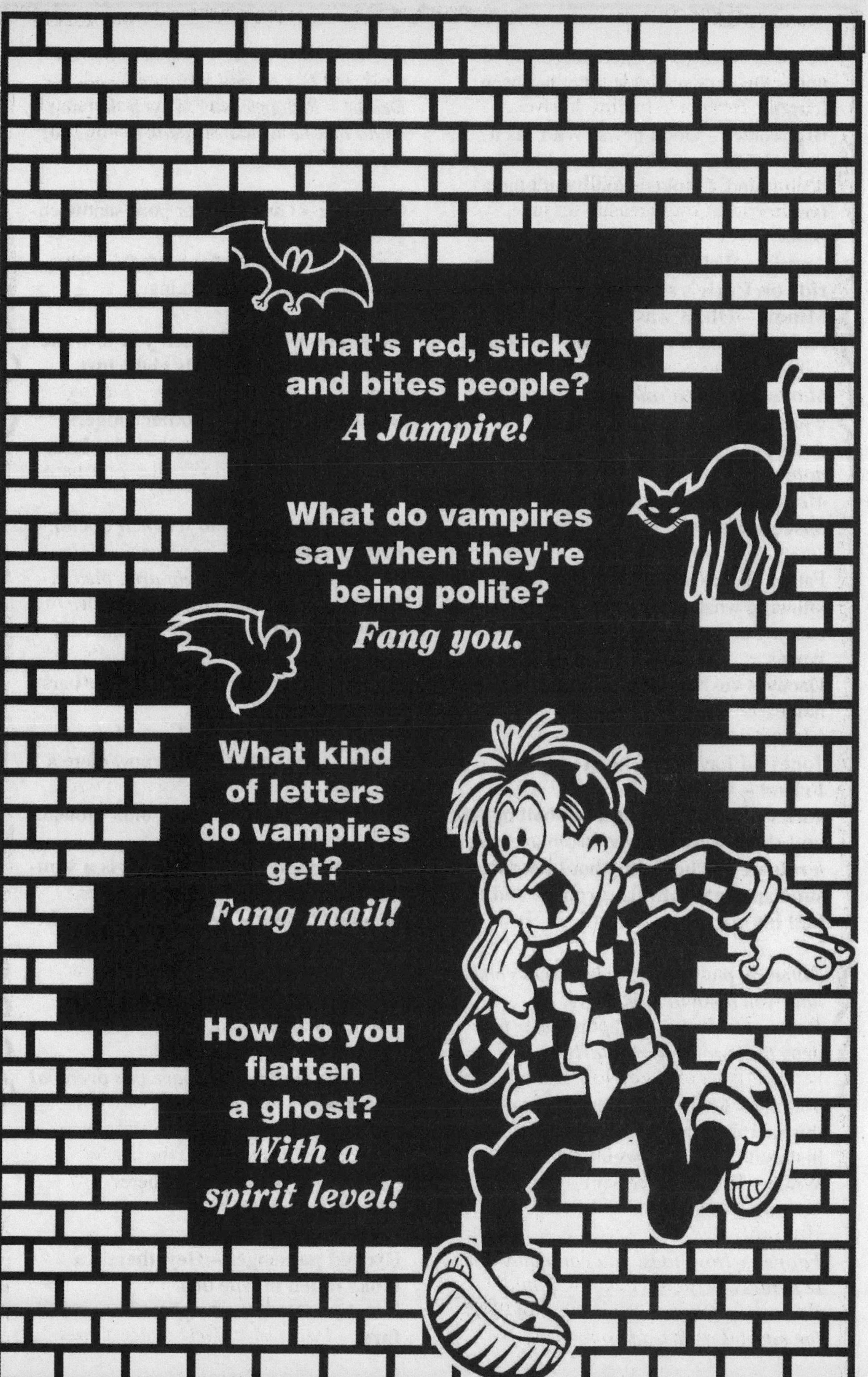

What's red, sticky
and bites people?
A Jampire!

What do vampires
say when they're
being polite?
Fang you.

What kind
of letters
do vampires
get?
Fang mail!

How do you
flatten
a ghost?
*With a
spirit level!*

Small brother – The skateboard you left under the park seat yesterday has been found.
Big brother – Good news! Who has it?
Small brother – I don't know, but it's been found. I looked, and it isn't there now.

Auntie – Well, how did you enjoy the ride on Uncle's shoulders?
Minnie – Oh, it was quite nice, but I had a ride on a real donkey yesterday.

Manager – I'm afraid that fellow I gave a job to last week is dishonest.
Assistant – You shouldn't judge by appearances.
Manager – I'm not, I'm judging by disappearances.

Father – You ought to be ashamed of not knowing what you learned at school today. Cuthbert Cringeworthy always knows.
Danny – Yes, but he hasn't so far to go home.

Jones – I have been born unlucky.
Friend – Why?
Jones – Well, I was at a football match, and there were twenty-two players and a referee on the field, about ten thousand spectators in the ground, and the ball hit me.

Judge (to pickpocket) – Just what good have you done to humanity?
Prisoner – Well, I've kept three or four detectives working regularly.

Tommy – I had a quarrel with Pug Smith this morning, and I would have punched his head if I hadn't been held off.
Willie – Who held you off?
Tommy – Pug.

Farmer – Now, lads, you can't play cricket here.
Batsman – Oh, can't we! Why, we're 69 for no wickets already.

Interested dog buyer – Yes, he looks all right, but has he any pedigree?
Dealer – Pedigree, sir? Why, if that dog could talk he wouldn't speak to either of us.

Customer – Give me four pork sandwiches to take away.
Assistant (speaking down tube) – Dress up four grunts to go walking.

Hotel guest – Didn't I tell you to wake me at nine, and it's only eight just now?
Boy – Yes, sir, but the other lodgers want their breakfast, and you're lying on the tablecloth.

Two grubby boys go to see their doctor.
Doctor – Ah! Let me see. Vaccinations for you two, isn't it? Right arm, please.
First boy – Just our luck, Jock. We've both gone and washed the left one.

Father – Where are those chocolate bars I left on the table?
Fatty – I haven't touched one of them.
Father – But I left five, and now there's only one.
Fatty – Yes, that's the one I didn't touch.

First student – Our professor is a wonderful man. He talks like a book.
Second student – Yes, but it's a pity he doesn't shut up as easily.

Jackson – I think we met in this restaurant last month. Your coat seems familiar to me.
Johnson – But I didn't have this overcoat last month.
Jackson – No, but I did.

Doctor – How did you get here?
Patient – 'Flu!

Excited passenger – Hey, there's a bloke fallen off the bus!
Conductor – It's all right, he's paid his fare!

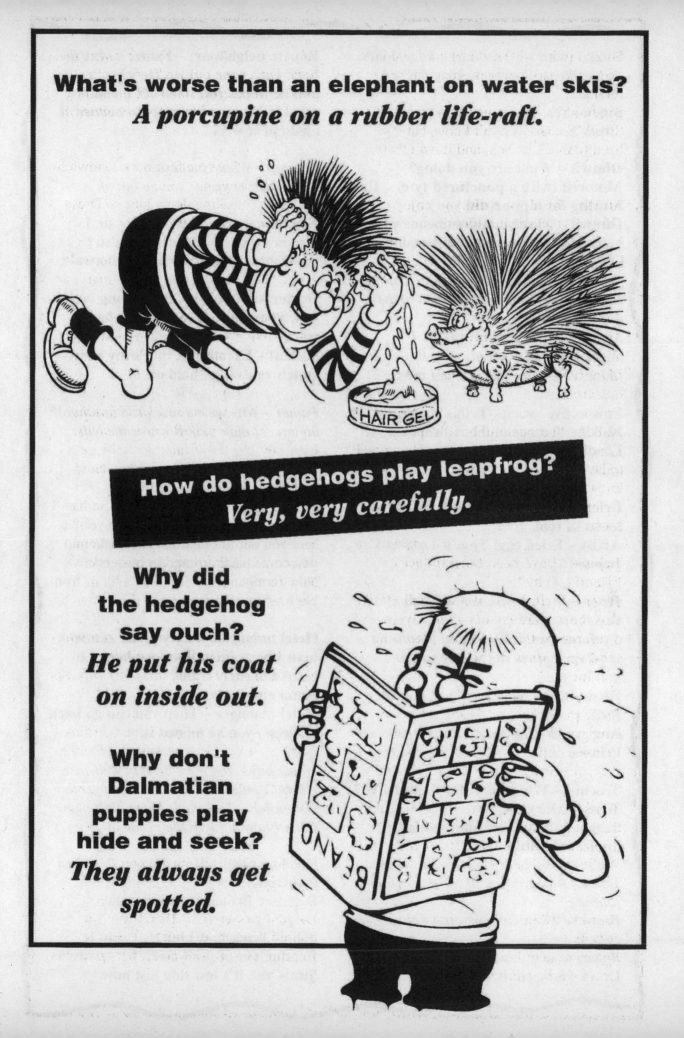

Brown (with wire netting) – I say, Jones, do you know how to make a chicken run?
Jones – Yes, clap your hands and say "shoo"!

Dimwit – What are you doing?
Motorist (with a punctured tyre) – I'm looking for a puncture.
Dimwit – Never mind; someone will come along soon and lend you one.

Walter – Would you mind taking that yellow tie with the green spots out of the window for me?
Shopkeeper – Certainly, sir.
Walter – Thanks awfully. The beastly thing bothers me every time I pass.

Prospective tenant – Is this cottage within walking distance of the railway station?
Landlord – Well . . . er ...how far can you walk?

Friend – I could eat that fried egg, it looks so real.
Artist – Fried egg! That's a sunset I've painted.

Passenger (on board ship) – Doesn't the vessel tip a lot?
Steward – Yes, it's trying its best to set a good example to the passengers.

Passer-by (to angler) – Good river for fish?
Angler – It must be. I can't persuade any to come out.

Teacher – Who succeeded Edward VI?
Toots – Mary, sir.
Teacher – And who followed Mary?
Toots – Her little lamb?

Jones – I always feel ill the day before a journey.
Brown – Why don't you go a day earlier?

Water, waiter, there's a fly in this soup!
Don't worry, sir. It won't drink much!

Boy (to neighbour) – Father's sent me back with your ladder. He's broken it, and he hopes you'll have it mended quickly because he wants to borrow it again next week.

Teacher – What is an exit?
Pupil – An entrance you go out of.

New apprentice joiner – Please sir, I couldn't get any two-inch nails, so I brought twice as many one-inch ones.

Doctor – There's nothing wrong with you. Your pulse is regular as clockwork.
Patient – Excuse me, that's my wrist watch you've got hold of.

Father – Why were you kept in at school?
Jimmy – I didn't know where the Nile was.
Father (angrily) – In future, you must remember where you put things.

Farmer – What's the matter with you? I sent you out to brand the livestock, and you come back covered in blisters!
New farmhand – Well, I had a lot of trouble branding the bees.

Hotel manager – Are you the gentleman who wanted to be awakened to catch the early train?
Hotel guest – Yes.
Hotel manager – Then you can go back to sleep , you've missed it.

Young boy – You must be very well-travelled, Captain.
Old sailor – Travelled! There ain't many ports I haven't seen the inside of.

Hotel manager – How did you sleep last night, professor?
Professor (irritably) – Lying down.

John – Look how high that ship is floating out of the water.
Jim – Yes, it's low tide just now.

Young boy – Why, you must know a lot about geography.
Old sailor – Yes, we did put in there once but only to coal the ship. 'Tain't much of a place, what I remember of it.

Terry – Have you improved your bicycle riding lately?
Jerry – On the contrary, I would say that I have fallen off a lot.

Jimmy – My history teacher is the meanest man I know.
Father – Why is that?
Jimmy – He borrows my sharpener to sharpen his pencil to give me bad marks.

New clerk – How long has that office boy worked for you?
Manager – About four hours.
New clerk – But I though he'd been with you a long time?
Manager – So he has, but he's only worked about four hours.

Mother – It's time to wake up, Jimmy.
Jimmy – I can't wake up.
Mother – Why not?
Jimmy – Because I'm not asleep.

Teacher – Can anyone tell me what is the highest form of animal life?
'Erbert – The giraffe.

Terry – I seemed to be always twisting and turning in my sleep last night.
Jerry – Ah, sleeping like a top, I suppose!

Mother – Sandy, stop pulling the cat's tail!
Sandy – I'm not pulling it. I'm only holding. It's the cat that's pulling!

Jerry – It's a twist! It's a twist!
Terry – What's a twist?
Jerry – A corkscrew.

Teacher – In what battle was General Wolfe killed?
Danny – His last one, sir.

Mother – Will you have a little of this steak pie, Jack?
Jack – No, thank you.
Mother – What? Then what will you have?
Jack – A lot, please.

Minnie – Dad, how long will that clock go without being wound up?
Dad – Eight days.
Minnie – And how long will it go when it is wound up?

Jim – What are you digging that hole for, Jim?
Bill – It's not the hole I'm digging. I'm digging the dirt and leaving the hole.

Lady – Those apples you sold me had a fishy taste.
Greengrocer – That's all right lady – they were crab apples.

Manager – And what is your father's walk in life?
Applicant – Er . . . one foot in front of the other.

Teacher – Wilfrid, what is a semi-circle?
Wilfrid – A straight line caught bending.

Father – Who is the laziest person in your class?
Sidney – I dunno.
Father – Well, who is it that watches the other hard-working pupils instead of working himself?
Sidney – Teacher.

Man (who has been knocked down by a motor car) – Where am I?
Enterprising street hawker – Here you are, sir; map of Glasgow, three pounds.

Bill – Hey, Sam, what are you putting on all those coats for?
Sam – It's like this, Bill, I'm going to paint my fence, and it says on the tin, "To obtain good results, put on three or four coats." And that's what I'm doing.

GNOCK! GNOCK!

Who's there?

Police.

Police who?

Police open the door.

Terry – I've just been having a tussle with the dentist.
Jerry – Who won?
Terry – It was a draw.

Which person always sticks up for his employer?
A billposter.

Street hawker – Want to buy a watch, old man?
Passer-by – What's the matter with it?
Street hawker – Nothing.
Passer-by – What are you selling it for then?
Street hawker – Nothing.
Passer-by – Righto. I'll buy it at that price.

Teacher – If ten men plough a field in six hours, how long will twenty men take to plough the same field?
Danny – They couldn't do it.
Teacher – Why not?
Danny – 'Cause the ten men have already ploughed it.

Terry – I know a man with over a thousand medals for sport.
Jerry – Some athlete!
Terry – No, but what a pawnbroker.

McTavish (victim of shipwreck) – Well, it might have been worse.
McTaggart (also a victim) – Yes, we might have bought a return ticket.

Dad – Jimmy, you are so naughty sometimes that I don't believe there's anything good in you.
Jimmy – Yes, there is, Dad. I've just eaten three mince pies, two bananas, and a chocolate bar.

Bobbie – Mother says these buns taste of soap.
Baker – Tell her they are bath buns.

Danny – A gallon of petrol, quick! The school's on fire.

Cricket fan – How many runs did you make?
Cricket player – I got twenty-four runs from one hit.
Cricket fan – How did you do that?
Cricket player – I broke a car window, and both teams and both umpires had to run for their lives.

Why is a cake like the sun?
Because it rises in the yeast and sinks beyond the vest.

Teacher – If I saw a boy beating a donkey, and I stopped him, what virtue should I be showing?
Plug – Brotherly love, sir.

Circus manager – The tent is on fire. What shall we do?
Attendant – Call the fire-eater.

Diner – Waiter, this soup isn't fit for a pig.
Waiter – Sorry, sir, I'll take it away and bring some that is.

Plug (on crowded train) – Isn't it rotten having to wait for a seat?
Fatty – You're lucky, I've to wait for two.

Polar explorer – Once we were nearly frozen to death, but we escaped.
Listener – How?
Explorer – We got into a heated argument.

Augustus Theodore d'Arcy – I want some peppah.
Store assistant – What sort? White, black or cayenne?
Augustus – Peppah, you fool, writing peppah.

Landlord (shouting upstairs) – Rent!
Tenant (shouting downstairs) – Spent!

Teacher – What is an organiser?
Minnie – The man that makes the music in church.

First author (reading) – The evening wore on.
Second author – Well, what did it wear?
First author – Oh, the close (clothes) of day, I suppose.

Boss – Have you got those tools sharpened?
Apprentice – Yes, but I can't get the nicks out of the saw.

Old lady – I thought you said this was a police dog?
Dog breeder – Yes, madam, but it's undercover.

Walter – Some powder please.
Chemist – The kind that goes off with a bang?
Walter – No, the kind that goes on with a puff.

Billy – Were you in the Ark, grandpa?
Grandpa – Of course not.
Billy – Then why weren't you drowned?

Old man -Excuse me, Mr Keeper, but does it cost very much to feed the giraffe?
Zoo keeper – Oh, no, sir. You see a little goes a long way with him.

Customer – Didn't you claim when you sold me this car that you'd replace anything that was broken or was missing?
Car salesman – Yes, sir. What is it?
Customer – Well, I want four front teeth and a collar bone!

Sharpe – Have you heard the tale of the three wells?
Smart – No, what is it?
Sharpe – Well! Well! Well!

Teacher – Can any boy give me a sentence with diploma in it?
Jimmy – Father heard a noise in the pipes, so he sent for di ploma (the plumber).

Guide – Yes, this is a marvellous echo. The people here shout out of their windows at night as they go to bed, and the echo wakes them in the morning.

Terry – Is McTavish any good at the high jump?
Jerry – No, he can hardly clear his throat.

Artist – Have you any camel hair brushes?
Village shopkeeper – No, sir, none of my customers keep camels!

Dick – I say, do you know the difference between "remember" and "recollect"?
Bob – None that I can see.
Dick – Well, I remember lending you five pounds last week, but I haven't re-collected it yet.

Pompous customer – I want two eggs, poached medium soft; toast, not too hard and buttered from edge to edge; and coffee, freshly ground Kenyan, not too strong and not too weak.
Waiter – Yes, sir, would you like any special design on the dishes?

Captain of team – Why can't you keep up with the other forwards?
Herbert – Because they didn't have to blow the ball up before we started.

Tommy had done something naughty and hid from his mother under the bed. When Tommy's father came home his mother told him what had happened. His father rushed upstairs and looked under the bed. Tommy looked at him, and then said – "Hello Dad, is she after you, too?"

Teacher -What is a niche in a church?
Boy – Well, it's just the same as an itch anywhere else – only you can't scratch it so well.

Horace – When I get old will the calves of my legs become cows?

Animal trainer – The leopard has escaped. Shoot him on the spot with the tranquilliser gun.
Circus hand – Which spot, sir?

Bandsman Bill – Our band was in a smash-up last night.
His friend – Any bones broken?
Bandsman Bill- Yes, two trombones.

Mother – What are you playing with?
Little son – A caterpillar and two little kittenpillars.

Father – I think my watch wants cleaning.
Jack – It should be really clean already. I had it in the bath yesterday.

Barber – Have I shaved you before?
Customer – No. I got these scars in the war.

Teacher – Where did King John sign the Magna Carta?
Smiffy – Please, sir, along the dotted line.

Professor Knowall is so absent-minded that he put his clothes to bed and hung himself over the back of a chair.

Billy – Why has your father such a large moustache?
Tommy – He put hair restorer on his sandwich in mistake for sauce.

Teacher – What is air?
Tommy – A balloon with the skin off.

Teacher – Smith, put what's in your mouth in the wastepaper basket!
Smith – I wish I could, sir. It's a gum-boil!

Tommy – Daddy, can you sign your name with your eyes shut?
Father – Why, that's easy!
Tommy – Well would you mind shutting your eyes and signing my school report card?

Teacher – What is wasted energy?
Bright lad – Telling a hair-raising story to a bald-headed man.

Bloggs – You should think of the future.
Noggs – I can't. It's my wife's birthday, and I'm thinking of the present.

Teacher – A fool can ask questions that wise people cannot answer.
Danny – No wonder we didn't pass our examination.

Singer – I'm afraid I wasn't singing very well tonight.
Wireless announcer – Oh, that's all right. You were announced as zoo imitations.

Boy (to teacher) – How did you like my essay on electricity?
Teacher – It was shocking.

Judge – You say Prisoner 66 brutally attacked you?
Warder – Yes, sir. He kicked me in the stomach while my back was turned.

Circus owner – Have you seen an escaped elephant round here?
Dimwit – No, but I've seen a grey rubber bull eating carrots with its tail.

Boy – Have you any broken biscuits?
Grocer – Yes, boy. Why?
Boy – Then here's some glue to stick them together again.

Salesman – Good morning. My name is Sparrow.
Customer – Oh? Well hop it.

Small boy (to mother) – Mother, all the boys at school call me "big head".
Mother – Never mind, Johnny; there's nothing in it!

Tommy – John plays the piano wonderfully by ear.
Freddie – That's nothing. My Dad fiddles with his whiskers.

Patient – Doctor, shall I be able to play the piano when my hand gets better?
Doctor – Why, certainly.
Patient – That's funny. I couldn't play it before.

Uncle – Jimmy, I'm going to give you a bright pound coin.
Jimmy – I'd rather have a dirty, old five pound note.

First boy – Coming out to play football?
Second boy – Can't. I broke a window yesterday, and Dad suspended me for the rest of the season.

Stranger – Boy, where does this road go to?
Dimwit – I don't think it goes anywhere. It's here every morning.

Motorist – Is the water very deep here, sonny?
Peter – No, sir, look it only comes up to the middle of that duck.

Barber – Do you want anything on your face when I've finished?
Smith – Well, I hope you'll leave me my nose.

Teacher – Tommy, why are your hands so dirty?
Tommy – Please, sir, I thought it was Saturday.

Auntie – Why, Fatty, you appear to eat very well.
Fatty – Yes, Auntie, you see, I've been practising all my life.

Gent (to a small boy fishing) – Have you caught anything yet?
Small boy – No, I don't believe my worm's trying!

Teacher – Billy Jones, how did you get that black eye?
Billy – Please, miss, I sprained it doing my homework.

Film actor – But look here, if he's going to throw me into the rapids, how am I going to get out?
Producer – Oh, that's all right – you don't appear again.

Tommy (to father) – Dad, I'm going to be a detective. Can you tell me a good disguise?
Father – Wash your face.

Second – You're all right, Bill. The crowd's with you.
Battered boxer – Wish I was with them!

Visitor – Is your father in, Tommy?
Tommy – Yes, but he is wrapped up in his work.
Visitor – Oh, I did not know he was so studious.
Tommy – He isn't, he's papering the parlour.

Gent – Waiter, I've been waiting half an hour for my turtle soup!
Waiter – Well, sir, you know how slow turtles are!

Teacher – If I said Plug's face was handsome, what tense would that be?
Fatty – Pretence.

Bill – Did you read about that burglar who stole a mile of elastic?
Jim – No, what happened?
Bill – He got a long stretch.

Gent – This soup's very thin, waiter.
Waiter – Yes, sir. The manager likes people to admire the design on the plates.

Man – Waiter, I have only five pounds and fifty pence. What do you recommend?
Waiter – Another restaurant, sir.

Angry grocer – Why did you run away when you broke my window?
Small boy – I couldn't bear to see my ball go through all that "pane".

Teacher – What made you so late this morning?

Tommy – I fell downstairs.

Teacher – That ought not to have taken you long.

First hiker – Go easy, we've got three miles before us.

Second hiker – That's why I'm hurrying. I want to get there before I'm tired out.

Burglar – Excuse me waking you up, but does this watch keep good time?

Small boy (in sweet shop) – How much is that big stick of toffee?

Shopkeeper – Thirty pence.

Small boy – How long will you let me lick it for five pence?

Cuddles – How do ghosts get through closed doors?

Dimples – They use skeleton keys.

Circus manager – What's the matter with your hand?

New lion tamer – I put it in the lion's mouth to see how many teeth he had, and he shut it to see how many fingers I had.

Customer – How the dickens do you open this tin of sardines?

Shopkeeper – There's full instructions inside the tin, sir.

Short-sighted golfer – Why didn't you tell me I was hitting a confounded toadstool?

Caddie – I never thought you would hit it, sir.

Customer – Are those eggs fresh?

Grocer – Fresh! Why, if I hadn't torn a leaf off the calendar too soon they wouldn't have been laid till tomorrow!

Terry – Are you superstitious?

Jerry – Not at all.

Terry – Well, lend me thirteen pounds.

Stage costumier – When are you going to pay me for those wigs you bought last year?

Actor – I'm an actor, not a prophet.

Old lady – I want a nice quiet dog that doesn't bite, bark or run about.

Dealer – Will you try a china one?

Ambitious young singer – And now that you've tested my voice, Professor, what d'you think it's best suited for?

Professor of music – A market stall!

Town boy (visiting cousin in country) – This stuff's just like grass.

Cousin – It is grass.

Town boy – No, it's not, because you don't have to keep off it.

First lodger (discussing new lodger) – He's either a political speaker or an actor.

Second lodger – What makes you think that?

First lodger – Didn't you see the way he ducked at dinner yesterday when you asked him if he'd have a tomato?

Grocer (to small boy applying for job as message-boy) – You ask high wages for a boy without experience.

Small boy – Well, sir, it's harder work when you don't know anything about it.

Customer – Do you exchange unsatisfactory goods?

Salesman – Certainly, sir.

Customer – Well, this is an overcoat I got here last year. I think your new style is much better.

Smith – Let me tell you, Brown, I've forgotten more than you ever knew.

Brown – I say, that's bad. Did you ever try tying a knot in your handkerchief?

Teacher – Can you give me a long sentence?

Pupil – No, but I'd like to!

Judge – And why do you think you should be let off this time?

Prisoner – Well, this is the fiftieth time I've been brought in, so I thought we might have a fiftieth anniversary celebration.

First burglar – If I can pick this lock, we can lay our hands on ten thousand pounds.

Second burglar – Well, see you don't break the blade of my pen-knife.

Man – In my job it's impossible to get a day's work.

Woman – How's that?

Man – Well, you see, I'm a night watchman by trade!

Customer – Didn't you snip off a little of my ear just now?

Barber – Yes, sir, a little bit, but not enough to affect your hearing!

Burglar (to partner who has just knocked a flower-pot over) – That's right, Bill. Deafen 'em so they can't hear us!

Artist – I've been working like a horse all day.

Friend – How?

Artist – I've been drawing a cart!

Terry – Someone told Jimmy that he could get his trousers pressed by letting a steam roller run over them.

Jerry – Well, what about it?

Terry – Jimmy forgot to take his pants off!

Landlady – How do you like your room, as a whole?

Lodger – As a hole, it is all right, but as a room it's rotten!

Sammy – Can you telephone from a submarine?

Sailor – Of course, anybody can tell a phone from a submarine!

Teacher – If I had ten potatoes to share equally among four boys, how would I do it?

Sidney – Mash them, sir.

Willie – Boo-hoo! I've lost the apple that teacher gave for the best boy in the class.

Kind man – Here's another; but how did you lose it?

Willie – I wasn't the best boy!

Johnny – My nerves are so bad that I cannot close my eyes at night.

Percy – Try boxing. After my first lesson, I couldn't open my eyes for three days.

Farmer – Catching my fish, eh?

Angler – Yes, I've just caught one of your big eels.

Farmer – Well, now you're going to catch one of my big toes.

Policeman – I'm looking for a small boy with only one eye.

Passer-by – Well, if he's very small, you'd better use both eyes, Constable.

Pat – That ten pound note you lent me yesterday was a fake one.

Mike – Well, didn't you say you wanted it bad?

Train guard – Keep your head inside the window there.

Passenger – Why?

Train guard – Because we don't want any of our bridges damaged.

Teacher – Can any boy tell me what nothing is?

Tommy – Yes, sir, it's what you gave me yesterday for minding your car.

Caddie (to player who has let his club slip from his hands about six times) – If you go on like this, you'll soon be champion of Britain.

Amateur – At golf?

Caddie – No, throwing the hammer!

Where do you put a criminal sheep?
Behind baas.

What do you get if you cross a werewolf with peanut butter?
A monster that sticks to the roof of your mouth!

Which farm animals talk too much?
Blah-blah-blacksheep.

What's got a screen and wobbles?
Jellyvision.

Visitor – What are you going to do when you grow up?

Burglar's son – Follow in my father's finger-prints.

Teacher – Aren't you sorry you hit Timmy under the chin? I'm sure it was a mistake.

Jimmy – Yes, miss; I meant to bash him on the nose.

First pickpocket – Here he comes now.

Second pickpocket – All right. You keep a watch on him while I take the watch off him.

Old man – Which is the quickest way to the hospital?

Constable – Poke me in the back with that stick again, and you'll soon find yourself there.

Teacher – There's only one trustworthy lad in the class.

Jones (in whisper) – That's me.

Teacher – Did you speak Jones?

Jones – No, sir.

Teacher – Would you like your son to learn the dead languages?

Smith – Certainly; he's going to be an undertaker.

Diner – Waiter, my bill should have been thirteen pounds, and you've made it fourteen

Waiter – Yes, sir. I thought you might be superstitious.

Angry man – I'll teach you to hit our cat with stones!

Tommy – I wish you would sir. I've had ten shots, and missed each time.

Customer – What! Four pounds for a shave? And such a shave, too! Why you've cut me three times.

Barber – Yessir! Three pounds for the shave, and one pound for the sticking-plasters.

Passer-by (to owner of antique car) – Engine trouble?

Owner – Well, I can't tell till I walk back and find it.

First kid – They tell me that in New York they have buildings twenty storeys high.

Second kid – My! What a time a kid could have sliding down the banisters!

Gent – Is the horse surefooted?

Horse dealer – Very! Why, he kicked me in the same place three times last week.

Teacher – Aren't you ashamed of yourself – hitting a smaller boy?

Jimmy – I'd rather be ashamed of hitting a smaller boy than sorry I hit a bigger one.

Boss – Look here, Tommy, I wish you wouldn't whistle at work.

Tommy – I'm not working. I'm only whistling.

First mechanic – Does the boss know this plane's crashed?

Second mechanic – He ought to; he's underneath!

Diner – Waiter, a little bird told me this coffee was not filtered.

Waiter – A little bird, sir?

Diner – Yes, a swallow.

Diner – I say, waiter, there's a dead fly in the soup.

Waiter – Ah, poor thing! It's the boiling that kills them, sir.

Briggs – Did you tell Jiggs that I had the biggest feet you had ever seen?

Griggs – No, I just said that if you took off your boots you would be half-undressed.

Motorist – Someone has stolen my car.

Cynical friend – These antique collectors will stop at nothing.

What do you get if you cross a ghost with a boy scout?
Someone who frightens old ladies across the road.

What happened when the boy monster met the girl monster?
It was love at first fright!

What's a ghost's favourite game?
Hide and shriek.

Suspicious character – What am I supposed to have stolen?
Policeman – A horse and van.
Suspicious character – All right, search me.

Hobbs – I'm thinking of raising turnips next year in my allotment. What's the best way?
Bloggs – Take hold of the tops and pull.

Teacher (pointing to the map) – Now, Plug, when you stand facing the north, you have on your right hand the great continent of Asia. What have you on your left hand?
Plug – A wart, but I can't help it, Teacher.

Old man – I want you to see to my piano. My son is learning to play the thing.
Workman – But I'm a carpenter, sir.
Old man – I know. I want you to nail the lid down.

Policeman (to man in stream) – Hey, you can't swim in there.
Man in stream – I know. That's why I'm calling for help.

Old man – Why are you continually throwing that coin in the air?
Small boy – Oh, I'm flipping it to see if I shall go to school or play truant, and sixty-eight times it has come down wrong.

Jim – I met Billy just now. He says you've fallen out with him.
Tim – He called me a fool.
Jim – How tactless! Just like him to blurt out the truth.

Railway passenger (shouting out of carriage window to porter) – Hi, there's a man in this carriage gone barmy! He says he's Napoleon.
Porter – Never mind. The next stop's Waterloo.

Hotel manager – Excuse me, sir, did you take a bath this morning?
Guest – No. Is there one missing?

Teashop domino player (to shortsighted opponent) – Here, you can't cheat me. That isn't a double five; you've got a currant stuck on it.

Small boy – Is that the sun or the moon up there?
Dimwit – Sorry, I don't know. I'm a stranger to this place.

Tom – That's an awful gash you have in your forehead.
Tim – Oh, it's next to nothing, next to nothing!

Horse dealer – This donkey will go twenty miles without stopping.
Buyer – But I only stay five miles away from here.

Villager – Are you painting those trees, sir?
Artist – I am; but it's no business of yours. Get on with your work instead of interrupting mine.
Villager – Well, my work is to chop them down. So you'd better hurry up with your painting.

Visitor (to prisoner in for life) – Congratulations, Spike! You've won a world cruise in that newspaper competition you entered!

First golfer (concluding fishing story) – And I'm telling you that fish was about as long as that last drive of yours.
Second golfer – Oh, I say, really!
First golfer – Yes, so I threw him back.

Driving instructor – Well, do you understand the car now?
Beginner – Perfectly! There's only one thing I should like to know. Do you put the water and the petrol in the same hole?

Employer – Mary, you are breaking more crockery than your wages will pay for! What's going to be done about I?
Maid – I don't know, madam. Maybe you could raise my wages.

Customer – What have you got in the shape of motor tyres?
Assistant – Children's hoops, lifebelts, quoits, curtain rings, CDs, and bicycle wheels!

Host (handing guest a cigar) – Now, that's something like a cigar!
Guest (after first few puffs) – Yes, but what is it?

Bobby (on visit from city to his uncle's farm) – My word, hasn't that cow a lovely coat?
Uncle – Yes, it's a Jersey.
Bobby – Oh, is it? I thought it was its skin.

Boss (finding office boy watching football match) – So this is your uncle's funeral, Tommy?
Tommy (after some quick thinking) – Looks like it, sir. He's the referee.

Boastful explorer – And there we stood – the tiger and myself in the thick of the jungle, face to face!
Listener – How terrible it must have been for both of you!

Smith – Where did you get that suit, old man? It fits you like a glove.
Friend – That's just why I don't like it. It should fit me like a suit.

American (gazing at the Forth Bridge) – Say, what's that bit of iron protruding over the waters there?
Scotsman – I've no idea. It wasn't there yesterday.

Landlady – I don't suppose you know what it means to starve?
Lodger – No, but I'm learning.

Visitor – And how old are you, my little man?
Young Freddie (indignantly) – I'm not old at all; I'm nearly new.

Film producer – In this scene you're blown up into the air, and caught by an aeroplane.
Film star – I see. But supposing the aeroplane isn't there?
Film producer – Oh, don't wait. Just come down again.

Black – They say that Smith is a terrible grumbler.
White – Yes, he's the kind of fellow who blames his hair for needing cutting.

Green – You're getting extravagant. Why did you tip the waiter five pounds?
Brown – Hush, man! He gave me ten pounds too much in change.

Uncle (sternly) – When I was a boy I was told that if I made faces like that my face would stay like it.
Nephew – Then why didn't you stop?

Bald man (in barber's chair) – Don't you think I should get some reduction? There's very little hair to cut.
Barber – Oh no, in your case we don't charge for cutting your hair. We charge for having to search for it.

Frenchman – Ah, so you have climbed the Matterhorn! That was a foot to be proud of.
Englishman – Pardon me, sir; you mean "feat".
Frenchman – So you climb it more than once, eh?

Professor Crumb – What struck you most at my lecture last night?
Professor Noodle – A bad egg that was meant for you.

What robbery is not dangerous?
A safe robbery!

Prospective purchaser of second-hand car – What's she like on hills?
Owner – Hills! Why, she's down them in a jiffy!

Tim – Say that I'm a fool again, and I'll knock your block off!
Billy – Consider it said again then!
Tim – Consider your block knocked off!

Second – Keep your eye on his left.
Battered boxer – I can't keep his left out of my eye.

Musician – Have you in stock a cylindrical flageolet?
Shop assistant – A what?
Musician – A thin whistle.

Mother – I hope your are sharing the scooter with Cyril?
Willie – Oh, yes. He has it going uphill, and I downhill.

Sergeant – When I say "one" stand to attention; at "two" jump in the air; and at "three" come down again.

Mum – Gracious me! Look at your face! Have you been fighting?
Dimples – Not me! The other boy was. I was only learning.

Professor (to student) – What are you laughing at? Me?
Student – Oh, no, sir!
Professor (absently) – Then what else is there in this room to laugh at?

Mother – I'll teach you to tie a kettle to the cat's tail!
Small boy – It wasn't our cat.
Mother – No, but it was our kettle.

Judge – You may as well just admit your guilt. This man recognises you as the burglar.
Burglar Bill – How could he recognise me? He had his head under the bedclothes all the time!

Lecturer (in village school) – Well children, what shall I talk to you about?
Small boy – About five minutes, sir.

Teacher – I've given you punishment exercises every day this week. What have you to say.
Pupil – Well, I'm glad this is Friday.

Auntie (to small boy at tea) – Why didn't you wash your hands, Harry?
Harry – I didn't think it mattered, seeing that we're having brown bread.

Father (to son) – Tom, go and fetch the old horse.
Tom – Why the old one, father?
Father – Wear out the old one first is my motto.
Tom – Well, Father, you fetch the horse.

Boss (as Jenkins comes in half an hour late) – Late again!
Jenkins – So am I!

Diner – Waiter, there's a fly at the bottom of my cup. What does it mean?
Waiter – Sorry, sir. I'm a waiter, not a fortune-teller.

First actor (speaking lines of play) – Psst! Are we alone?
Second actor – Yes, we certainly are. The last member of the audience has just gone.

First lawyer (to second lawyer) – Sir, you are the biggest ass I've ever seen.
Judge – Order, order gentlemen! You seem to forget that I am here.

Jones (to boy) – Could you direct me to the boarding-house called Pleasant View?
Boy – Yes, sir, it's just round the corner, facing the gasworks.

Courtier – Hail, O mighty King!
King – I can't. My job is to reign, and I am doing it.

Grocer – What was that woman complaining about?

Assistant – Because she had a long wait.

Grocer – Humph! Some people are never pleased. She was complaining about the short weight yesterday.

Butler – Yes, sir, Mr Smyth is at home. What name shall I give?

Visitor – Professor Gottfried von Vandersplinkenheimer.

Butler – Er . . . have you got a visiting card, sir?

Fussy diner (after altering his choice several times) – Yes, waiter, I'll have mutton chops and chip potatoes. And make the chops lean.

Fed-up waiter – Yes, sir. Which way, sir?

Mother – I am glad you are keeping quiet boys, while Dad's having his nap.

Bill – Yes, Mum, we're watching his cigar burn down to his fingers.

Centre-half – It's a coach we're needing.

Manager of the team – No! A hearse!

Falling man – Take this mirror, Joe! If I break it, I'll get seven years' bad luck!

Teacher – Now Smiffy, who discovered spots on the sun?

Smiffy – My mother!

Teacher – Really!

Smiffy – Yessir, when I had measles.

Customer – You said that this dog was fine for rats. Why, it won't even go near them!

Shopkeeper – Well, that's fine for the rats, isn't it?

Landlady (to visitor) – Good morning. Did you sleep well, sir?

Visitor – Not very well. I am not used to a three-season bed.

Landlady – Three-season?

Visitor – Yes, one that has no spring in it!

Sea cook – Ever been on a ship before?

New helper – Sure, I was a gunner in the Royal Navy.

Sea cook – Champion. Start right in and shell the peas.

Customer – You barbers always seem to have plenty of news.

Barber – Yes, sir, we always know what's in the 'air.

Newspaper editor (to visitor) – What is the best thing you have seen in my paper?

Visitor – Fish and chips.

Teacher – Your son spells atrociously.

Smiffy's dad – Splendid! That's a very difficult word to spell.

Captain – Have you cleaned the deck and burnished the brass?

Seaman – Ay, ay, sir, and I've swept the horizon with a telescope.

Pa – Failed again. You must be a wooden head.

Tommy – Yes, Pa, I'm afraid I'm a chip off the old block.

Patient (with large lump on his head) – I seem to have had a nasty blow on the head during the operation.

Nurse – Oh, that's all right; we ran short of anaesthetic, that's all.

Doctor – Now, Tommy, put your tongue out.

Tommy – No jolly fear. Ma gave me a telling off for doing that yesterday!

Stranger (pointing to cats round goalkeeper) – Are they the club's mascots?

Local supporter – No. The goalie is a fishmonger.

Diner – This lobster has only one leg.

Waiter – Yes, sir, lost it fighting.

Diner – Then take it away and bring me the winner.

DOCTOR, DOCTOR. I THINK YOU'RE A VAMPIRE!
Necks, please!

DOCTOR! I KEEP HEARING NUMBERS INSTEAD OF WORDS.
It must be something you eight!

WHAT FRUIT DO VAMPIRES LIKE BEST?
Blood oranges and necktarines.

DOCTOR, DOCTOR. I THINK I'M A BRIDGE.
What's come over you, man?
THREE BUSES, FOUR CARS AND A LORRY.

WHAT GOES ALONG THE WASHING LINE AT 100 MILES PER HOUR?
Honda pants!

Teacher – What is a zebra?
Bobby – A donkey wearing a football jersey.

Pierre- Bonjour!
Pat – What does that mean?
Pierre – Good day, in France.
Pat – Well, Hot Cross Buns.
Pierre – What does that mean?
Pat – Good Friday in England.

Barber – How shall I cut your hair, sir?
Customer – Off!

Terry – I'm awfully worried. I think I'm losing my memory.
Jerry – Oh, forget all about it!

Mother – Don't drink out of your saucer, Billy. Use your cup.
Billy – But the spoon sticks in my eye.

Visitor – Have you any brothers or sister?
Bobby – No. I'm all the children we've got.

Lady – Call your dog off! It will bite me.
Boy – Sorry but his name is Caesar (sieze her)!

Customer – Are these fish quite fresh?
Shopkeeper – Fresh? Why, they're still warm!

Passer-by – Had any bites?
Angler – Yes. One mosquito and a couple of gnats.

Jinks – Lend me a fiver for a week, old man?
Binks – Certainly. Who is the weak old man?

Brown – Take no notice of advertising slogans. I know a man who took the advice of one of them and got ten years in prison for forgery.
White – Which was that?
Brown – "Make money at home"!

Passenger – Do I take this train to Leeds?
Guard – No. Get in, and it will take you.

Tommy – Hello! What's the matter with your thumb?
Billy – I hit the wrong nail.

Cuddles – Sorry I stood on your feet.
Dimples – That's all right! I usually walk on them myself.

Teacher – So, your father is a vegetarian.
Tommy (proudly) – Yes, sir, as he has carrot red hair, a cauliflower ear, a beetroot face, and a fountain pen that leeks.

Bobby – I hear Willie is greatly troubled with noises in the head.
Nobby – Yes, it's the band on his hat.

Bill – So you've got back from your holiday. Any change?
Jim – Not a penny.

Passenger – Can you take a joke?
Taxi driver – Yes. Where do you want to go?

Teacher – Name three kinds of nuts.
Boy – Monkey nuts, chestnuts and forget-me-nots.

Dennis – What would you do if you were in my shoes?
Walter – Clean them.

Milly – Why does Arthur work as a baker?
Jilly – I suppose he kneads the dough.

Teacher – Tell me the largest island in the world.
Toots – Australia.
Teacher – Right. Now the smallest?
Toots – A brick in a puddle.

Doctor (answering call at midnight) – Well?
Caller – No, I'm ill.

Customer – A cake of soap, please.
Shopkeeper – Do you want it scented?
Customer – No, I'll take it with me now.

Hawker – Buy a paper barometer, madam; only a pound each.
Lady (after buying one) – How does it work?
Hawker – Just put it on the window-sill, and when it's wet you'll know it's raining.

Small boy (to crashed motorist) – Do it again mister; my little brother didn't see you!

Falling man – I'd like to get hold of the fool who sold me a knapsack instead of a parachute!

Sidney – Dad, what are the Russian Steppes?
Dad – Ask your sister. She knows all the new dances.

Soldier – Why do you tar your ships?
Sailor – Because you pitch your tents.

Assistant – This suit is very much worn, sir.
Mr Newrich – Well, give me something new. I don't want second-hand goods.

First lodger – I'll bet the new arrival is or has been an actor.
Second lodger – What makes you thinks so?
First lodger – Haven't you noticed the way he ducks when asked if he will have a tomato?

Customer – Waiter, this portion of roast chicken is very small.
Waiter – Yes, sir; but you wait and see how long it takes you to eat!

Doctor – What is the matter with you?
Patient – Pains in my joints. I can hardly raise my arms above my head, and it is just the same with my legs.

Doctor – Well, Mr Brown, are you feeling all right now?
Patient – Much better, doctor, but my breath is always coming in little short pants.
Doctor – Well, what do you expect it to come in – flared trousers?

Jones – I thought you hated the saxophone?
Bones – I do.
Jones – Then why did you buy your son one?
Bones – Because I hate the neighbours more.

Tourist (to policeman with extra large feet) – Can you tell me where Trafalgar Square is?
Policeman – Yes, I'm standing on it.
Tourist – No wonder I couldn't find it.

Dodgy Den – Hey, Ken, I think honesty is the best policy.
Crafty Ken – What for ?
Dodgy Den – You know that dog I pinched last night? Well, I tried to sell it, and nobody would give me more than ten pounds for it, so I took it back to the owner and got fifty pounds for it.

Artist – Yes, many a time my poor old mother implored me not to become an artist.
Critic – Don't worry, old man. You didn't.

Gent – What are you doing, barber? You're lathering my bald head.
Barber – Very sorry, sir. Force of habit. I used to whitewash ceilings before I worked here.

Artist – I'm proud of my paintings. I shall soon be able to give an exhibition of my work.
Critic – Well, take my tip and see that you don't get rheumatics through sitting on the cold pavement.

Electric company's clerk – You are not always bothered with poor light, are you?
Householder – Oh, no, not always.
Clerk – Ah, I thought not. It's only at certain times you notice it, eh?
Householder – Yes, after dark.

Diner (finally) – Anyhow, waiter, I won't eat such food. You'd better fetch the manager.
Waiter – That's no good, sir. He won't eat it.

First Cockney – Ever seen 'am growing?
Second Cockney – 'Am doesn't grow.
First Cockney – Ain't you never 'eard of an 'ambush?

Toots – Are you still looking for your dog?
Smiffy – Yes.
Toots – Why don't you put an advert in the paper?
Smiffy – What's the use? The dog can't read!

Dad – Where are you going?
Minnie – Oh, just for a stroll.
Dad – Then stroll about the lawn, and take the mower with you.

Fatty – May I have those three apples off the table?
Mother – Yes, certainly.
Fatty – Oh, that's all right, then. You see, I've already had them.

Brown – Did you go anywhere for your holiday last summer?
Jones – Yes, I went to Venice, and the beastly place was flooded.

Policeman – Lights out, no number plate, no licence, and doing sixty in a forty-mile-an-hour zone.
Motorist – While you're about it, I stole this car.

Teacher – Danny, will two go into one?
Danny – Yes, sir – two halves.

Magistrate – How is it that you managed to take the man's watch from his waistcoat pocket when it was secured by a patent safety chain?
Prisoner (with dignity) – Sorry, Your Worship, but my fee is fifty pounds for the full course of six lessons.

Manager – Henry, you wear a very old-fashioned coat in the office.
Henry – Yes, it is a bit out of date. I bought it the last time I got a rise.

Mistress – And, remember, we have breakfast at seven.
New cook – All right, madam; but if I ain't down, you needn't wait for me.

Teacher – You have a lot of history to make up now, Tommy. How long have you been absent?
Tommy – Since the French Revolution, sir.

Lady – Why didn't you come yesterday to mend my bell?
New workman – You must have been out when I called, madam. I rang three times and got no answer.

First burglar – What about the burglar alarm, Bill?
Second burglar – Oh, shove it in the sack. The bells might fetch a copper or two.

Guide – This is the battleaxe of Robert the Bruce.
Traveller – Is that so? It looks quite modern.
Guide – Well, it's had five new heads and seven new shafts since he used it.

Admiral – Captain, is there no way in which the ship may be saved?
Captain – None at all, sir. We are going to the bottom. But I would not worry about the ship, sir, if I were you, she is fully insured. You'd better find a lifebelt.

Magistrate – You are accused of stealing a chicken. Have you anything to say?

Thief – I only took it for a lark.

Magistrate – A lark! No resemblance whatever. Ten days!

Jim – Please, sir, can you change five pound note?

Old gentleman – Why, certainly.

Jim – Well, please change this one into a ten pound note.

Gordon – Gilbert's just told me I look like you.

Graham – Where is he? I'll punch his head.

Gordon – I've just punched his head.

Old man – What's the matter?

Youngster – Boo, hoo! I have lost a pound coin.

Old man- A pound does not go far nowadays.

Youngster – Mine did. It fell down the drain.

Sidney – Please, sir, Danny says he knows a baby that was fed on elephant's milk and it gained ten pounds a day.

Teacher (severely) – Danny, you should not tell lies. Whose baby was it?

Danny – The elephant's, sir.

Showman – This man can pick up a needle with his toes.

Disgusted visitor – That's nothing. I've often picked up carpet tacks with my heels.

Bystander – That's nothing. I pick up five nails every time I lift my foot.

Driver of car (going downhill) – The steering wheel's busted, the brakes won't act, but thank goodness the horn still toots.

Mike – Do you rise early?

Millie – Early? If I rose much earlier I'd meet myself going to bed.

Teacher – What is a mountain, Tommy?

Tommy – A great big lump of earth sloping straight upwards.

Mistress – Jane, I've told you over and over again I will have cleanliness; yet why is it I am always finding cobwebs on the drawing-room ceiling?

Maid – I think it must be the spiders, miss.

Jenny – Came in last night and fell against the piano.

Penny – Hurt yourself?

Jenny – No. I struck the soft pedal.

Customer (who has ordered a pancake half an hour previously) – Er . . . I say, will that pancake be long?

Waitress – No, sir, it'll be round.

Captain – Well, Private Smith, what did you have for dinner?

Private – Taters, sir.

Captain – What does he mean by taters, Sergeant?

Sergeant – It's only his ignorance; he means spuds.

Office boy – A young man called to see you, sir.

Clerk – What was he like? Tall or short?

Office boy – Both.

Clerk – What do you mean?

Office boy – Well, he was tall, and wanted to borrow fifty pounds.

Sailor – I joined the navy to see the world.

Gentleman – Did you see it?

Sailor – No, they put me in a submarine.

Teacher – Why are you so late for school this morning?

Johnny (breathless) – Please, sir, I dreamt I was at a football match that ended in a draw, and the referee ordered extra time to be played, so I stopped to see the finish.

School inspector- Can you tell me where Ben Nevis is?

Jackie – I couldn't tell you, sir. He's not at this school.

Smiffy – What have I learned today, Teacher?

Teacher – Why, that's a funny question to ask.

Smiffy – Well, they are sure to ask me when I get home.

Joe – I say, Bill, if it takes a man an hour to walk a mile, how long will it take a fly to go through a barrel of treacle?

Bill – I'm stuck.

Joe – So was the fly.

Smiffy (writing composition) – The streets of Venice are noiseless, for they are canals; boats called gorgonzolas take the place of cabs.

Delivery boy – Does Mrs Jack live here?

Lady – No, my boy. It must be a case of mistaken identity.

Delivery boy – No, Mrs; it's a case of lemonade.

Tommy (crying) – Mother, Johnny Jones hit me.

Mother – Well, don't come in here crying. Hit him back.

Tommy – I did, I hit him back first.

Jones – Did you settle with Brown about his dog barking at night?

Smith – Oh, yes.

Jones – Buried the hatchet?

Smith – No, buried the dog!

Smiffy's dad (to his son) – Don't stand there walking about. Get up and sit down.

Teacher (to class in natural history) – What kind of birds are frequently kept in captivity?

Wilfrid – Jailbirds.

Impatient passenger – How long is the next train?

Porter – About three carriages.

Impatient passenger – Smart, ain't you?

Porter – No, I'm Jenkins; Smart's gone to dinner.

Mother – Jimmy, you're a bad boy. You can just go to bed without your tea.

Jimmy – But, Mother, what about the medicine I've got to take after meals?

First prisoner – How often have you been in prison?

Second prisoner – This is the first time.

First prisoner – Huh, you're lucky.

Second prisoner – I don't know so much about that – I'm here for life.

Jones – You remember that watch I lost five years ago?

Smith – Yes.

Jones – Well, yesterday I put on a waistcoat I had not worn for years, and what do you think I found in the pocket?

Smith – Your watch – splendid.

Jones – No, I found the hole it must have dropped through.

Old man – Could you tell me where the other side of the street is, my boy?

Boy – Over there, sir.

Old man – That's funny. Another boy told me it was over here.

Old man- Oh, so you've fallen down and hurt your leg, have you, my poor little man?

Cheeky boy – Well, did you think I'd fallen up and bashed my head against a cloud?

Smith – Airmen can do anything birds can do.

Brown – I'd like to see one sleeping in a tree standing on one foot.

Teacher – What is a cannibal?

Smiffy – A thing shot out of a cannon.

Judge – Did you steal the tortoise?
Lazy Len – No, sir, it followed me home.

Professor's wife – You've got your hat on the wrong way round, dear.
Professor – Now, how do you know which way I am going?

Young boy (watching painter) – How many coats of paint do you give a door?
Painter – Two, my boy.
Young boy (brightly) – Then, if you give it three coats, it would be an overcoat.
Painter – Yes, my lad, and a waste coat.

Captain (to new sailor) – Now what is the first thing you do when you fall into the sea?
New sailor – Get wet.

Warder – Owing to economy, three of us are being sacked tonight.
Prisoner – Any chance of it spreading to our department?

Old man – I dropped a shilling. If you find it give it back to me; if you don't, keep it.

Teacher – Now, then, Dennis, what countries are on the other side of the Atlantic?
Dennis – Er . . . it all depends what side you stand on, sir.

Bill – That a nasty hole you have in your umbrella.
Tom – Oh, that? I put that hole there purposely.
Bill – Whatever for?
Tom – So that I can see when it's stopped raining.

Visitor – Are there many fools in this part of the world, my lad?
Dimwit – Not as I know of, sir. Why? Do you feel a bit lonesome like?

Teacher (giving a lesson on Norsemen) – Smiffy, what is a Norseman?
Smiffy – A man who rides an 'orse.

Examining admiral (to naval candidate) – Now mention three great admirals.
Candidate – Drake, Nelson, and – I beg your pardon, sir? I didn't quite catch your name.

Teacher – What's this? You haven't put answers to any of these sums.
Sandy – No, sir, I left that part out purposely. You see, I always get them wrong.

Teacher – What is a man called who speaks and nobody listens to him?
Dennis – A teacher, sir.

A family went away for the holidays and left a note on the door saying, "Don't leave anything."
When they came home they found a note saying. "We haven't! – Burglar Bill and Co."

Customer – Give me another half-pound of your insect powder.
Shopkeeper – I'm glad you like it, sir. Good stuff, isn't it?
Customer – Yes. I've made a cockroach very ill, and if I give him another half-pound I think he'll die.

Teacher – What are gladiators?
Minnie – Please, sir, things that give out heat.

Dad – If you want to get on, you must have push and go, my boy.
Son – I've got it. The boss gave me the push this morning, and I'm going on Saturday.

McWhirter – What do you do with your old razor blades, McHaggis?
McHaggis – I throw them on the lawn, and the grass comes up already cut.

Tom – I heard something this morning that opened my eyes.
Ted – Oh! What was it?
Tom – An alarm clock.

What games do horses like playing best?
Stable tennis!

What do you call a chicken in a shell suit?
An egg.

Which famous painter always had a cold?
Van cough.

What do you call an inquisitive pig?
A nosey porker.

Doctor, doctor! I keep seeing into the future!
When did this first happen?
Next Thursday!

When is the cheapest time to phone a friend?
When they're out.

What happened to the man who stole a calendar?
He got twelve months.

Tom – Do you see all those blackbirds up in that tree?
Johnny – Yes.
Tom – Well, my dad has a name for every one.
Johnny – What! Every one?
Tom – Yes. Crows!

Charles – My dad bought a horse and trap for ten pounds.
Bertie – You sure?
Charles – Yes. A clothes-horse and mouse-trap!

Nervous passenger – Oh, I've pulled the communication cord by mistake! What shall I do? I'll be fined £100.
Crafty Ken – Give me £50 and I'll pretend to have a fit.

Two boys were fighting in the pouring rain. They fought till one boy got the other on his back and held him there.
First boy – Will you give up?
Second boy – Never.
First boy – Then will you get on top a while; I'm getting wet through.

Airman – If you use your parachute, count ten before you pull the cord.
Passenger – B-b-but, I s-s-s-stutter w-w-when I'm afraid.

Teacher – Tommy, do you know the present tense of knew?
Tommy – No, sir.
Teacher – Correct.

Passenger (in taxi) – There's only one thing I worry about in a car, and that's the brakes.
Taxi driver – Then you've nothing to worry about, sir; this car hasn't got any.

Doctor – Well, how are you this morning, Harry?
Harry the hypochondriac (mournfully) – Oh, I'm so ill I've been looking in the papers all morning to see if my death was in.

Little boy (to capsized canoeist) – While you're there, mister, you might have a look at my hook and see if the worm's still on.

Cannibal king – What did I have for dinner?
Waiter – Grilled chauffeur.
Cannibal king – What did the servants have?
Waiter – Pneumatic tyre in oil and vinegar.

Agent – You want your office furniture insured against theft?
Manager – Yes, all except the clock; everybody watches it.

Mother – Have you given the goldfish some fresh water this morning, Smiffy?
Smiffy – No, Mum, they haven't drunk the water I gave them last week.

Kevin – What's the lump on your head for?
Colin – My father's portrait fell on my head.
Kevin – Hah! Struck by the family likeness!

Magistrate – So this is the fourth person you have knocked down this month.
Speed fiend – Excuse me, it's the third. One of them was the same person twice.

Angry grocer – What do you mean by throwing that brick at my window?
Little boy – How was I to know the wasp was on the inside?

Customer – I want a hat to suit my head.
Milliner – Try a soft one, sir.

Farmer (roused at one a.m.) – Well, what's the matter?
Tramp – Sorry to trouble you, but I'm sleeping in your barn tonight, and I want to be wakened at seven sharp.

First boy – I'll bet I've got a brother bigger than yours.
Second boy – I'll bet you haven't. I've got one twelve feet high.
First boy – I don't believe you.
Second boy – Well, you see, I've two half-brothers each six feet tall.

Prospective tenant – Does the chimney always smoke like this?
Landlord – Oh, no; only when the fire's on.

Billy – My father gets a warm reception wherever he goes.
Tommy – He must be very popular.
Billy – No, it's not that. You see, he's a fireman.

Bore – Yes, cricket is a frightfully dangerous game. Why, last year I was knocked senseless while playing in bat.
Bored listener – When do you expect to recover?

Nature study teacher – Remember, you reap what you sow. If you sow poppy seed you get poppies, and grass seed you get grass, and so on.
Pupil – If I sow bird seed will I get a canary, please? I'm wanting one.

Auntie – What are you going to be when you grow up?
Nephew – I'm going to be an Arctic explorer. And now, will you give me five pounds?
Auntie – Gracious! What do you want five pounds for?
Nephew – I want to get five ice-creams and find out how much cold I can stand.

Doctor – How did you break your leg?
Patient – I threw a cigarette down a manhole and stood on it.

Shoeshine boy – My father works on a farm, sir.
Mr Jones – That's rather funny. He makes hay while the son shines!

Smiffy was reading a book, and was astounded at the description of the hero. It said he had a brass neck, a lantern jaw, his eyes flashed fire, and he had nerves of steel.
"Amazing," said Smiffy, "they must feed him on screwnails and matches."

Amateur gardener – What's the best way to grow potatoes?
Dimwit – Plant onions above them. The onion will make the potatoes' eyes water, and that'll save you a lot of work with the watering-can.

Patient – Doctor, while I was playing a game last night, spots kept coming before my eyes.
Doctor – What game were you playing?
Patient – Dominoes.

"The thing for you to do," said the doctor to the man who was suffering from nervousness, "is to stop thinking about yourself and bury yourself in your work."
"Oh dear!" exclaimed the patient. "I'm a grave digger!"

Teacher – What is torture?
Roger – Death in instalments, sir.

Lodger – Only cheese for lunch?
Landlady – Yes. The cutlets caught fire and it spread to the apple tart, so I had to use the soup to put it out.

Teacher – Tommy, give me a sentence containing the phrase "chop and change".
Tommy – The waiter brought the chop and change.

Auntie – What's that lump on your head, Georgie? Been fighting again?
Georgie – No, that was an accident.
Auntie – How?
Georgie – Well, I was sitting on Jimmy Brown's chest, and I forgot to hold his feet.

A man was being shown around a carpenter's shop. "By the way," he remarked, picking up a plank, "what are these holes in this wood?"

"Those are knot holes," explained the carpenter.

"They are holes," insisted the other angrily. "Do you think I don't know a hole when I see one?"

Danny – Does your watch tell you the time?

Smiffy – No; I have to look at it.

Man – Boy, where does your father work?

Boy – At the zoo?

Man – What doing?

Boy – Sandpapering elephants down to greyhounds.

Old man (to bricklayer) – Did your fall hurt you?

Bricklayer – No, it was the sudden stop that was most painful.

"You idiot!" said the teacher. "Write 'I have gone' fifty times on the board. Perhaps that will teach you not to use 'I have went'."

When the teacher came back some time later he found the following note: "Please, teacher, I have written 'I have gone' fifty times, and I have went home."

Old sailor – How did that new cabin boy do last trip?

His friend – Clumsy young hound! He broke all the saucers, and we had to drink out of the cups.

Customer (to barber who has accidentally clipped his ear) – Say, what do you think you're doing – fretwork?

Leader of band – Hush, man! Doesn't your music say "rest"?

New drummer – Sure! But I'm not a bit tired yet.

Nature lover (gazing at tree) – Oh, great oak tree, if you could only speak, what would you say to me?

Gardener – If you please, sir, it would say it was a sycamore, not an oak.

John – Stop rubbing your hands like that. The weather isn't cold.

Jim – I'm not trying to warm the weather – I'm trying to warm my hands.

Teacher (to Jock) – What do two and two make?

Jock (keen football fan) – Please, miss, a draw.

Prison chaplain – So you were a musician, were you? Well, I'm afraid we won't be able to give you much comfort in a musical way.

Prisoner – If you could only get me a file, sir, I think I could manage a few bars for myself.

Smith – It's going to rain, according to the radio.

Jones – I thought you didn't believe in the weather forecasts?

Smith – I didn't use to, but we've got a better set now.

Teacher – That boy of yours seems bright. He'll carve out a name for himself some day.

Father – He's done it already – on our new piano!

Stout man – You look as if there's been a famine.

Thin man – And you look as if you'd caused it.

Guest – These cakes are lovely, Mrs Brown. I don't know how many I've had.

Johnny Brown – You've had six!

Teacher – Give a sentence with the word "fascinate" in it.

Roger – My waistcoat has nine buttons, but I can only fascinate.

Polite but annoyed youngster (to man in front of him in cinema) – Please, sir, would you mind taking off your hat? I can't see the screen.
Man – Never mind, my boy; just you laugh when I do.

Locksmith – Morning, sir! I believe it was you who telephoned for the locksmith?
Smiffy's dad – Yes, that's right. Come inside, please. We've lost the key of our tin of sardines.

Burglar – Come on, let's figure up and see how much we made on that haul.
Mate – Oh, I'm tired. Let's wait and look in the morning papers.

A boastful American walked up to a British fruit seller's stall and picked up a large melon.
"Is that the largest apple you fellows can grow over here?" he asked.
"Put that grape down!" snapped the fruit seller.

Barber – And how do you find the razor?
Customer – Didn't know I was being shaved.
Barber – Very glad, I'm sure, sir.
Customer – I thought I was being sandpapered.

Optician – Weak eyes, have you? Now, sit here and tell me how many lines you can read on that chart.
'Erbert – Chart? I can't see any chart.

Admiral (testing new recruit) – What must a man be before he can be buried at sea with full naval honours?
Recruit – Dead, sir.

Mother – Sandy, take these matches back to the shop, and say they are no use. They won't light.
Sandy – But they will light, ma. I tried them all before you came in.

Motorist (with punctured tyre) – I'm looking for a puncture.
Yokel – Never mind. Someone will come along soon and lend you one.

Tim – Don't come down that ladder. I've taken it away.
Tom – Too late. I'm halfway down.

MacWhirter – These trousers seem to be rather baggy at the knees.
Tailor – Well, you see, sir, I used to make concertinas!

Optician – Has your little boy got used to his glasses?
Lady – I can't get him to wear them in the daytime, but I manage to slip them on when he goes to sleep.

Hotel guest – I tell you I won't have this room! I'm not going to pay good money for such a small room. You think that just because I am from the country ...
Bellboy – Step in, sir. This isn't your room. It's the lift.

Prisoner – Say, warder, when is the fun gonna start?
Warder – What do you mean, fun?
Prisoner – Why, the judge said that I was to be sent here for the time of my life.

Toots (to Plug with bandaged head) – What's wrong with your head, Plug?
Plug – Some water fell on it.
Toots – But surely that wouldn't hurt it?
Plug – No; but this water was in a jug.

Doctor – There's not many people live through this operation. Is there anything I can do for you before we begin?
Patient – Yes, get me my coat.

Teacher – You don't know what the word thief means? Well, if I were to put my hand in your pocket and take a pound away what would I be?
Smiffy – A conjurer, sir.

Gnock! Gnock!

Who's there?

Disguise.

Disguise who?

Disguise the limit.

Recruit – Shall I mark time with my feet, Sergeant?
Sergeant – Did you ever hear of marking item with your hands, you idiot?
Recruit – Well, I understand that clocks do, Sergeant.

Teacher – Give me a sentence with the word "centimetre" in it.
Wilfrid – My aunt arrived yesterday, and I was centimetre.

Old man – Your father is entirely bald, isn't he, Jack?
Jack – Yes, I am the only heir he has left.

Angry customer – I can't find words to express my feelings towards you.
Smart assistant – That's all right, sir. We sell dictionaries here.

The boss – Now, James, we've forgotten to get stamps.
Office boy – There, sir, aren't we a couple of thickheads!

Teacher – I once found a fossilised fish in a rock. What could be more wonderful than that?
Quick pupil – Please, sir, a ship in a current.

Terry – You still take your morning bath, I suppose?
Jerry – Never miss it. Sometimes I take it hot, sometimes I take it cold and when I'm in a hurry I take it for granted.

Fortune-teller (to football referee) – I see you as leader of a large crowd.
Referee (worried) – Have I got a good start?

Father (angrily) – Bobbie, didn't you hear me call you?
Bobbie – Yes, Father, but you always tell me not to answer back.

Parent – My son has many original ideas.
Teacher – Yes, especially in arithmetic.

Wilfrid – Do you know Francis?
Spotty – What Francis?
Wilfrid – Francis not far from England!

Bill – I had a lot of money left me yesterday.
Bob – Really! How was that?
Bill – Well, I had a hole in my pocket, and it fell out.

First wrecked motorist – I tell you I came round that corner in my car like a tortoise.
Second wrecked motorist – So that's why my car turned turtle.

Lady – Why is your little brother crying?
Jimmy – He isn't crying – he's been playing football with an onion.

Teacher – Billy, which is the more useful – the sun or the moon?
Smiffy – The moon.
Teacher – Why?
Smiffy – Because the moon comes out at night and gives us light, and the sun comes out in the daytime when we don't need it.

Little boy – I wish I was old enough to wash my own face.
Mother – Why?
Little boy – 'Cos I wouldn't wash it at all.

Diner – Waiter, there's a fly in my soup.
Waiter – Catch it yourself. I'm not a spider.

Mother – Johnny, Auntie won't kiss you with a dirty face like that.
Johnny – That's what I thought.

Dr Dosem – One dose to be taken after each meal.
Fatty – Yes, but where do I get the meals?

First pickpocket – Why are you reading a fashion magazine, Bill?
Second pickpocket – Well, if we're to do well in our profession we must know where pockets are worn.

Jim – I took all the prizes at the racing contest the other day.
Jack – Really?
Jim – Yes, with a camera.

Lazy Len – I had a fall last night which rendered me unconscious for six hours.
Weary Willie – Really! Where did you fall?
Lazy Len – I fell asleep.

Danny (trying to buy a dog) – No, I don't care for that fox terrier. His legs are too short.
Dog dealer – You couldn't have them any longer. They reach right down to the ground!

Old gent (to policeman blocking his view of the football match) – Can you play draughts? Because it's your turn to move.
Policeman – When I move I usually take a man with me.

Boss – Now, my boy, are you boss of this business or not ?
Office boy – No, sir.
Boss – Then don't talk like an idiot!

Jones – Can you give anyone something you haven't got?
Brown – Yes, a black eye.

Passer-by – What are you digging for?
Workman – Money.
Passer-by – And when do you expect to get it?
Workman – Pay-day.

Smiffy (after being given a detention) – I knew that note Danny wrote for me wouldn't fool Teacher. He only put one "g" in excuse.

Jimmy – How are you getting on at school, Johnny?
Johnny – First rate. I can wiggle my ears now, and stand on my hands without leaning against the wall.

Fran – What's the crowd looking at?
Dan – A man tried to cross the bridge.
Fran – Well, what about it?
Dan – There isn't any bridge.

Teacher – Well, Smiffy, can you tell me what chivalry is?
Smiffy – It's when you feel cold all over.

Buyer of rather thin cow – How much do you want for this cow?
Farmer – Thirty pounds.
Buyer – I asked the price, not the weight of it.

Teacher (at swimming class) – Danny, that's not a swallow dive.
Danny – Isn't it? Why, I thought I'd swallowed the whole pool.

Teacher – Give a sentence with the word "analyse" in it.
Billy – My sister Anna lies in bed till ten o'clock.

Talkative barber (about to lather customer for a shave) – Do you mind shutting your mouth?
Tired customer – No, do you?

Mac – Are you musical, Sandy?
Sandy – Am I musical? Why at the age of two I used to play on the linoleum.

Diner – Waiter, this steak is only half the size of the one I had yesterday.
Waiter – But you're not sitting beside the window today, sir.

Man – And how are the fish biting today boy?
Small boy (fishing) – With their mouths.
Man – I mean, how are they coming out.
Small boy – Head first, sir.

Binks – I hear Brown is travelling in gas ovens.
Jinks – Why? Can't he afford a car?

Foreman – Now, then, Jock, what about carrying up some more bricks?
Jock – I am not feeling very well, boss. I'm trembling all over.
Foreman – Very well, then – get busy with the sieve.

Terry – How is it you know all about the Smiths' private affairs?
Jerry – We looked after their parrot during the summer holidays.

A man dashed onto the quayside, threw his bag aboard the boat, and jumped on. "A narrow squeak!" he said. "Nearly missed it!"
"Sorry mate, " said a passenger. "The boat's just coming in."

Sergeant – What was all that noise you were making in the dormitory last night?
Private – I was only dragging Brown's trousers about the room, sir.
Sergeant – Surely that wouldn't make all that noise?
Private – But Brown was in them, sir.

Villager – It was 'ere that Catherine of Aragon was bitten by a mad dog.
Tourist – Tudor?
Villager – Yes, chewed 'er something 'orrible.

Grocer – You want a pound of ochre? Is it red ochre for cleaning brick?
Willie – No, it's tappy ochre – the stuff Mum makes the pudding with.

Mac – What is hand painting?
Geordie – I don't know.
Mac – Two lovely black eyes!

Teacher – What is space?
Smiffy – Space is nothing. I can't explain it, but I've got it in my head all right.

McTavish – I got this cup for running.
McNab – Oh! Who did you beat?
McTavish – The owner, four policemen, and a crowd of sixty men.

Tom – What is the most useful purpose of cow's hide?
Dick – Why, to make leather, of course.
Tom – No, to keep the cow together.

Old man – What are you crying for, my little man?
Billy – My b-big b-brother d-dropped a b-big b-box on his toe.
Old man – That surely is nothing to cry about. I should have thought that you would have laughed.
Billy – I did!

Inquisitive pedestrian – What is the matter, Constable?
Constable (fed up) – Bus ran over a cat.
Pedestrian – Was the cat in the road?
Constable – Oh, no, the bus chased it up a lamppost.

Employer – I'll pay you one hundred pounds a week, starting now, and in three months I'll raise your salary to three hundred pounds a week.
Applicant – Righto! I'll look in again in three months.

Diner – Waiter, bring me a knife for the butter.
Waiter – Very good, sir.
Diner – Oh, and a revolver for the cheese.

Smiffy's mum – Did Fatty enjoy the party?
Fatty's mum – I think so. He wasn't hungry again till five o'clock next day.

Customer – Do you make life-size enlargements from photographs?
Photographer – Yes, sir. That's one of our specialities.
Customer – Well, will you do this for me? It's a snap I took of a whale.

Gnock! Gnock!

Who's there?

Disk.

Disk who?

Disk is a recorded message,

please leave your message

after the beep.

Teacher (giving astronomy lesson) – Now, Bobby, give me the names of some stars.
Bobby (brightly) – Football or film, sir?

Jimmy – How are you getting on at your work, Jock?
Jock – Fine. I've got five men under me now.
Jimmy – Really?
Jock – Yes, I work upstairs.

Old man – Why is the railway station so far from the village?
Smiffy – I don't know, sir, unless it's so that it's near the railway line.

Old man – You mustn't say, "I ain't going"; you must say "I am not going," "he is not going," "we are not going," "they are not going."
Little boy – Ain't nobody going!?

Dud footballer – I was transferred for ten thousand, and now fifty thousand won't buy me.
Manager – And I'm one of the fifty thousand.

Aunt (listening to bird singing) – Listen, Danny! Don't you wish you were able to sing like a robin?
Danny – I'd sooner be able to squirt water through my nose like an elephant.

Doctor – Did you open both windows in your room, as I told you to?
Patient – Well, not exactly. You see, there is only one window, so I opened it twice.

Salesman – Yes, sir, this car is so economical to run that it simply pays for itself.
Buyer – Then send it along when it has.

Diner – Do you see that waiter over there? They call him "Tomorrow".
Friend – Why?
Diner – Because he never comes.

Teacher – What animals eat less than others?
Wee Jean – Moths, because they only eat holes in things.

Young man – How did you lose your hair?
Bald man – Worry.
Young man – What did you worry about?
Bald man – Losing my hair.

Sandy – Did you call me a blockhead?
Jock – No, I told you to keep your hat on; there are woodpeckers flying around!

Plug – What's the weather like, Smiffy?
Smiffy – I couldn't say yet; it's too foggy.

Prisoner (to warder) – You'd better have a key made for me. I never know what time I'll be in at night.

First salesman – Your firm can't hold a candle to mine.
Second salesman – What is your firm?
First salesman – Oh, we manufacture gunpowder.

Fussy old man (as radio announcer sneezes) – There! That's how colds spread.

Teacher (pointing to a sweet wrapper on the floor) – Wilfrid, is this yours?
Wilfrid – Not at all, sir. You saw it first.

Waiter – Eggs, sir? How will you have them cooked?
Customer – I don't mind. Any difference in the price?
Waiter – None whatever, sir.
Customer – Then have them cooked on a large rasher of ham.

Plug (sarcastically to Wilfrid) – You are so short that if you pulled up your socks you'd be blind-folded!

Weary Willie – What are you doing now?
Tired Tim – Imaginative work.
Weary Willie – What is imaginative work like?
Tired Tim – Imagining what work is like.

Youngster – Grandpa, can I ask you a question?
Grandpa – Yes. What is it?
Youngster – Did you comb your hair with a razor?

First workman – Hard lines on Jock being shortsighted, isn't it?
Second workman – Why? You don't need good eyesight for this job.
First workman – But he can't see when the foreman isn't looking, so he has to keep on working all the time.

Foreman (to workman on ladder) – Mind you don't fall.
Workman – That's all right. I'm holding on.
Foreman – I don't mean fall down; I mean fall asleep.

Benny – Hello, Roger, have you come back for something you've forgotten?
Roger – No, I've come back for something I've remembered.

Teacher – Toots, put the word "social" in a sentence.
Toots – Dennis says he'll be glad when the holidays come, and social I!

Magistrate (to offender) – The constable says you put out your left hand and turned to the right.
Offender – Yes. You see, I'm left-handed.

Snooty (at football match) – I could kick myself for missing that penalty.
Scrapper – You'd better let me do it; you might miss again.

Teacher – Tell me, Dennis, who first invented underground tunnels?
Dennis – The worms, sir.

Teacher – Now, Danny, do this subtraction mentally. Six of your friends went to the river, but two had been told not to go into the water. Now tell me how many bathed?
Danny (promptly) – Six, sir.

Foreman – What's all the arguing about down the road?
Labourer – Why, the bloke driving the steamroller wants us to call him "chauffeur".

Mum – Goodness, Minnie, where's the canary?
Minnie – I dunno, Mum. It was there when I started cleaning its cage with the vacuum cleaner.

Pedestrian – Hi, up there! You dropped a brick that nearly hit me on the head.
Workman – All right, you can keep it. I've got plenty up here.

Election candidate – Really, gentlemen. With all this uproar, I can hardly hear myself speak.
Critic – Well, cheer up! You ain't missing much!

Uncle – Are you able to keep your position in class?
Smiffy – Certainly! I started at the bottom, and no one has been able to take my place from me.

Old lady (to street musician) – Do you always play by ear?
Musician – Yes, lady, 'ere or 'ereabouts.

Merchant – Here, you told me this safe was burglar-proof, and I found it cracked and the contents stolen.
Agent – Well, isn't that proof you had burglars?

Customer – Are you sure your milk is pure?
Milkman – Oh, yes. Every drop of water we put in is filtered.

Roger – How much will it cost to take me and my luggage right to my door?
Taxi driver – Five pounds. The luggage goes for nothing.
Roger – Right! Take my luggage and I'll walk.

Teacher (to Toots who is laughing) – What are you laughing at?
Toots – Nothing, sir.
Teacher – Then why are you laughing?
Toots – I can't help it sir. I've got on a new shirt, and it tickles me.

Diner (who has had a long wait) – I suppose I will sit here till I starve?
Waiter – Hardly that sir. We close at eleven.

Tobacconist – Try these cigars, sir. You can't get better.
Customer – I know. I had one last week, and I'm still ill.

Jimmy – Who cut your hair, Jock?
Jock – Father did, but he couldn't find the scissors, and the bread knife was a bit blunt.

Sidney – That kid lives in a sweet shop. Isn't he lucky?
Wilfrid – Rather! That's what you call "Home, sweet home".

First shipwrecked sailor – I say, where are we?
Second shipwrecked sailor – I don't know. I'm a stranger here myself.

Roger (in butcher's shop) – I suppose you have joints to suit everybody's pocket?
Butcher – Yes, my man, I have.
Roger – Well, what have you got to suit an empty pocket.
Butcher – The cold shoulder.

Teacher – Now Smiffy, what do we get from India?
Smiffy – I know: India-gestion!

Traveller (on spotting a bad-tempered-looking dog) – What's the matter with that dog?
Rustic – Laziness.
Traveller – How's that?
Rustic – He's sitting on a thistle, and he's too lazy to get off.

Waiter – Thank you very much, sir.
Gent – What do you mean? I haven't given you anything.
Waiter – No, sir, but I had bet a fiver with another man that you wouldn't.

Old man – What are you digging for, Johnny?
Johnny – Lemonade. Teacher says that minerals are found in the earth.

Spotty – I know something that doesn't weigh an ounce yet I'm certain you couldn't hold it for ten minutes.
'Erbert – What's that?
Spotty – Your breath.

Judge – Have you anything to say before I sentence you?
Prisoner – No. Get it over quickly, guv'nor, or I won't be at the jail by dinner time.

Visitor (to local) – It's been glorious weather here since I came. Doesn't it ever rain here?
Boastful local – Rain? Why, there's frogs in this town over five years old that ain't learned to swim yet.

Stage manager – You handle millions of pounds in this play. Try to look as if you were used to it.
Hard-up actor – I see. Could you let me have fifty pounds to rehearse with?

Customer (to shoemaker) – What I complain of in these boots is that the soles are too thick.
Shoemaker – Oh, just put on the boots and the objection will gradually wear away.

Stage manager – You received a tremendous ovation. They're still clapping. What did you say?
Actor – I told them I would not go on with my act until they quietened down.

New tenant – The roof is so bad that it rains on my head. How long is this going to continue?
Landlord – What do you think I am – a weather prophet?

Roger – Look, the man behind has been looking for a pound coin for ages.
Dennis – How do you know it was a pound coin?
Roger – I picked it up.

Jock – I have an awful cold in my head.
Tom – Well, that's better than nothing.

Scene-shifter (called in at the last moment to take the place of an actor who has not turned up) – The police have discovered everything, my lord, and are at the gate.
The wicked earl – 'Tis false, knave! 'Tis false!
Scene-shifter – All right, go and ask the manager yourself. 'E told me to say it.

Gamekeeper – Now, you young rascal, I've caught you. You weren't fishing with a permit, I bet.
Roger – No, sir. I was fishing with a worm.

Professor – Now, Jenkins, what is your opinion on this point?
Jenkins (nervously) – The same as yours, sir.

Customer – Let me see. How much do you want for that dog?
Dealer – Forty pounds.
Customer – I thought you said thirty yesterday?
Dealer – Yes, but he swallowed a ten pound note last night.

Doctor (to patient) – It's nothing to worry about. Just a little boil on the back of your neck. But you must keep your eye on it.

Manager – Why do you keep saying "Bah!" while you're acting?
Villain – Well, you see, I'm the black sheep of the family.

Sam – I caught a snake forty-eight inches long this morning.
Joe – Why do you always measure snakes by inches?
Sam – Because they haven't any feet.

Visitor – So they call this the Black Mountain? Is there any legend about it?
Guide (bored stiff) – Yes, sir. Two men went up it and never returned.
Visitor – Awful! Wonder what happened to them.
Guide – Oh, they went down the other side.

Teacher – Smiffy, how many letters are in "blackbird"?
Smiffy – Four letters?
Teacher – What?! You silly boy. Spell it please.
Smiffy – C-R-O-W?

Doctor – Can you tell me how you felt when you first took ill?
Dennis – Yes. Very pleased because I didn't have to go to school.

Actor – Did you see the audience cry when I played the death scene?
Critic – Yes, they knew you weren't really dead.

Jock – I once had a parrot for five years, and it never said a word.
Sandy – It must have been tongue-tied.
Jock – No, it was stuffed.

Old man – So you are an exporter?
Young man – Yes, the railway company sacked me.

Visitor – How is your new man getting on?
Farmer – Well, he broke two spade handles yesterday.
Visitor – Working hard?
Farmer – No, leaning on them.

Wilfrid – How would you like to drop two hundred feet with a parachute?
Plug – I'd hate to drop that far without one.

Teacher – What's wrong with your brother?
Pupil – Please, sir, he's broken his leg, and the doctor says it's one of those compound fractions.

Optician (testing Smiffy's eyesight) – Can you read that?
Smiffy – Yes, but I can't pronounce it!

District nurse – Do your twins make much noise?
New mum (stressed) – Not really. One makes so much racket that you can't hear the other.

Sergeant – You've only one shot out of ten on the target.
Recruit – It isn't my fault. The bullets left this end all right.

Teacher – Anybody know anything about alabaster?
Sidney – Yes, sir. He was the chap who outfoxed the forty thieves.

Fortune-teller – Do not worry, the dark clouds will soon roll by.
Old gent – Look here, I want to know my fortune, not the weather forecast.

Gent (who has fallen) – Help! Help! I've broken my leg.
Shop assistant – Walking stick department, third floor, sir.

Motorist – My car will do ninety.
Friend – Per hour, per litre, or perhaps?

Foreman – I see you are coming earlier of late. You used to be behind before, now you're first at last.

Old lady (at first football match) – Why have they had that player framed?
Spectator – That's not a frame; that's the goal.

Sergeant – If you could only shoot as well as you can eat you'd be OK.
Recruit – Well, I've been practising eating for twenty-six years, but I've only had this gun a fortnight.

Teacher – Strange as it may seem, quite a number of flowers have the prefix "dog". For instance, the dog-rose and the dog-violet. Can you name any more, 'Erbert?
'Erbert – Yes, Teacher, the collie-flower.

Host (to guest) – Would you like to sit on my right hand at supper?
Guest – I don't mind at all. But can you eat all right with your left?

Indignant householder (holding up a dead cat) – Here, constable, look what I found in my garden. What are you going to do about it?
Constable – Well, you know the law. If it's not claimed in six months it's yours.

Sandy – Lend me ten pounds.
Jock – Can't. I've only got eight pounds.
Sandy – Well, lend me that, and owe me two pounds.

Chairman (at concert) – Miss Screecher will now sing, "Had I the wings of a dove I'd flee."
Jimmy (nudging his dad) – Dad, what kind of a thing is a dove-eyed flea?

Salesman – These shoes are the finest quality. They will last a lifetime.
Smiffy – Then I'll have two pairs.

Country greyhound (as hare runs past) – That's a big hare.
Town greyhound – That's not a real hare. A real one has wheels and runs on a line.

Two motorists met in a narrow lane, which was too narrow to allow two cars to pass at the same time. Neither would go back until one shouted, "I never go back for a fool!"
The other said, "I do!" and he backed his car.

Professor – What is the result when a patient's temperature gets dangerously low?
Student doctor – Why . . . er . . . he gets cold feet!

Teacher – It is well known that heat expands and cold contracts. Give me an example of this.
Danny – Please, sir, holidays. In summer they last six weeks, but in winter only two.

Teacher – Tell me, Dennis, what is silence?
Dennis – Something you don't hear when you listen.

Dad – Minnie, if you eat too much pudding you will be ill.
Minnie – All right, Dad, give me a piece more and send for the doctor.

Teacher – What is a primeval forest?
Tommy – A place where the hand of man has never set foot.

First motorist – How did you get on at the police court?
Second motorist – Fine.

Doctor – How did you get your nose smashed up like that?
Patient – Well, I had a terribly red nose, and when I put it through a hole in the boiler for a sniff of fresh air the man with the hammer mistook it for a red-hot rivet.

Toots – Where are you going, Sidney?
Sidney – I'm not going anywhere, Toots
Toots – Yes, you are.
Sidney – No, I'm not. I'm coming back.

Teacher – Give me a sentence using the word "miniature".
Dennis – The miniature asleep you begin snoring.

Teacher – Now I have an impression in my head. Can any of you children tell me what an impression is?
Dennis – Yes, sir. An impression is a dent in a soft place.

Traveller (with hours to wait at small country station) – Any cinema here, or billiards hall, or library?
Railway porter – No, nothing like that here.
Traveller – Well, how do you spend the evenings?
Railway porter – We go down to the village store. They've just got a new bacon slicer – it's wonderful!

Father – If you want a thing done well you must do it yourself.
Wee Jock – How about a hair-cut?

Tim – Look there's Giles Miles the actor.
Jim – Does he act tragedy or comedy?
Tim – Both. He's tragic in comedy, and comic in tragedy.

Sandy – I work in a shirt factory.
Mac – Well, why are you not working today?
Sandy – Because we are making night-shirts.

Teacher – What king is said to have never smiled again?
Sidney – Charles I. After his execution.

Jim – Did you ever feel that the whole world was against you?
Tim – Yes, this morning when I slipped and fell on the pavement.

Bill (in new car) – I passed a car going at ninety miles an hour the other day.
Bob – You must have been going fast.
Bill – I wasn't. I was going the other way.

Young boy – Dad, what's a family tie?
Dad – Mine. Every time I want it one of your brothers is wearing it.

Theatre producer – Couldn't the villain shoot himself instead of taking poison?
Writer – Why?
Theatre producer – Well, the bang would wake the audience up.

Diner – Hey, waiter, there's a fly in my soup.
Waiter – Well, you don't want me to jump in and rescue it, do you?

Clarke – You say your business is picking up. What is your job?
Sparke – Picking up wastepaper in the public park.

Landlady – Mary, the new lodger is a sword-swallower at the circus. Be sure to count the knives when you clear the table.

Drummer – I'm the fastest man in the world.
Runner – How do you make that out?
Drummer – Time flies, doesn't it?
Runner – So they say.
Drummer – Well, I beat time.

Policeman – Now then, what's your name?
Culprit – John Smith.
Policeman – I want your proper name!
Culprit – William Shakespeare.
Policeman – That's better. You can't pull that "Smith"' stuff on me!

Warder – There's talk of us getting our wages reduced.
Prisoner – Any chance of it spreading to our sentences?

Teacher – And now I have told you the uses of measures of length, Tommy, can you tell me anything which we buy by the metre?
Tommy – Yes, miss. Gas.

Mum – Our little Smiffy shows great determination.
Dad (proudly) – Yes?
Mum – Yes, indeed! He spent the whole day making soap bubbles and trying to pin one to the wall.

Teacher – Danny, you mustn't laugh like that in the classroom.
Danny – I didn't mean to do it. I was smiling, and all of a sudden the smile burst.

Terry – What did you give me that nasty look for?
Jerry – Well, you have a nasty look, but I didn't give it to you.

Teacher – Aren't you ashamed of yourself, being at the bottom of the class?
Smiffy – No, it's warmer near the radiator.

First boy – My dog went to the dog show, and got two firsts and a second and was highly commended.
Second boy – Well, my dog stayed at home and got two fights and a feed and was highly delighted.

Dougal – Sorry I'm late, sir. I slipped and sprained my ankle.
Teacher – Another lame excuse!

Teacher – Do you know, Billy, that a grasshopper is so strong that it can jump a hundred times its own length?
Billy – Why, that's nothing. I once saw a wasp lift a twelve-stone man two feet into the air.

Visitor to hospital – Have you been under an operation?
Patient – No, under a car.

Terry (during a quarrel) – Well, I'm not two-faced.
Jerry – No; if you were you wouldn't be wearing that one.

Captain – What is strategy in war?
Sergeant – Well, strategy is when you don't let the enemy discover you are out of ammunition, but keep firing on.

Barber – You say you've been here before for a shave? I don't remember your face.
Victim – Probably not. It's all healed up now.

Voice from radio – Will Mr John Brown, who is believed to be on a pleasure cruise, return home at once?

Mother – Dennis, didn't I tell you to count fifty before fighting with Walter?
Dennis – I am counting, mother. I'm just sitting on him to make sure he's here when I've finished.

Teacher – Name a popular general?
Pupil – General holiday.

Man (with very big feet) – I should like to see some boots that would fit me.
Assistant – So would I, sir.

Magistrate – Didn't I tell you I didn't want to see you here again?
Prisoner – Yes, but the policeman wouldn't believe that.

Maid – When shall I waken you, sir?
Absent-minded master – I'll ring when I want wakened.

Tourist – And is the chin-strap to keep the helmet on?
Policeman – No, mister, it's to rest the jaw after answering foolish questions.

Roger – I always do my hardest work before breakfast.
Dad – What's that?
Roger – Getting up.

Mother – Why don't you give your brother a bite of your apple?
Sandy – I've given him the seeds. He can plant them, and have a whole orchard to himself.

Teacher – Putting a tin tack in a teacher's chair is a stupid old joke.
Dennis – Yes, but it hasn't lost its point yet, sir.

Dad – Roger, I hear you had detention at school today. Why was that?
Roger – Teacher told us to write an essay on laziness, and I sent in a blank sheet.

Spectator – I'll be mighty surprised if that referee doesn't get into hot water after the match.
Country chap – Then you'll be surprised. He's going in the horse trough.

McHaggis – That new florist certainly believes in the slogan, "Say it with flowers".
McTaggart – Why?
McHaggis – Well, he sent me a bunch of forget-me-nots with my bill last week.

Sam – I thought my rich uncle would leave me some money, but all I got was a rotten old flowerpot.
Jim – That must have been a nasty jar.

Jones – Who was that man you just raised your hat to?
Bones – Oh, that was my barber. He sold me a bottle of hair restorer a month ago, and whenever I meet him I let him see what a fraud he is.

Dentist – Have you seen any small boys ring my bell and run away?
Policeman – They weren't small boys – they were grown-ups.

Sailor (on sinking ship) – Say, mate, give us a read of that book on How to Swim when you've finished with it!

Porter (cheerfully) – Miss the train, sir?
Passenger (sarcastically) – No. I didn't like the look of it, so I chased it out of the station.

Jim – I've got the sack, Tom. I dropped a brick, and it broke.
Tom – That's nothing to get the sack for.
Jim – But it broke on the foreman's head.

Teacher (explaining a hard sum to class) – Now, watch the board carefully, boys, and I'll run through it again.

Old man – Where did you catch that nice string of fish, my boy?
Boy – You go down that lane marked "Trespassers Will be Prosecuted", keep right on till you come to a field with the notice, "Beware of the Bull", go right across till you come to a stream where there's another notice saying "Fishing Forbidden", and there you are!

Dud golfer – Notice any improvements since last year?
Caddie – You've had your clubs cleaned, haven't you?

Joe (from the top of a high building) – How do I get down?
Bill – Same way as you went up.
Joe – No fear! I came up head first!

Diner – Waiter, take away this egg.
Waiter – What shall I do with it, sir?
Diner – Wring its neck!

Teacher – Stand up, John. Did you give Jack this black eye?
John – No sir; he had the eye – I simply blackened it for him.

Workman (after digging hole in ground) – Where shall I put this pile of earth I have left?
Foreman – Use your sense, man – dig another hole and put it in.

Teacher – What is the difference between "goose" and "geese"?
Minnie – Why, one "geese" is a "goose" and a whole lot of "gooses" are a "geese".

Shopkeeper (to boy assistant) – Now look what you've done. You've knocked the arm off the Duke of Wellington's statue.
Boy assistant – It doesn't matter. Knock his eye out too, and call him Nelson.

Roger – Those eggs I bought is no good.
Shopkeeper – Why, what's the matter with it?
Roger – I've dropped them on your step.

Office boy (about to ask for increase in wages) – I tell you I'm going to get a rise or know the reason why.
Friend (later) – Well, did you get your rise?
Office boy – N-no, but I know the reason why.

Judge – You tell me you have no present occupation. What did you do last?
Prisoner – Six months, your Honour.

Father – So you are president of your bicycle club. That's nice. Why did they choose you?
Jimmy – Well, you see, Dad, I'm the only one that has a bicycle.

Smiffy's dad – Would you be good enough to look after my car, please?
Mayor – Sir, I'm the mayor of the town!
Smiffy – That doesn't matter. You look honest enough.

Gunfighter – See that fellow? He's the best gunman in town, and he's never killed a man yet.
Stranger – How's that?
Gunfighter – Well, he shoots so fast the second bullet catches up with the first and pushes it out of the way.

Bill – How long did it take you to learn to roller-skate?
Bob – Oh, about a dozen sittings.

Old man (to small youngster fishing) – Did you catch all those fish by yourself?
Youngster – No, sir. I had a worm to help me.

Angry gentleman – Porter, call me a taxi!
Porter – Yes, sir, you're a taxi.

Walter – Say, Dennis, I can trace my ancestry way back through my family tree.
Dennis – Well, there are only two things that live in trees, birds and monkeys, and I don't see any feathers on you.

Jock – What sort of a boat would you take to shoot rapids?
Sandy – A gunboat.

Sergeant (on rifle range) – This new bullet will penetrate nearly two feet of solid wood, so remember to keep your heads down.

Mrs Green – Did the burglars waken you last night?
Mrs Brown – Oh, no! They took things very quietly.

Teacher – Why are you boys arguing?
Sidney – There's no argument, sir. We're in agreement. Fatty thinks I'm not going to give him half this chocolate bar – and I think the same.

Prisoner – What are you doing?
Reporter – I'm taking notes.
Prisoner – Umph! That's what brought me here.

Jack – Brown fell asleep in his bath this morning with the water running.
Jock – Did the bath overflow?
Jack – No; fortunately he sleeps with his mouth open.

Minnie – Dad, are you still growing?
Dad – No, my girl. What makes you ask?
Minnie – Because the top of your head is coming through your hair.

Old man – Can you direct me to the Bank of England?
Little boy – I'll tell you for a fiver.
Old man – Isn't that rather a lot?
Little boy – Well, bank directors are always well paid.

Visitor (listening to an old sailor's tall tales) – You say you killed a whale, how inhumane. What did you do with it?
Old sailor – Why, miss, we ate him.
Visitor – Really, how horrible! And what did you do with the bones?
Old sailor – We left them on the sides of our plates.

Father (to young son) – Where are you going, Jock?
Son – I'm going fishing, Dad.
Father – But what about school?
Son – There! I knew I'd forgotten something!

Prisoner 99 – I say, mate, when is your time up?
Prisoner 66 – In ten years' time.
Prisoner 99 – Well, I'm in for twenty. Will you post this letter for me when you get out?

First burglar – Any luck lately, mate?
Second burglar – None! Worked all night on a butcher's safe, and when I got it open I found it was a refrigerator.

Caller – Are you sure the manager is not in?
Dignified office boy – Do you doubt his word, sir?

Terry – You say your brother is a leading light in the cinema?
Jerry – Yes; he shows the people to their seats.

Prison visitor – And what sort of man will you be when you leave prison?
Prisoner – An old one!

Barber – Haircut, sir?
Sarcastic old man – No, part it in the middle, then do it up in a bun on top, and tie it with pink ribbons.

Mum – Eat your rice up, Minnie.
Minnie – Don't like rice.
Mum – Well, eat it and pretend you like it.
Minnie – Ah, I know! I'll pretend I've eaten it.

Mum – Dennis! Don't you dare shoot that arrow at Walter's stomach!
Dennis – But we're playing at William Tell, and he's swallowed the apple.

Dad – Who gave you that black eye, Dennis?
Dennis – Nobody. I had to fight for it.

Trainer (to boxer who is being continually hit) – Why don't you stop them lefts, Bill?
Bill – Well, none have passed me yet, have they?

Prospective employer – I advertised for a strong office boy. Do you think you'll suit?
Applicant – I guess so. To get here first I knocked twenty-four applicants down the stairs.

Terry (in café, examining bill) – What? Five pounds fifty! Look here, waiter, I had sardines on toast, not goldfish.

Diner – Waiter, I want some chicken. The younger it is the better.
Waiter – How about an egg, sir.

Terry – My uncle died of music on the brain.
Jerry – How's that?
Terry – A piano fell on his head.

A passenger in an aeroplane was far up in the sky when the pilot began to laugh hysterically.
Passenger – What's the joke?
Pilot – I'm thinking what they'll say at the asylum when they find out I have escaped!

Acrobat (on flying trapeze, to partner who is flying towards him with outstretched hands) – You'll have to excuse me a minute, old man; my back feels itchy.

Explorer (speaking on advance of civilisation) – In the past, the Eskimos used to eat candles.
Old lady (seriously) – And now I suppose they eat electric bulbs?

Film director – The lion will pursue you for a hundred yards; no farther, understand?
Actor – Yes, I do, but does the lion?

Officer (to new recruit during manoeuvres) – Hi! Do you realise you're exposing yourself to an imaginary enemy five hundred yards away?
Recruit – Yes, sir. But I'm standing behind an imaginary rock thirty feet high.

The village team were getting severely beaten on their own ground.
Visitor – Do you ever score any goals?
Local – Dunno. I've only watched them for two seasons.

Binks – I've a pair of golf socks.
Jinks – Golf socks?
Binks – Yes. There's eighteen holes in them.

Poet – So you think I ought to give up writing poetry?
Editor – No, you ought to begin.

Bill – What fish can't live in water?
Harry – I dunno.
Bill – Dead ones, of course.

Gnock! Gnock!

Who's there?

Dinah.

Dinah who?

Dinah shoot until you see the whites of their eyes.

Customer – Can you recommend this hair restorer?

Barber – Yes, I know a man who pulled out the cork with his teeth, and in twenty-four hours he had a moustache.

First cannibal – And what makes our Royal Highness so full of laughter?
Second cannibal – Oh, he must have swallowed that last gent's funny-bone.

Judge (to witness, for fifth time) – Did the bus run over the man?
Weary witness – No, the conductor leaned out and bit him as the bus passed by.

Visitor – So you own a pet store? Do you have any trouble in selling parrots?

Store owner – Oh no, they speak for themselves.

Why did you give up your position in the choir?
I was ill last Sunday, and didn't go, and after the service someone asked if the organ had been mended.

Mr White – Excuse me, sir, are you Mr Green?
Mr Brown – No, sir. I'm Mr Brown.
Mr White – A thousand pardons! You see, I'm colour-blind.

Boss – Has the foreman told you what to do?

New watchman – Yes; I've to wake him up when the boss comes.

Freddie – My father is a mounted policeman.
Visitor – Is that better than being a foot policeman?
Freddie – Course it is. If there is any trouble he can get away quicker.

Fireman – Hi, what are you going back for?
Rescued person – I just love sliding down this chute.

Pat – I'd sooner be in a collision than an explosion.

Mike – How's that?

Pat – Because in a collision there you are, but in an explosion, where the dickens are you?

Uncle – What's etiquette, Bobby?
Bobby – Oh, that's the noise you mustn't swallow your tea with when there's company.

Teacher – Tommy, why did the boy stand on the burning deck?
Tommy – Because it was too hot to sit down.

Plumber (to applicant) – Got any references?

Boy – Yes, but I left them at home.

Plumber – You'll do.

Jack – I've never seen a dog marked like yours before, Bobby!
Bobby – Well, Dad is an artist, and he never looks where he wipes his brush.

Doctor – What you need is an iron tonic to sharpen your appetite. By the way, what is your profession?
Patient – I'm a sword-swallower at a circus.

Politician (at a party rally) – My friends, if we were to turn and look ourselves squarely in the face, what should we find we needed most?

Voice from the crowd – A rubber neck!

Mr Smith – Your son threw a potato at me.
Mr Jones – Did it hit you?
Mr Smith – No.
Mr Jones – Then it wasn't my son.

Teacher – What are weights and measures?
Smart boy – Waits are people who sing carols round this time, and measures are what father takes to stop them.

Brown – Where have I seen your face before?
Stranger – Same place as you see it now.

Teacher – Johnny, your mouth is open.
Johnny – Yes, I know; I opened it.

Boss (to office boy) – Why is it that every time I come into the office I find you reading a book?
Office boy – Because you wear rubber soles.

Office boy (to employer) – Can I take a day off, sir?
Employer – Yes; off that calendar.

Damaged boxer – Am I doing him any damage?
Second – No, but swing your arms and make a draught. It might give him a cold.

Jim (to Bill who has already been asked the question fifteen times) – Who gave you that black eye?
Bill – No one. I was looking at a football match through a hole and my eye got sunburnt.

Jim – Gracious me! Look at your face! Have you been fighting?
Bill – Not me. The other bloke was; I was only learning.

Mother – Billy, why is the baby crying like that?
Billy – There was a naughty fly biting him on the head, so I killed it with my spade.

Foreman – There goes Mr Twister. He twists so much that if he swallowed a nail it would become a corkscrew.

Jimmy (as his mother dishes out the Christmas pudding) – Is that big bit of pudding for Mary?
Mother – No, it's for you.
Jimmy – Crumbs, what a tiny bit!

Mother – If you eat any more plum pudding, Billy you'll burst.
Billy – Pass over the dish then, and stand out of the way.

Two boys were passing a ruined castle on Christmas Eve.
Darren – They s-say them castles a-are haunted. A-are you s-scared of g-ghosts?
Derek – N-n-no.
Darren – N-n-neither am I.

Teacher – What are weights and measures?
Smart boy – Waits are people who sing carols round this time, and measures are what father takes to stop them.

Burglar (caught in cupboard) – If you p-please, sir, I've called for my Christmas box.
Bashem Billy (drawing on his boxing gloves) – Righto! Come out here and get it!

Kevin (to uncle who has just been thrown from his horse) – Uncle Dave, has your horse thrown you?
Uncle Dave – No. Just as he kicked up his hind legs, I gently dismounted over his head.

Passenger – Hi, captain, one of the nails on your seat has torn my trousers.
Captain – Well, that's what we advertise. Cheap sea trips (seat rips).

Teacher – Now, the cow is a very useful animal. Can anyone tell me what is made from its horns?
Danny – Yes, sir – hornaments.

Uncle – How can you eat so much?
Nephew – I don't know; but I'm always empty when the table's full.

Billy – Didn't you tell me that if I ate the rest of the turkey it would make me ill?
Mother – Yes. Why?
Billy – Well, er, it hasn't.

Terry – How did you get on at the skating rink?
Jerry – All right.
Terry – Did you fall?
Jerry – No, but my neck changed places with my feet several times.

Youngster (calling in at shop door) – Please, sir, your wife sent me to tell you that the chimney of your house is on fire, the dinner is all spoilt, the baby's having a screaming fit, and the water pipe's busted, and before I forget, sir, allow me to wish you a merry Christmas!

Policeman – Come on, now, you must not stand there singing.
Carol singer – Thanks! You're the first one to admit that I can sing.

Teacher – Well, my boy, what are you going to give your little brother for his Christmas?
Jimmy – I don't know. I gave him measles last year.

Terry – What kind of Christmas did you have?
Jerry – Same as last year, twenty minutes of turkey and mince pies, and a week in bed.

It was the day after Christmas, and the two chums were comparing how they spent Christmas:
Jock – I bet you didn't have a good time yesterday.
Wullie (angrily) – I bet I did.
Jock – Then why aren't you ill to-day?

Mother – Surely you're not hanging a stocking up with a large hole in it?
Willie – Oh, that's all right, Mum. I'm going to put your largest clothes basket under it.

What did the baby light bulb say to its mother?
"I love you watts and watts!"

Jimmy – Did you get many Christmas presents?
Johnny – You bet I did. More than my brothers and sisters.
Jimmy – Did you? You're lucky.
Johnny – Yes, you see I got up two hours before them.

Minister – You like going to Sunday school, don't you, John?
John – Yes, sir.
Minister – What do you expect to learn there today?
John – The date of the Christmas party, sir.

Father – Did you hear Father Christmas this year, Sandy?
Sandy – No, it was too dark to see him, but I heard what he said when he knocked his toes against the bedpost.

Is a graveyard like a herring because it's full of bones?

"How time flies!" as the husband said when his wife threw the clock at him.

"Drop me a line," remarked the sailor as he fell overboard.

When the storm is brewing, what does it brew?

Can a drink be got from a tap on the door?

Is an angle a triangle with only two sides?

Smiffy wrote in his history exam: Boney Prince Charlie got his name because he was so thin. Another famous thin man was Napoleon, who was nicknamed Boney Pat.

Wilfrid wrote in his history exam: The Romans made their roads straight so that the Britons could not hide round the corners.

Is a quack doctor one who looks after ducks?

Father – Well, Alfie, what were your end-of-term marks like?
Alfie – Underwater!
Father – What do you mean?
Alfie – Below "C" level!

Busy man – I really can't see you today.
Salesman (eagerly) – Well, I'm the very man you want to see, sir. I'm selling spectacles.

Aunt – Do you know what toffee does to your teeth, Tommy?
Tommy – No, Auntie. But I know what my teeth do to toffee.

Andrew – My brother's so thin he looks just like a garden rake.
Bobby – That's nothing. My brother's so thin that if you see a door open and nothing comes in, that's him.

Teacher – Are you sure your father didn't do these sums for you, Alex?
Alec – Quite sure, sir. He did have a try, but he got into such a muddle that Grandad had to do them all over again.

Fred – Do you know, when I was young I couldn't walk for a whole year?
Old lady – Oh, you poor boy. Why was that?
Fred – I wasn't old enough!

What's a barbecue?
A line of people waiting for a hair cut!

What kind of job did the lazy man get?
He stood around for so long, he became a dust collector!

Did you hear about the werewolf's party? It was a howling success!

Jane – Why was the farmer hopping mad?
Jill – Someone stepped on his corn!

Bill – What do hedgehogs eat?
Bob – Prickled onions!

What do birds eat between meals?
Tweets!

Ship's officer – Oh, there goes eight bells. Excuse me, it's my watch below.
Old lady – Gracious! Fancy your watch striking as loudly as that!

Angry diner – Look here, waiter, there's a button in my salad!
Waiter – Yes, sir, that's part of the dressing.

Salesman – This bicycle is a very sound model.
Customer – I know that. I heard that when I tried it.

Lazy man – I dreamed last night that I was working.
Workmate – I thought you looked tired this morning.

Sergeant – How did the prisoner get away from you?
Policeman – Well, you see, on the way to the police station we were chased by an angry bull, and the prisoner stood still.

Teacher – Now, tell me the names of any wild animals found in this country – beginning with Danny.

How do you send a baby astronaut to sleep?
Sing him a luna-by!

If you cross a dog with a cat, what do you get?
An animal that chases itself!

What goes fast around castles?
Moat-a-boats!

Patient – Doctor, doctor, I keep stealing things.
Doctor – Have you taken anything for it?

Bill – What kind of make-up do ghosts use?
John – Vanishing cream!

**What's black when it's clean, and white when it's dirty?
A blackboard!**

*What nail should you never hit with a hammer?
Your fingernail!*

What lives under the water and wears a cowboy hat?
Billy the squid!

**Teacher – Sidney, you give me a sentence using the word "gruesome".
Sidney – Er, my mum's plants grew some in the past two weeks!**

*First workman – Poor Bill. He's working himself to death.
Second workman – How's that?
First workman – He's so short-sighted he can't see when the boss isn't looking.*

Host (absent-mindedly, to singer) – Will you sing your song now, or shall we let the guests enjoy themselves for another half-hour?

**Visitor (in deserted Scottish village) – Where are all the people today?
Grocer – The laird's out shooting.
Visitor – Ah – everyone has gone to watch, then?
Grocer – Not likely! They're all indoors out of his way.**

*Uncle – Did you have measles worse than Pete Smith?
Jimmy – Much worse. I had them during my holidays.*

Bill (at Scout camp) – Is Jack a good cook?
Sam – I don't think so. The last time I saw him he was trying to open an egg with a tin-opener!

**What did the alien say to the petrol pump?
Take your finger out of your ear when I'm talking!**

*What do you get when you cross an insect and a rabbit?
Bugs Bunny!*

Girl – A packet of helicopter flavoured crisps, please.
Shopkeeper – We have no helicopter flavour left, only plane (plain)!

**Why do bees buzz?
Because they can't whistle!**

*Customer – I want three lawnmowers.
Assistant – You must have a large lawn, sir.
Customer – No, no. I have two borrowing neighbours.*

Local – Hello! Caught anything yet?
Angler – No, not yet.
Local – I thought not. There was no water in the pond till it rained last night.

**Seaside visitor (whose wig has blown into the sea) – Lifeguard! Lifeguard! Get my wig!
Lifeguard – Excuse me, sir, but I'm a lifeguard, not a hair-restorer.**

*Smiffy – Fancy going to bed with shoes on!
Toots – Who does?
Smiffy – A horse.*

What happened to the snake with a cold?
She adder viper nose!

**What happened to the boy who ran away with the circus?
His parents made him bring it back!**

*Man (waiting for change) – You don't seem very quick at giving change.
Waiter – I'm a bit out of practice, sir. Most folk tell me to keep it.*

Gnock! Gnock!

Who's there?

Diploma.

Diploma who?

Diploma to fix the leak.

Did you hear about the scientist who crossed a parrot with a crocodile?
It bit off his leg and said, "Who's a pretty boy, then!"

Customer – Will the band play anything I ask?
Waiter – Yes, sir.
Customer – Well, ask them to play cards!

Boy – Dad, I can't eat this hamburger. It's awful!
Dad – Shall I call the waiter?
Boy – No, I don't think even he'll be able to eat it!

Motorist (stopped for careless driving) – What I know about driving would fill a book.
Constable – And what you don't know will fill mine.

Patient – Doctor, doctor, I feel like a bell.
Doctor – Take some of these pills, and if they don't work, give me a ring.

Ian – When I'm grown up, everybody will be scared of me.
Pa – What'll you be – a boxer or a wrestler?
Ian – None of them. I'm going to be a dentist!

Teacher – Give me a sentence using the word "pasture".
Bobby – On the way to school yesterday, I pasture house!

Son – Mum, can I get 50p?
Mum – Do you think money grows on trees?
Son – 'Course it does. Otherwise why would banks have so many branches?

Customer – I ordered a dozen oranges and you only sent eleven.
Grocer – Well, sir, one was bad so I didn't send it.

How do you stop a cold going to your chest?
Tie a knot in your neck!

Where do sheep like to do their shopping?
Woolworths, of course!

Why did the boy not hurt himself when he fell on a pin?
Because it was a safety pin!

Where can you find a rubber trumpet?
In an elastic band.

Dennis – How do you cure a cold?
Minnie – Drink a glass of orange after a hot bath.
Dennis – Does it work?
Minnie – I don't know. I haven't finished drinking the bath yet!

Jim – Do you like the dentist?
James – No, he's a real bore!

The Dachshund is so long and thin,
You pat its head on Sunday.
And though the message travels fast,
Its tail won't wag till Monday.

Dennis – I want to thank you for that woolly vest you sent me.
Auntie – Were you pleased with it?
Dennis – Pleased? I was tickled to death!

Tim – Funny, isn't it?
Jim – What's funny?
Tim – Well, this year will be last year next year.

Mum – Jack, why are you buttering both sides of your bread?
Jack – I'm going to eat both sides, Mum.

Householder (to burglar) – Put all that stuff back in the safe at once. Do you hear?
Burglar – Gosh, not all of it! Half of it belongs to next door.

What do you call a man covered in beef, vegetables and gravy?
Stu?

Why didn't the monkey hurt himself when he jumped from 1,000 metres into a glass of lemonade?
Because it was a soft drink!

Man – You've been working in your garden for ages. What are you growing?
Gardener – Tired!

Why is a lion in the desert like Father Christmas?
Because it has Sandy Claws!

What do you get if you mix the white of an egg with a pound of gunpowder?
A boom-meringue!

Captain – Haven't you got that rope untangled yet, my man?
Sailor – No, sir.
Captain – You're very slow.
Sailor – Not really, sir, I'm doing thirty knots an hour.

First cricket captain – Our best batsman can't play, he has measles.
Second cricket captain – That's no excuse, our fast bowler would have knocked spots off him!

Diner – I want a dozen oysters – not too large, not too small. Don't bring me any that are not plump and fresh. Choose them carefully.
Waiter – Er – with or without pearls, sir?

Very lazy, slow plumber – Yes, I remember your little boy, ma'am. When I was working at the school, he was in the infant class.
Woman – And what class was he in when you finished?

What wears shoes, but has no feet?
The pavement!

Gent – So you have a cottage for sale. Is it within walking distance of the railway station?
Landlord – Well, it all depends on how far you can walk!

What do you get if you cross a horse with a football player?
A centaur-forward!

Teacher – What comes before seven, boy?
Sidney – Er, the milkman!

What is it that lives in winter, dies in summer, and grows with its roots upwards?
An icicle!

Patient – Doctor, I've got a sore stomach.
Doctor – What have you been eating?
Patient – Yesterday I had three black snooker balls. Today for breakfast, I had two white snooker balls, and for dinner, I had five reds!
Doctor – Ah, yes, I see the problem. Not enough greens!

Doctor – Why have you got a fried egg on your head?
Patient – Because a boiled one keeps rolling off!

Manager – I want to post a notice where all the men will see it.
Foreman – That's easy. Paste it up on the face of the clock!

Dad – Your teacher has written to me saying it's impossible to teach you anything.
Dennis – There you are, I always said he was no good.

Dennis – Dad says will you lend him your gardening tools?
Polite man – Haven't you forgotten something, young man?
Dennis – Oh yes, he said if the old miser refuses, try next door.

Foreman – Look here, that man's doing twice the work you are!
Lazy workman – That's what I keep telling him, but he'll not slow down.

Customer (to baker) – Are you sure this loaf is today's – because yesterday's wasn't.

Dave – Jimmy told me you told him that secret I told you not to tell him.
Andy – He's the limit! I'll have to talk to him about it.
Dave – All right, but don't tell him I told you because he told me you told him what I told you!

Teacher – Dennis! You can't sleep in my class.
Dennis – Please, sir, if you didn't talk so loudly I could.

Doctor (to patient) – Did you take your two-mile walk every day last week?
Patient – Yes, but I was very giddy after it.
Doctor – Giddy? Why?
Patient – Well, I'm a lighthouse keeper.

Why was the clock nervous?
Because it was all wound up!

Doctor, doctor, I feel like a car!
Stop driving me round the bend!

What is flat as a pancake, round as a berry, has the head of a woman, and the tail of a lion?
A ten pence piece!

What must you do if you break your leg?
Limp!

Heard about the two peanuts walking down the road?
One was a salted!

What do you call a man who can chop down twenty trees a day?
A good feller!

When does it rain money?
When there's a change in the weather!

What gets dirty by washing?
Water!

My brother gets a warm reception wherever he goes.
He must be very popular.
No, he's a fireman!

Lecturer – Will the members of the audience who keep on interrupting please be quiet. I can hardly hear myself speak.
Voice – Cheer up – you're not missing much.

McAndrew – It's no use. I can't talk to a fool.
McPherson – Well, I can. Listen ...

Jock – Hector and Hamish had a terrible row last night.
Alec – I thought they were inseparable friends?
Jock – That's right. It took six of us to separate them.

Doctor – What's this? You've sent a letter saying you had smallpox, and I find you have rheumatism.
Patient – Well, doctor, no one in the house could spell rheumatism.

Tommy – My father can write with both hands at the same time.
Hamish – How does he manage that?
Tommy – He uses a typewriter.

What has six legs and would kill you if it jumped out of a tree on top of you?
A snooker table!

Teacher – If there were ten sheep in a field and two got out through a hole in the hedge, how many would be left?
Angus – None, miss.
Teacher – Nonsense! The answer is eight.
Angus – You may know arithmetic, miss, but you don't know sheep.

Jack – Did you hear about the man who knocked down a house with one blow of his hammer?
Jill – No.
Jack – Yes, he was the auctioneer!

Terry – A man was walking down the road stealing all the garden gates.
Jerry – What did you do
Terry – I didn't say anything, in case he took offence!

Customer – Can I have my milk bill?
Shopkeeper – Excuse me, sir, my name isn't Bill, it's Colin.

Dennis – I fell off a sixty-foot ladder yesterday.
Minnie – It's a wonder you weren't killed.
Dennis – Not really. I fell off the first rung.

Smiffy (in bed) – Gosh! It's quarter to eight! If Mum doesn't wake me up soon I'll be late for school!

Teacher – Now look at the map, Harry. Which is the warmest side of Scotland?
Harry – The east.
Teacher – And why do you say that?
Harry – Because it's nearest the radiator.

Alistair – Ma, am I rude if I speak with my mouth full?
Ma – Yes, Alistair.
Alistair – And am I polite when I say, "Thank you"?
Ma – Why, yes.
Alistair – Well, what am I if I say "Thank you" with my mouth full?

Diner – Why is my food all mashed up?
Waiter – You did ask me to step on it, sir!

Jim – Do fish sing?
Tim – Only when they have musical scales!

What does an invisible baby drink?
Evaporated milk!

What kind of an ant can count?
An accountant!

Why should you never trust a shepherd?
Because he's always walking around with a crook!

What do you get if you cross a load of diamonds with a road?
A jewel carriageway!

Jill – I bumped into an old friend today.
Bill – Was she pleased to see you?
Jill – Not really; we were both in our cars at the time!

Jock – Jamie's not such a big fool as he used to be.
Alistair – Is he getting wiser, then?
Jock – No – thinner.

Dad – How many sums did you have wrong in your arithmetic test?
Smiffy – One.
Dad – And how many did you have to do?
Smiffy – Twelve.
Dad – So you had eleven right?
Smiffy – No, I didn't do the rest.

Officer – Sergeant, where have all these silly asses in our company gone?
Sergeant – I don't know, sir. It seems we're the only two left.

Tommy – I'll bet you won't go into that haunted room alone, Andy.
Andy – Oh, won't I? You just come with me and I'll show you.

Boatman – Come in, number 91, your time is up!
Boss – Hang on! We haven't got a number 91!
Boatman – Oh, sorry! Are you in trouble, number 16?

Jim – Nick was very confused yesterday.
Joe – What happened?
Jim – The foreman gave him five shovels, and told him to take his pick!

Piano tuner – I've come to tune your piano.
Man – But I didn't send for you.
Piano tuner – No, but your neighbour did!

What would be worse than finding a maggot in an apple you're eating?
Finding half a maggot!

How do you make a bandstand?
Take away their chairs!

Sword swallower – I'm off my food.
Pal – Really?
Sword swallower – Yes, I can only eat razor blades!

Zoo keeper – Now then, keep away from that lion, sonny.
Smiffy – I'm not hurting him!

Absent-minded professor (caught in revolving doors) – I can't remember if I'm going out or coming in!

Cuddles – I saw a funny thing the other day.
Dimples – You shouldn't go looking in mirrors!

Slow barber – Your hair is turning very grey, sir.
Customer – Quite possibly, but do you think you could finish cutting it before it becomes white!

Old man – Where's your brother, Charlie?
Charlie – He's in the house playing a duet on the piano with me, but I finished my part first.

What is a frog's favourite flower?
A croak-us!

First farmer – Do you own a lot of land?
Second farmer – Not really, my farm's so small, the cows give condensed milk!

Susan – Everything ends in "ing".
Annie – Don't be silly – of course it doesn't!
Susan – Yes it does – everything!

Judge – You've been up before this bench seven times – I fine you £200!
Prisoner – Can I get a discount for being a regular customer?

Jill – Have you heard the joke about the eggs?
June – No!
Jill – Two bad!

Why did Mickey Mouse go on a journey to Outer Space?
He wanted to find Pluto!

Boss – Everything in this office is worked by electricity.
Office boy – I know, sir. Even the wages give you a shock!

Old lady (visiting prison) – How long are you in for, my man?
Prisoner – Two years.
Old lady – What is the charge?
Prisoner – Oh, there's no charge. Everything's free.

Jockey – That horse you sold me dropped dead this morning.
Dealer – That's strange. He never did that before.

Chief of village fire brigade – I want a shave, Joe. And make it fast. I'm on my way to a fire.

What do you get if you cross a bee with a giant ape?
Sting Kong!

Why do lions eat raw meat?
Because they can't cook!

Old man – Which way do you go from here to see the football match?
Billy – Straight up.
Old man – Straight up this road?
Billy – No, straight up this tree.

Ma – Goodness, Jimmy, how can you eat so much?
Jimmy – I don't know, I suppose it's just my good luck!

Waiter – Wasn't your egg cooked long enough, sir?
Diner – Oh, yes – but not soon enough.

What do you get if you cross a parrot with an elephant?
Something that tells everything that it remembers!

Patient – Doctor, doctor, my legs feel like jelly.
Doctor – Don't worry, they'll be better in a trifle!

What do you get if you cross an elephant with a goldfish?
Swimming trunks!

What is the speed limit in Egypt?
Six Niles an hour!

Mum – Where have you been?
Charlie – Helping Mr McKay to look for a five pound note he'd lost.
Mum – Did you have any luck?
Charlie – No – he found it himself.

Shopkeeper – That man tried to cheat me with a dud pound coin yesterday.
Friend – Did you give it back to him?
Shopkeeper – Yes, I mixed it up with his change today.

Patient – Doctor, doctor, I feel like a thermostat.
Doctor – Oh control yourself, man!

What do bees do with their honey?
They cell it!

Customer – Can you give me a really good shave?
Barber – Yes, sir. Satisfaction guaranteed or whiskers returned.

Archie – That's a very short coat you're wearing.
Angus – Maybe so, but it'll be long enough before I get another.

What is the best cure for a splitting headache?
Glue and an aspirin!

What do you call a monkey born on 1st April?
An Aperil fool!

What is a snake's favourite football team?
Slitherpool!

Which members of an orchestra are most untrustworthy?
The fiddlers!

How does a robot stand?
Bolt upright!

MacDonald – Why are you pulling the wallpaper off the walls? Are you spring-cleaning?
MacDougal – No, we're moving house!

Mum – Do you know your alphabet yet, Angus?
Angus – Yes, Mum.
Mum – Well, what comes after T?
Angus – Supper.

Poet – What do you think of my last poem?
Editor – Well, I'm glad to hear it's your last.

Gamekeeper – Fishing is not allowed in this steam, sir. I'm afraid you must give me what you've caught.
Angler – Well, I've caught the cold so far; you're welcome to it.

Smiffy – Do you always walk as fast as this, Uncle?
Uncle – No – I walk a lot faster when I'm by myself.
Smiffy – Gosh! I wouldn't like to be with you when you're by yourself.

Colonel (inspecting barracks) – If the barracks caught fire, Sergeant, what order would you give?
Sergeant – Cease fire, sir!

What is rhubarb?
Celery with a high temperature!

Teacher – Why were you so late for school this morning?
Danny – I squeezed too much toothpaste onto my brush, and it took me ages to get it back into the tube.

What did the rake say to the hoe?
"Hi, hoe!"

What nut has no shell?
A dough-nut!

Mum – I thought I told you to watch when the milk boiled over.
Dennis – I did. It was exactly two o'clock!

Where do monsters travel?
From ghost to ghost!

Which king of England first introduced wine into the country?
Alfred the Grape!

What do Martians eat for breakfast?
Unidentified frying objects!

Prison visitor – It must be terrible to be shut up all the time in a small room like this. What were you before you came here?
Prisoner – A lift attendant.

Sergeant – What are fortifications?
Recruit – Two lots of twentifications!

Mum – My pastry brush is very stiff today!
Dennis – That's funny – it was OK yesterday when I varnished Gnasher's kennel with it.

Butler – There's a man wanting to see you, sir.
Absent-minded professor – Tell him I'm not in.
Butler – I told him, but he won't go away, sir.
Absent-minded professor – Oh well, I'd better go and tell him myself!

Passer-by – What's that lamp on top of these stones for?
Workman – So that no one will tumble over them.
Passer-by – But what are the stones for?
Workman – Why, to hold the lamp up, silly.

Dentist – Which is the sore tooth?
Patient (who is cinema attendant) – Balcony, third from the left in the front row.

Why couldn't the little boy go to his friend's birthday party?
Because the invitation said for 3 to 5, and he was 7!

What kind of animals can jump higher than a house?
All animals – houses can't jump!

What's a frog's favourite television programme?
Top of the Hops!

What has one horn and gives milk?
A milk delivery van!

Joe – My uncle's very absent-minded.
Moe – Is he?
Joe – Yes. He thought he had left his watch at home yesterday, and then he took it out of his pocket to see if he had time to run back and get it.

Visitor – When I saw your circus last year you had a very good ventriloquist. What has become of him?
Attendant – He's left us. He found he could make more money selling parrots!

Andy – Will you please come at once, doctor? Our door's jammed.
Doctor – It's a joiner you want then, sonny, not a doctor.
Andy – But Dad's fingers are in it!

Doctor – I don't like that cold of yours.
Dennis – I'm sorry, but it's the only one I've got.

Lift boy – There you are, son – the fourth floor.
Old man – Who are you calling "son"?
Lift boy – Well, I brought you up, didn't I?

Employer – The man who can't make himself understood is a fool. Do you understand?
Clerk – No, sir.

What did the mummy bee say to the naughty baby bee?
"Go home and behive yourself!"

What do you get if you cross a sheep with a thunderstorm?
A wet blanket!

First naturalist in jungle – I've just spotted a leopard!
Second naturalist – You can't fool me! They're born that way!

Where do sick gnomes go to be cured?
A national elf service hospital!

Terry – Why are you eating all these cheese biscuits?
Jerry – Because I'm crackers about them!

What is easy to get into, but hard to get out of?
Trouble!

Judge – The next person who raises his voice in this court will be thrown out!
Prisoner – Hip, hip, hooray!

Diner – Look here, waiter, first I found a splinter in this pie, then I found a button.
Waiter – I suppose you haven't seen anything of a fork, have you? One went missing the other night.

Teacher – What is 1314?
Toots – The Battle of Bannockburn.
Teacher – What is 1066?
Cuthbert – The Battle of Hastings.
Teacher – Good. Now, Smiffy, what is 1215?
Smiffy – Quarter past twelve!

Slow waiter – How did you order your steak, sir?
Weary customer – I ordered it by word of mouth, but I suppose I ought to have sent you a postcard two weeks in advance!

Why was a shellfish driving a getaway car?
It was a smash and crab raid!

Doctor – Have you been taking that medicine I prescribed?
Patient – No, I tried it, but I decided I'd rather cough!

Doctor – Please breathe out three times.
Patient – Is that so you can check my lungs?
Doctor – No, it's so I can clean my glasses!

Did you hear about the man who crossed a snail with a dog?
He sent it down to the newsagent's, and it came back with last week's papers!

What do you get if you cross an octopus with a sheep?
A jumper with eight arms!

Which monkeys like eating sweet cakes?
Meringue-utans!

Teacher – Now, Danny, can you tell me how many days there are in a year?
Danny – Seven, sir.
Teacher – I said a year, not a week
Danny – It's still seven, sir. Monday, Tuesday, Wednesday, Thursday, Friday, Saturday and Sunday. If there are any others, I've never heard of them!

Where do you go to get a stopper for your bottle?
Cork!

First mother – My daughter is only two, and she can spell her name backwards.
Second mother – Really? What is her name?
First mother – Anna.

Comic artist – Has the editor seen the joke I left last week?
Office boy – Not yet, sir, but he's trying hard.

Pa – Do you know what's happened to my shaving brush?
Bobby – No, Pa, but Jimmy's wooden horse has a new tail.

Andy – Dad, I've just saved you a pound!
Father – How?
Andy – Remember you said you'd give me a pound if I behaved at Billy Martin's birthday party?
Father – Yes.
Andy – Well, I didn't.

Danny – Smiffy, you've got your trousers on inside out.
Smiffy – Yes, I'm saving the outside for Sundays!

Old man – I take a walk every morning to get an appetite for my breakfast.
Poacher – I take one every morning to get a breakfast for my appetite!

What do you call a man in between two houses?
Alley!

How does a skeleton eat his dinner?
Off bone china!

What makes Donald Duck fall over?
Disney spells!

First farmer – I've just bought a piece of land ten miles long and an inch wide.
Second farmer – What are you going to grow on it?
First farmer – Spaghetti!

Film actor – But look here, if I'm to be thrown into the rapids, how am I going to get out?
Producer – Don't you worry about that – you don't appear again in the film!

Customer – Hey, waiter, there's a caterpillar on my plate.
Waiter – Oh, no, sir – that's a sausage.

Diner (suspiciously) – Why do you call this "enthusiastic" stew?
Waiter – Because the cook put everything he had into it.

Brown – I say, old man, will you push me or give me a kick.
Jones – What on earth for?
Brown – Well, I've just bought this dog, and I want to see if he's fierce.

Showman – Two pounds to see the acrobats. Come along, sonny – only two pounds.
Davie – I've only got one pound, mister – but if you let me in, I'll only open one eye.

What is oval and wears a kilt?
A Scotch egg!

First postman – Why don't you go in, Sam? The dog's wagging his tail.
Second postman – Yes, and he's growling too. I don't know which end to believe.

What flower spreads?
A buttercup!

Why are opticians such nice people?
They see eye to eye with all their patients!

What's the difference between an elephant and a banana?
Try picking them both up!

What's a volcano?
A mountain with hiccups!

Farmer – Gosh, you must be brave to come down by parachute in a gale like this.
Stranger – I didn't come down by parachute. I went up with a tent.

Lady (to train conductor) – I'm afraid my little dog has eaten the ticket.
Conductor – Well, lady, you'll have to buy him a second helping.

First man – Why do you sleep with a parrot beside your bed?
Second man – Because I want to know what I say in my sleep.

Angry passenger – Here, what's happened to my clothes?
Ship's steward – Where did you put them last night?
Passenger – In that cupboard.
Steward – That's not a cupboard – that's a port hole.

Patient – Doctor, doctor, I keep thinking I'm a dog!
Doctor – Just lie on the couch!
Patient – I'm not allowed up on the furniture!

Why was the dentist thrown out of the army?
Because he didn't know how to drill!

Why did the horsebox?
Because it saw the wire fence!

When is a car not a car?
When it turns into a garage!

What is the best day for cooking bacon and eggs?
Fry-day!

Cat – When are you going on holiday, mousey?
Mouse – Next squeak!

Andy – What kind of car have you got now, Sandy?
Sandy – Oh, a runabout. You know, it'll run about a mile then stop.

Old lady (on ship) – What's the matter, Captain?
Captain – The rudder's broken.
Old lady – But that won't matter, will it? It's always under the water and no one will notice it.

Conductor – A lady has left a pint of milk in the bus.
Inspector – Take it to the office, and if nobody claims it in six months you can have it.

Patient – Doctor, doctor, what will you give me for my sore throat?
Doctor – Nothing, I don't want one!

King to Queen – What's that rabbit doing in there?
Queen to King – That's not a rabbit – it's the "hare" to the throne!

First boy – Do you know the difference between an elephant and a Post Office?
Second boy – No.
First boy – Well, I won't send you to buy a stamp!

Who tells jokes about knitting?
A nitwit!

Lazy Len – Can I have a shave please?
Barber – You'll have to hold your head up if you want a shave, sir.
Lazy Len – Will I? Oh well, make it a haircut.

Dad – How did that window get broken?
Dennis – I was cleaning my catapult, and it went off!

Father (to Tommy) – You're going to take your medicine like a man, aren't you, Tommy?
Tommy – No fear! It says double dose for adults!

Prospective house buyer – Yes, it's a good house, but why are all the windows broken?
Landlord – That's nothing serious. I was only convincing a few inquirers that it was a stone's thrown from the beach.

Why did the Romans always build straight roads?
Because they didn't want to drive their soldiers round the bend!

What is the difference between an angry rabbit and a counterfeit £10 note?
One's a mad bunny, and the other's bad money!

What walks on its head all day?
A drawing pin stuck in your shoe!

Gas man – What's this Irish coin doing in your meter, madam?
Lady – Oh, I was cooking Irish Stew!

What did one cucumber say to the other cucumber?
"If you had kept your big mouth shut, we wouldn't be in this pickle!"

Thief – Pardon me, sir, but have you seen a policeman around here?
Pedestrian – No, I'm sorry.
Thief – Thank you. Now will you kindly hand over your watch and wallet?

Teacher – Now, what's wrong with this sentence, "The toast was drank"?
Smiffy – It should be "The toast was eaten"!

Bill and Bert paid a visit to a court while a trial was in progress.
Bert – I've no doubt about this case. One glance at that fellow over there tells me he's guilty.
Bill – Sssh! That's the judge!

Dramatist – In the third act there is an earthquake.
Manager – Well, that ought to bring down the house!

Visitor (speaking of little boy) – He has his mother's eyes.
Mother – And his father's mouth.
Boy – And his brother's trousers.

What does a winner lose in a race?
His breath!

What would you get if you crossed a gorilla with a skunk?
I don't know what you would call it, but it'd have no trouble getting a seat on the bus!

Car salesman – This car has had one careful owner.
Customer – But it's all smashed up.
Car salesman – The others weren't so careful!

Teacher – If you add 387, and 769, then double it and divide by 5, what do you get?
Smiffy – The wrong answer!

What do you get when you cross a carrier pigeon with a woodpecker?
A bird who knocks before he delivers his message!

Teacher – Now, boys, if I drop this pound coin into this chemical, will it dissolve?
Boy – Not likely, sir, or you wouldn't risk it.

What's worse than a crocodile with the toothache?
A centipede with bunions!

Jones – Once I was glad to be down and out!
Green – When was that?
Jones – After my first trip in an aeroplane!

First travelling salesman – I travel in toothpaste.
Second travelling salesman – By tube, I suppose?

Tom – Why are you walking so slowly?
Bill – I've got toothache.
Tom – What's that got to do with walking?
Bill – Nothing, but I'm going to the dentist.

Bill – What moves faster, heat or cold?
Ben – I don't know.
Bill – Heat, of course – you can catch a cold!

Which birds are religious?
Birds of pray!

Mean Marty – I've just saved seventy pence running home behind a bus.
Friend – Really, how daft!
Mean Marty – Yes! Then I realised I could have saved five pounds running home behind a taxi!

What time is it when the clock strikes thirteen?
Time the clock was fixed!

Man – Do you have a good memory for faces?
Wife – Yes, but why?
Man – I've just broken your make-up mirror!

What did Robin Hood have when the arrow fired at him just missed?
A n-arrow escape!

Did you hear about the man who had two left ears?
He couldn't hear right!

What kind of fish make shoes?
Soles and eels!

What makes the Tower of Pisa lean?
It never eats!

What did the big Christmas cracker say to the little Christmas cracker?
"My pop's bigger than your pop!"

What do short-sighted ghosts wear?
Spooktacles!

Customer – Waiter, waiter, there's a fly in my alphabet soup!
Waiter – Maybe it's learning to read!

Son – If I didn't have more brains than you, I'd –
Father – Listen, lad, if your brains were dynamite and they doubled every second for a hundred years, and then exploded, they wouldn't blow your hat off on a windy day!

Manager – Who was that on the phone, Jock?
Office boy – Someone who said it was a long-distance from Paris?
Manager – Yes?
Office boy – So I said, "Any fool knows that", and rang off.

Teacher – What are you crying for, Smiffy?
Smiffy – My boots are hurting me.
Teacher – Why, you've got them on the wrong feet.
Smiffy – Don't be daft, I haven't got any other feet.

Customer – I must say, waiter, this is the first time I've ever had a really tender steak here.
Waiter (horrified) – Gosh, I must have given you the boss's dinner!

What is green and jumps out of the soup pot?
Spring cabbage!

Teacher – What is your favourite subject Danny?
Danny – Latin.
Teacher – But you're not learning that.
Danny – I know, that's why it's my favourite.

Haughty lady – Can you tell me where I can find my son, Algernon Fitzgerald Popplethwaite Fitzroy?
Schoolboy – Hey, Butch, your mother wants you.

Old gent (to small boy) – Well, sonny, what are you crying for?
Small boy – I haven't a pond to sail my boat on.
Old gent – Keep on crying and you'll soon have one.

What bird does a happy dog represent?
A wag-tail.

The pianist thumped and pounded his way through his piece at the concert.
First music lover – Wonderful! Wonderful!
Second music lover – How he plays, you mean?
First music lover – No. How the piano stands it.

Boastful man (telling the story of an accident in his car) – There I was on a lonely road, miles from anywhere, with a blazing car. What do you think I did?
Bored listener – Took a deep breath and blew it out.

Diner – Look here, this will never do. That man over there has got much more to eat than me. Where's the manager?
Waiter – That man is the manager.

Mother – Danny, how was the test?
Danny – Oh, fine.
Mother – Then why did Teacher send this note home with you?
Danny – I said the test was fine, I said nothing about the answers.

There are two flies in the airing cupboard. Which one is in the army?
The one on the tank!

First man – Five of my friends went fishing and fell in the river, but only one got his hair wet.
Second man – That's amazing!
First man – Not really – four of them were completely bald!

What is a minimum?
A little mother!

How do chickens communicate?
They use fowl language!

Doctor – What seems to be the trouble?
Patient – I swallowed a clock last week.
Doctor – Good grief! Why didn't you come to see me before?
Patient – I didn't want to alarm anyone!

Why did the boy push his father into the fridge?
Because he wanted ice-cold fizzy pop!

What fish sings?
A tuna fish!

What do you call a foreign body in a chip pan?
An unidentified frying object!

What do musicians like to wear best?
Cords!

Sergeant (in army camp) – Why haven't you shaved this morning?
Private – Well, there were eight of us using the same mirror, and I must have shaved the wrong face.

Teacher – Give me an example of a collective noun.
Danny – Vacuum cleaner, sir.

What do you call a class of university students on the underground?
A tube of smarties!

Absent-minded professor – Who's there?
Burglar – No one.
Absent-minded professor – That's funny, I was certain I heard something.

Customer – If this is an all-wool jersey, why is it marked "cotton"?
Shopkeeper – That's to deceive the moths, sir.

Jerry – How did you get on when you asked the boss for a rise?
Terry – Aw, he was like a lamb.
Jerry – What did he say?
Terry – Bah!

Passenger – Why are we late, porter?
Railway porter – The train ahead is behind and we were behind before besides.

Wilfrid – I wonder what time it is?
Smiffy – Well, it can't be four o'clock yet because my mum said I was to be home then, and I'm not!

Dud singer – I will now sing "On The Banks of Allan Water".
Voice from audience – Thank goodness! We thought you were going to sing here.

Teacher – Sidney, spell "wrong".
Sidney – R-O-N-G.
Teacher – That's wrong.
Sidney – Well, that's what you asked me to spell.

Bill – You know, Tom, I sent a shirt to the laundry and it came back with the wrong buttons on.
Tom – I sent one as well, but the buttons came back with the wrong shirt on.

Teacher – What is a worm?
Sidney – A caterpillar that has been shaved, sir.

How does an octopus go to war?
Well armed!

Old lady (in museum) – Don't be afraid sonny. That lion is stuffed.
Little boy – But maybe he's not stuffed so full that he can't make room for a little boy like me!

Bald man – I'd like to buy that wig, please.
Shopkeeper – That will be £50 with tax, sir.
Bald man – It's all right. I'll glue it on!

Where do cows go in the evening?
To the moovies!

Fatty – They say that travel broadens a man.
Plug – Oh, my goodness, you must have been round the world!

Patient – Doctor! Doctor! I feel like a ladder!
Doctor – Keep calm, and let me take this one step at a time!

Diner – Waiter, this fish is awful! Why did you tell me to try it?
Waiter – Well, if you hadn't taken it, sir, it would have been served to us in the kitchen!

Teacher (on a winter morning) – Smiffy, correct the following sentence. "It am very hot."
Smiffy – It am very cold.

Barney – I was born in New York, but I went to school in Scotland.
Jock – Gosh, what a long way you had to go every day!

Businessman – If you want to get on, you must wrap yourself in your business.
Listener – That doesn't suit me. I'm a manufacturer of sticky tape.

Spotty – Why do you sleep with your spectacles on?
'Erbert – I'm so short-sighted I can't recognise the people I dream about.

John – Joe's feeling sore today.
Dick – Why? What happened to him?
John – He was in a restaurant with Bill, who found a fly in his soup. Bill called the waiter and said – "Waiter, please remove this insect!" and the waiter threw Joe out on his bottom in the street.

Police sergeant – How do you account for having all this silverware in your pockets?
Suspect – Well, you see, we've got no sideboard at home.

A diner at a restaurant saw at another table a man whom he thought he had met before and went across to speak to him. "Excuse me, but are you Dunn?" he asked.
"Done?" he said, "No, I've only just started!"

George – I made two trips from London to New York and didn't even have time to take a bath.
Jim – You dirty double-crosser!

Visitor to new housing estate – I didn't expect to hear mice in a new house like this.
Tenant – That's not mice. That's the man next door eating celery.

What would you call a mischievous egg?
A practical yolker!

Terry – What hand do you stir your tea with?
Jerry – I stir mine with a spoon!

Why did the weight-lifter eat bricks?
To build himself up!

Why did the snake walk out of his maths lesson?
Because he'd adder-nough!

Patient – I snore so loudly, I keep myself awake.
Doctor – Sleep in another room, then!

Ghoul – My goodness, hasn't your little ghoul grown!
Ghoul mother – Yes, I must say she's certainly gruesome!

Smith – Jones is going to retire from business for five years.
Brown – Oh, I've heard him say that before.
Smith – This time the judge said it.

Customer – That bacon I bought from you last week was bad.
Shopkeeper – Impossible, madam. Why, it was only cured last week.
Customer – Then it must have had a relapse.

Speaker (after a very boring lecture) – Now is there anybody who has a further question to ask about the railways of Great Britain?
Angus – Yes. What time does your train leave?

Dad was talking to little Bobby when they were out for a walk.
Dad – Just fancy, Bobby, at one time these fields were covered by the sea, and fish were swimming about on the very spot where we stand.
Bobby – Yes, Dad. Look! Here's an empty salmon tin!

Prison Governor – We must set you to work. What can you do?
Forger – Give me a week's practice and I'll sign your cheques for you.

Farmer (to carpenter) – I want this ladder mended. It needs new sides and new rungs, but the same holes will do.

Where do frogs hang their coats?
In the croakroom!

Winston the cat (visiting sick pal) – Did you eat your dinner today?
Sick moggy – No, I could only manage a little swallow!

How do you start a jelly race?
Just say, "Get set!"

First boy – Why do you call your lizard Tiny?
Second boy – Because he's my newt (minute)!

Daddy Bear, Mummy Bear and Baby Bear all came back from their walk.
"Who's been eating my porridge?" asked Daddy Bear.
"And who's been eating my porridge?" said Mummy Bear
"Never mind about that!" said Baby Bear. "Somebody's stolen the video!"

Son – I am sure Dad gets more absent-minded every day.
Mother – What makes you think that?
Son – Well, when I met him today, he shook hands with me and said: "Pleased to meet you, my boy. And how's your father?"

Golfing beginner – I always seem to strike the ball on the top. How can I put that right?
Caddie – What about turning the ball upside down?

Tom – You don't look well, Tim. Why don't you take a holiday?
Tim – I should very much like to, but I couldn't stay away from the office.
Tom – Couldn't the firm do without you for a week?
Tim – Quite easily. That's the trouble. I don't want them to find out.

Naturalist – There I was, face-to-face with a lion and only five feet between us.
Friend – How unusual! A three-legged lion!

Why can't a car play football?
Because it's only got one boot!

What date is a command to go forward?
March 4th!

Petshop owner – Would you like to buy a budgie? They're only £12 apiece.
Customer – How much is it for a whole one?

Teacher – Sarah, what was the first thing James did on coming to the throne?
Sarah – He sat down!

What do you call a polite spy?
A-gent!

Teacher – A biped is anything that goes on two feet. Toots, can you give me an example?
Toots – Yes, Teacher, a pair of shoes.

Uncle – Good gracious, Minnie, that's your third helping of pudding! You do eat a lot for a little girl!
Minnie – Oh, I'm not as little as I look from the outside!

Footballer (to spectator) – Do you know enough about football to referee?
Spectator – I know enough about football not to.

Jones – My son wants to be a racing driver. What shall I do?
Smith – Whatever you do, don't stand in his way.

Two insurance agents were boasting of their quickness.
"Why," said the first, "one man had an accident and we handed the insurance money to him within an hour."
"That's nothing," said the second. "A man fell from the top storey of our building, and I handed him his money as he passed my window."

How do you know if there's an elephant in your bed?
He has an E on his pyjamas!

What has 45 heads, but can't think?
A box of matches!

What is the definition of an archaeologist?
A man whose career is in ruins!

What do you call a Stone Age cowboy?
Flint Eastwood!

Teacher – Gary, did your sister help you with your homework?
Gary – No, miss. She did it all.

Tourist – How many sheep do you have here?
Shepherd – I can't say exactly. Every time I start to count them, I fall asleep.

Injured man (to workman who had dropped a hod of bricks) – Confound you! One of those bricks hit me on the head.
Workman – My word! You're lucky. Look at all the bricks that didn't!

Doctor – Stop smoking, and you will live to be eighty.
Old man – It'll be too late.
Doctor – It's never too late to mend.
Old man – But I'm eighty-eighty now!

Crystal-gazer – I'm afraid someone very near to you is going to be very disappointed.
Client – You're right. I've forgotten to bring my money.

First student – I wonder if Professor Smart meant anything.
Second student – What about?
First student – He advertised a lecture on "Fools", and when I bought a ticket it said "Admit one".

What is round and red and goes up and down?
A tomato in a lift!

Bad golfer – Why has that man with the tin been following us all afternoon?
Caddie – Oh, he's after worms to go fishing, sir.

Diner – Hey, waiter!
Waiter – Yes, sir!
Diner – Bring me a saw for this pudding and an axe for this meat.
Waiter – Anything else, sir?
Diner – Oh, yes. A hammer to mash the potatoes!

Mother – Why don't you sing to the baby when it cries?
Father – I did, but the neighbours said they'd sooner hear the baby cry!

If King Kong went to Hong Kong to play ping-pong and have a sing-song and then died, what would they put on his coffin?
A lid!

Shall I tell you the story about the red-hot poker?
No, I'd never be able to grasp it!

What's long and thin and goes "hith, hith"?
A snake with a lisp!

If I cut three bananas and four oranges into ten pieces each, what would I have?
A fruit salad!

Is your new car fast?
Fast? Why, when I want to go from Dundee to Glasgow I have to start putting on the brakes halfway.

Gipsy – Tell your fortune, mister.
McWalter – How much?
Gipsy – A pound!
McWalter – Quite correct.

Teacher – I was very angry yesterday when I heard a boy snoring during my lesson.
Pupil – Yes, so was I. The noise woke me up!

Danny – Why are you running?
Sidney – To stop two boys fighting.
Danny – What two boys?
Sidney – Billy Smith and me!

What happened to the first chair made for the king?
It was throne out!

What did the ground say to the rain?
If you keep this up, my name will be mud!

What does a geometry teacher like when he's hungry?
A square meal!

Why did the tea bag go to hospital?
Because it was under a strain!

Why was the crab arrested?
He kept pinching things!

Teacher – Toots, say something beginning with "I".
Toots – I is . . .
Teacher – No, "I am" not "I is".
Toots – Right, I am the ninth letter of the alphabet!

What is a sick crocodile called?
An illigator!

One day I saw a man pouring a bowl of broth into the radiator of his car.
"What are you doing?" I asked.
He said, "I'm trying to soup it up!"

Boss – Did you put those circulars in the post?
Secretary – No, sir, I couldn't find any round envelopes for them.

Bore – Talking about Africa makes me think of the time –
Friend – Good gracious you're quite right. I had no idea it was so late. Goodbye!

Why do people laugh at fish?
Because they think they are finny!

What do you get if you cross a quarter pound of mince with a bee?
A humburger!

Variety agent – You say you're a magician?
Applicant – Yes.
Variety agent – Well, vanish!

Teacher – Don't bother me now Dennis, I have a good deal on my hands.
Dennis – So I notice. Why not try soap and water?

Farmer Jones – That's the third time in six months you've gone and cut off your whiskers.
Farmer Brown – Yes. My wife is stuffing the sofa!

Stranger – Have you had much rain?
Farmer – Yes, but my neighbour had more.
Stranger – How was that?
Farmer – He has more land than me.

What do you call a flying pig?
Piggles!

What do you get if you cross a kangaroo with a chicken?
Pouched egg!

Barry – Why do you call your dog "Locksmith"?
Garry – Because every time I open the door he makes a bolt for it.

Who makes a success loafing at his job?
A baker!

Terry – Did you buy that second-hand car, or do you still have to walk to and from your work?
Jerry – The answer to both of your questions is, yes.

Algernon – Your father's a cobbler, yet your boots are full of holes.
Albert – That's nothing. Your father's a dentist, yet your little brother has no teeth!

Jack – Would you please open the gate for me?
Old man (opening the gate) – Yes, but why don't you open it yourself?
Jack – Because it's just been painted!

Angry diner – You're not fit to serve a pig.
Waiter – I'm doing my best, sir!

Terry – Have you heard the joke about the empty house?
Jerry – No.
Terry – There's nothing in it to tell!

Why is your heart like a policeman?
It follows a regular beat!

What happened to the wasp that got run over?
It was taken to waspital!

"Tough luck," said the egg in the monastery. "It's out of the frying pan, and into the friar!"

What part of a clock is always old?
The second hand!

What did the Spanish farmer say to his hens?
"Olé!"

Landlord – You aren't always bothered with poor light, are you?
Tenant – Oh, no, not always.
Landlord – I thought not. It's only at certain times you notice it, eh?
Tenant – Yes, after dark!

Teacher – If I said a man was creating a stir, what would he be doing, Hamish?
Hamish – Making porridge, miss.

What does a kettle suffer from?
Boils!

What did the bell say when it fell in the water?
I'm wringing wet!

Mum – Quick, Garry, run for the doctor! Baby's swallowed one of your marbles!
Garry – That's all right. I've got plenty more!

Guide – This, ladies and gentlemen, is the room where Sir Walter Scott wrote Ivanhoe.
Tourist – But last year you said it was written in the room over there.
Guide – Yes! But we can't get in there just now. It's being cleaned.

Dud actor – You know, when I'm acting I'm carried away by my feelings. I forget everything but the part – the very audience seems to vanish.
Manager – You can't blame them.

Judge – After the prisoner put his fist through the window did you observe anything?
Witness – Yes. There was a hole in the glass.

Inspector – You're late. Don't you have a watch?
Detective – No – One of the pickpockets I was after pinched it from me!

If Shakespeare were alive today he'd be looked upon as a very wonderful man. Yes, he'd be over 300 years old!

Terry – Briggs says he's the big noise at the factory.
Jerry – So he is. He's the fellow who blows the hooter at stopping time.

Applicant for a job in a music shop – I've a marvellous ear for music. I can pick up anything musical.
Boss – All right. Help me shift this piano.

Jenny – I believe Freddie was caught cheating at an examination?
Penny – Yes, he went in for the botany exam with twenty-four flowers in his buttonhole.

Clerk – I can't read this letter. The writing is too bad.
Employer – Nonsense! Any fool can read it. Pass it over here!

Dougal – I'm thinking of raising turnips next year. What's the best way?
Donald – Take hold of the tops and pull.

Would-be comedian – Well, you've seen my act. What sort of clothes should I wear on the stage?
Stage manager – Armour!

Policeman – Now then, what's your name?
Speeding motorist – Demetrius Aloysius Fortescue.
Policeman – None of that, now. It's your name I want, not your family motto.

Actor – On my first appearance, the people stormed the box office.
Friend – And did they get their money back?

Sid – Bill, there's a hole in the boat, and water's coming in.
Bill – Never mind. I'll drill another hole to let the water go back out!

Customer – I wish to return this cricket bat. It's useless.
Shopkeeper – What's wrong with it?
Customer – Every time I've been in to bat with it, I've been out first ball!

A dog and a porcupine had a boxing match. The porcupine won on points!

Boy – Do you like baked apples, Mr Bloggs?
Farmer – Yes, boy, I love them! Why?
Boy – Your orchard is on fire!

What would you do if you're alone in a jungle and an elephant charges you?
Pay it!

How do porcupines kiss?
Very carefully!

Patient – Doctor, I'm afraid my wife mistook that medicine you gave me for furniture polish.
Doctor – So you want me to give you some more?
Patient – No, I want you to come and shake our table!

New neighbour – Have you a large family to support, Mr Green?
Mr Green – Yes, and if they didn't earn their own livings I don't know how I'd do it.

Patient – My head is like a lump of lead, my neck is as stiff as a poker and I feel as if I have bands of iron round my chest.
Doctor – It's not a doctor you want, it's a blacksmith!

First lodger – This cheese is so strong it could walk over and say "Hello" to the coffee.
Second lodger – Yes, and the coffee is too weak to answer it.

Angry customer – Look here, that honey you sold me was full of hairs.
Shopkeeper – Well, it came straight from the comb!

Mum – Now, then, take your dinner and grow up big like Dad.
Dennis – Has Dad stopped growing?
Mum – Yes.
Dennis – Well, why do you still feed him?

Salesman – I am working for the support of literature.
Customer – Oh, what are you doing?
Salesman – Selling bookcases.

Did you hear about the man who always wore sunglasses?
He took a very dim view of things!

Did you hear about the pharaoh who had Egyptian 'flu?
He caught it from his mummy!

What sits at the bottom of the sea and laughs?
A merrymaid!

What runs around a house, but never moves an inch?
A fence!

Why do you forget a tooth when the dentist pulls it out?
It goes right out of your head!

What did people wear at the time of the Great Fire of London?
Blazers!

Jock – How much are these handkerchiefs?
Shopkeeper – Four pounds a pair, sir.
Jock – How much for one?
Shopkeeper – Two pounds fifty.
Jock – Right, I'll take the other one!

For a long time the visitor to the museum stood gazing at the Egyptian mummy, swathed in bandages.
"Tell me one thing," he ventured.
"What is it, sir?" asked the guide.
"Was he in a car accident?"

Inquisitive man – How much do you get paid for banging that hammer down?
Workman – Nothing. It goes down itself. I get paid for lifting it up.

Bobby – Pa, does a cup of coffee do any harm?
Pa – No, Bobby.
Bobby – That's lucky! I've just spilled one over your new suit.

Barber (giving bald customer hair restorer) – Now don't go putting any on until you get home. You don't want your hair to push your hat off in the street.

Old man – How old are you sonny?
Little boy – Eight, sir.
Old man – Eight? And you're not as big as my umbrella!
Little boy – How old is your umbrella?

First boy – Here's a bull coming.
Second boy – Well, don't just stand there! Help me to climb this tree.

Teacher – Can you give me the name of an underground creature?
Boy – A worm.
Teacher – Another underground creature?
Boy – Another worm!

What has sixty keys, but can't open a door?
A piano!

What do you get two of in every corner?
The letter R.

What do you get if you cross a mouse and a bar of soap?
Bubble and squeak!

Teacher – What is the meaning of this, Minnie? I told you to write an essay on the funniest thing you've ever seen and you handed me a blank page.
Minnie – Well, sir, the funniest thing I've ever seen was too funny for words.

Absent-minded professor – I say, Mary, bring my hat.
Maid – It's on your head, sir.
Absent-minded professor – Don't bother, then. I'll look for it myself.

Landlady – How did you like my cake? I took great pains with it.
Lodger – So did I!

Teacher – Walter, what do two tens make?
Walter – Twenty, sir.
Teacher – Correct. Now, Dennis, what do two elevens make?
Dennis – A football match, sir.

Willie – There was a fly in that currant bun you sold me yesterday.
Grocer – Well, sonny, you bring the fly back and I'll give you a currant for it.

Policemen – Lost your way, sonny?
Little boy – No, but I've found a street I don't know.

What is a vampire's favourite game?
Bat-minton!

Why is it hard to talk when a goat is around?
Because it always butts in!

How can you tell the difference between a stoat and a weasel?
A weasel is weasily recognised because a stoat is stoatally different!

What do you call a man with a spade?
Doug.
And what do you call a man without a spade?
Douglas!

Why is the letter "A" like a sweet-smelling flower?
Because a bee always comes after it.

Passenger – Porter, porter, I've lost my luggage.
Porter – Well, you won't need me then, will you?

Teacher – Can you give me a proverb?
Harry – Yes, miss. A sock on the foot is worth two on the nose!

Bob – Who do you think you're pushing?
Bully – Dunno. What's your name?

Visitor – Is this place good for rheumatism?
Local inhabitant – I think so. I got mine here!

How do you make anti-freeze?
Hide her coat!

Boxing instructor – Well, now that your first lesson is over, have you any questions?
Dazed novice – Er . . . how much is your postal course?

Terry – Did your grandfather remember you when he made his will?
Jerry – He must have – he left me out!

Patient – Doctor, doctor, I feel like a snooker ball.
Doctor – Go to the end of the cue!

First golfer – How long have you been playing golf?
Second golfer – Two months!
First golfer – You're terrific for someone who's only been playing for two months!
Second golfer – Yes, but I've been learning for ten years!

Diner – Waiter, waiter, what kind of soup is this? I ordered pea soup – this tastes like soap!
Waiter – My mistake, sir. That's tomato soup. The pea tastes like petrol!

Dennis – Please, Mum, may I have two pieces of cake?
Mum – Certainly. Cut the piece you have in half.

Bus driver – I don't have much time for meals, so I generally have a bite at the wheel.
Passenger – That's a bit tough, isn't it?

Father – What can you do that no other boy at school can do?
David – Read my writing!

Sandy (in shop) – Mum wants a tape measure.
Assistant – Certainly. How long does she want it?
Sandy – She wants to keep it.

What do you call a sleeping bull?
A bulldozer!

Why is a clock a shy piece of furniture?
Because it covers its face with its hands!

Mary – How come you never passed the maths exam? I thought you had all the answers written on your sleeve!
Julie – I did, but I put on my biology blouse by mistake!

Patient – Doctor, doctor, I keep thinking I'm a bee!
Doctor – Well, go home, and if it gets worse, give me a buzz!

Which cheese is made backwards!
Edam!

Cabbie – Where to, sir?
Customer – Waterloo, please, driver.
Cabbie – Is that the station?
Customer – Well, I'm too late for the battle!

Who played at Hampden Park and didn't get a kick at the ball?
The pipe band!

What is never seen, but often changes?
Your mind!

Who wrote Great Eggspectations?
Charles Chickens!

What did the rolled-up piece of string with fuzzy hair say when it was asked if it was a piece of elastic?
"No, I'm a frayed knot!"

How can you get out of a locked music room?
Play the piano until you find the right key!

Man – What's your cat called?
Boy – Felt-tip.
Man – Is that his real name?
Boy – No, just his pen name!

Where do pilots keep their money?
In air pockets!

Terry – What's your idea of an optimist?
Jerry – A fellow without any money going into a restaurant and ordering oysters in the hope he can pay for his dinner with a pearl.

Dave – That's a very mean boss I'm working for.
Dan – Oh, why is that?
Dave – He's cut the legs off the wheelbarrow so I can't put it down and have a rest.

What do you get if you cross an ocean with a crook?
A crime wave!

What colour is the wind?
Blew, of course!

What is the perfect cure for dandruff?
Baldness!

What do you get if you cross a rag with a skeleton?
A rag and boneman!

What is small, brown and carries a suitcase?
A handle!

If a magician brought you a cup of tea, what would you have?
A cuppa and a sorcerer!

Traveller – I say, can you tell me where I am? I'm lost.
Local – Is there a reward out for you?
Traveller – No.
Local – Then you're still lost.

Old gent – How old are you, my boy?
Billy – Six
Old Gent – And what are you going to be?
Billy – Seven

Teacher – Now, Wilfrid, tell me what a grape is.
Wilfrid – A bald gooseberry.

Cabin boy – Is a thing lost if you know where it is?
Captain – Of course not.
Cabin boy – Well, I've dropped your gold watch to the bottom of the sea!

Pat – So you're distantly related to the Jones family, are you?
Tim – Yes. Their dog is our dog's brother.

Stranger – Are there any clever crooks in this town?
Local – Clever crooks? Why, someone stole my trousers and hung weights on my braces so that I wouldn't miss them.

Mother – Was the conjurer good at the party last night?
Dick – Rather! I gave him a dud pound coin to do a trick and he gave me a good one back!

Why did the chewing gum go across the road?
It was stuck to the chicken's foot!

Teacher – Late again! What's the excuse this time?
Minnie – Sorry, miss the bus said "Dogs must be carried", and I couldn't find one anywhere!

What has no legs and runs down hills?
Water!

What do you call a policeman ghost?
Chief-in-spectre!

What did the flour say when it fell off the table?
"Don't pick me up, I'm self-raising!"

Teacher – What were you saying, Tommy?
Tommy – Nothing, miss.
Teacher – But I saw you speaking to Johnny.
Tommy – Yes, miss. He asked me what I had in my pocket, so I said "Nothing".

What do you get if you dial 666?
A policeman standing on his hands!

Father – Why didn't you tell me the truth when I asked who broke the window?
Son – I thought my story was more interesting.

What can make a cow fly?
The letter "R" because it makes a cow into a crow!

Woodwork teacher – What are you making John?
John – It's a collapsible, sir.
Teacher – A collapsible what?
John – I don't know. I've only got as far as the handle!

What flies under water?
A bird in a submarine!

What is the most common illness amongst spies?
A code in the nose!

McDuff – Did you have much trouble with your French when you went to Paris?
Mcleod – No, But the Parisians did!

Ted – How did you get that bump on the head?
Fred – Playing a saxophone.
Ted – I don't understand.
Fred – Well, you see, I was sitting in front of the trombone player.

What did the mouse do when the other mouse fell in the river?
Gave him mouse-to-mouse resuscitation.

Dick – I'm positively finished with gambling.
Chick – For ever? I don't believe it.
Dick – Oh, no? I'll bet you fifty pence I stop.

When does a doctor get angry?
When he loses his patients!

Brown – I hear that Green's in hospital suffering from shock. His business partner let him down.
Smith – What was his profession?
Brown – A trapeze artiste.

Teacher – Now, Smiffy, will five go into one?
Smiffy – Yes, Teacher.
Teacher – How do you make that out, you stupid boy?
Smiffy – Well, I put five toes into one sock every morning.

Did you hear about the man arrested for stealing luggage?
He asked for forty other cases to be taken into consideration!

What did the cobbler say to the flock of geese that walked in?
Shoo! Shoo!

Dan – My girlfriend's one of twins.
Dave – How can you tell them apart?
Dan – Her brother's got a beard!

What do you get if you cross a sheep with six radiators?
Central bleating!

Sid – My feet are always frozen when I wake up in the morning.
Billy – If they're so cold, why don't you try a hot water bottle?
Sid – I tried that.
Billy – Didn't it work?
Sid – No, I couldn't get my feet in the neck of the bottle.

Waiter – Don't you like our college pudding' sir?
Diner – No, there's an egg in it that should have been expelled.

Toots – I hear your father is a very smart man.
Smiffy – Yes. He walks in his sleep, so he can get rest and exercise at the same time.

Hector – Who are we playing next week, Hamish?
Hamish – Auchentogle Gasworks Football Club.
Hector – Are they good?
Hamish – Not half. They've got a football!

Patient – Doctor, Doctor, I've been stung by a bee. Shall I put some cream on it?
Doctor – Don't be silly. It'll be miles away by now.

What are pupils at ghost schools called?
Ghoulboys and Ghoulgirls!

Why did the dinosaur cross the road?
Because there were no chickens in those days!

Where does a king go to buy a new house?
Newcastle!

What never asks questions, but usually gets an answer?
A telephone!

Knock, Knock!
Who's there?
Alison.
Alison who?
Alison to my radio in the morning!

Cuthbert – Smiffy, why do you not put your hand in front of your mouth when you yawn?
Smiffy – No fear! I bit myself last time.

Visitor – What's the name of that river?
Local – Wye, sir.
Visitor – Because I want to know.

Fat uncle – Alex, take the cat out of the room. I can't stand the noise it's making.
Alex – No wonder. You're sitting on it.

Teacher – Can you read French?
Minnie – Yes, if it's written in English.

Patient – I have a terrible corn on the bottom of my foot.
Doctor – That's a good place to have it. Nobody can step on it but you.

Mother – Oh, dear! Did you fall down the stairs?
Bertie – Yes, but it didn't matter – I was on the way down anyway.

Uncle – How did you like your first day at school, David?
David – Oh, it wasn't bad, but there was a big man in front who kept spoiling all the fun.

Policeman – This man is charged with stealing an elephant, sir.
Judge – Search him!

Naturalist – How did you make fifty lions run?
Explorer – Well, I ran, and they all ran after me!

Old lady – What sort of man will you be when you come out of prison?
Prisoner – An old one, madam.

Sandy – That star up there is larger than the earth.
James – Then why doesn't it keep off the rain?

Boaster – I've got the most wonderful family tree.
Fed-up listener – And what are you – the sap?

Ma – You shouldn't make faces at the bulldog, Bertie.
Bertie – Well, he started it.

Diner – These oatcakes are terrible.
Waiter – They're not oatcakes, they're cork tablemats.

Judge – You say the stone was as big as my head?
Constable – Yes, but not so thick.

Joe – Do your glasses magnify, Mum?
Mum – Yes, Joe.
Joe – Well, please take them off when you cut me my piece of tart.

Judge – Why did you put your hand in the man's watch pocket?
Prisoner – I wanted to know the time, your honour.
Judge – Well, it's six months!

Excited maid – Oh, sir, there's a burglar in the kitchen.
Absent-minded professor – Tell him I can't see him.

Uncle – Well, Tommy, what did you get on your birthday?
Tommy (tired of answering questions) – A year older.

Tim – Coming out to play football?
Tom – I can't. I broke a window yesterday, and Dad's suspended me for the rest of the season.

Diner – Waiter, I can't eat this food. Fetch the manager.
Waiter – That's no use, sir. You can't eat him either.

Teacher – Why are you always late for school?
Danny – Because you always ring the bell before I get here.

Teacher – You used to be as good at sums as Cuthbert.
Danny – Yes, but I don't sit beside him now!

Sandy – If a farmer raises wheat in dry weather, what will he raise in wet weather?
Hector – I don't know!
Sandy – His umbrella!

Teacher – How many seasons are there in the year?
Sandy – Two, sir: football and cricket.

Lady (at lunch) – This isn't a clean knife, Jennie.
Maid – Well, it ought to be, because the last thing it cut was soap.

McDonald – I know a man who shaves more than twenty times a day.
McDougall – Who?
McDonald – A barber.

Policeman (after accident) – This man says you used your right indicator then turned left.
Motorist – Ah, well, you see, I'm left-handed.

Waiter – What? No tip! Why, the champion miser of the world once gave me a five-pence tip!
Diner – Then gaze upon the new champion.

Jones (showing off new suit) – I've got a suit for every day of the week now.
Smith – Really!
Jones – Yes, this is it.

Salesman – Ladies and gentlemen, I'm selling a wonderful comb that will stand any amount of rough handling. You can bend it, hit it with a hammer, twist it, bite it, and you can . . .
Listener (interrupting) – Can you comb your hair with it?

Magistrate – You say the defendant struck you? Have you any witnesses to prove it?
Plaintiff (pointing to black eye) – I have an eye-witness, your honour.

Old man – Haven't I seen your face somewhere else, sonny?
Donald – No, it's always here, between my ears.

Diner – Give me something to eat, and make it snappy.
Waiter – Will a crocodile sandwich do, sir?

Foreman – Why do you always pull your barrow instead of pushing it?
Workman – Because I hate the sight of it.

Danny – I dreamed last night that I was talking to the wisest man in the world.
Cuthbert – What did I say?

Old lady in department store – I want to buy enough wool to knit a sweater for my dog.
Saleswoman – How big is he?
Old lady – Oh, dear! It's hard to say exactly.
Saleswoman – Why not bring him in, and I'll be able to see how big he is, and tell you how much wool you will need.
Old lady – I couldn't do that – it's meant to be a surprise for him!

Why were the flies playing football on the saucer?
Because they were playing for the cup!

Diner – This restaurant must have a very clean kitchen.
Owner – Thank you, sir, but how did you know?
Diner – Everything tastes of washing-up liquid!

What is the best way to light a fire with two sticks?
Make sure one's a match!

What did the big tooth say to the small tooth?
"Get your coat on, the dentist is taking us out!"

Did you hear about the sheepdog trials?
Three of the dogs were found guilty!

Dennis – You should keep your eyes open this afternoon, mister.
Man – Why, sonny?
Dennis – You won't be able to see if you don't.

Terry – Why does that man keep staring at every garage and car park he passes?
Jerry – Because he's a nosey parker!

Teacher – Now, if I have ten tennis balls in one hand and eight in the other, what do I have?
David – Big hands, sir!

Sister – How did Mum find out you hadn't washed yourself?
Brother – I forgot to wet the soap!

One thousand bars of soap have been stolen from a warehouse.
Police say the thieves made a clean getaway.

Chris – I'm glad I wasn't born in France.
Louise – Why?
Chris – I don't speak French!

How do you get rid of a boomerang?
Throw it up a one-way street!

What happened to the hyena who ate a box of beef cubes?
He became the laughing stock!

Mum – Well, Jane, how does your teacher like your work?
Jane – I think she likes it. She puts little kisses beside all my sums.

Weary mother (to a group of wild children at a birthday party) – There is a special prize for the one who goes home first!

What does a skeleton serve his food on?
Bone china!

What do snowmen sing at parties?
"Freeze a jolly good fellow!"

New bricklayer (working on scaffolding) – How can I get down?
Foreman – Shut your eyes and walk about.

What sort of a boat would you take to shoot rapids?
A gunboat!

Minnie – Why are you going bald, Dad?
Dad – Oh, that's because my mother used to pat me on the head so much for being a good boy.

Doctor (to midnight visitor) – Well?
Visitor – Of course not – I'm ill!

Teacher – Now, Hamish, can you tell me why swans have long necks?
Hamish – To keep them from drowning at high tide.

Big brother – What's the idea of wearing my raincoat?
Little brother – Well, you don't want your shirt to get wet in the rain, do you?

Minnie – Please, Mum, may I have two pieces of cake?
Mum – Certainly. Cut the piece you have in half!

Plug – Let's see who can make the funniest face.
Wilfrid – No fear!
Plug – Why?
Wilfrid – Well, look at the start you've got.

What fish terrorises other fish?
Jack the Kipper!

Jenny – What is the most common parting gift?
Jill – A comb!

Why is a duck always in debt?
Because it always has a bill in front of it.

Farmer – Do you know it takes three sheep to make a sweater?
City man – Goodness! I didn't even know sheep could knit!

What do rabbits do when they get married?
They live hoppily ever after!

Knock! Knock!
Who's there?
Yvonne.
Yvonne who?
Yvonne though it is cold, I'm not wearing gloves!

Mum – Would you like a duck's egg for tea?
Billy – Only if you quack it for me!

Woman – I bought a carpet that was in mint condition.
Neighbour – What do you mean?
Woman – It had a hole in middle of it!

Teacher – Give me the name of an underground creature.
Smiffy – A worm.
Teacher – Any other creature?
Smiffy – Another worm!

Maggie – B-Bert! There's a cow in the garden!
Bert – Well, don't stand there stammering, lass! Get a pail and milk it before it runs away!

Spectator at a football match – Go on! Shoot, Bill!
Second spectator – Why pick on Bill?

Passenger (in train) – I wish I had my piano with me!
Ticket collector – What for?
Passenger – I've left my ticket on it!

Teacher – You mean to tell me you don't know where your tonsils are?
Danny – That's right. You see, they were taken out over a year ago!

Teacher – Give me a sentence with the word "omnivorous"!
Fatty – Omnivorous happy as when I'm eating toffee apples!

Cuddles – Why are you washing your feet with your socks on?
Dimples – The water's cold!

Guide – I'm sorry I can't show you round the castle just now. Food and drink aren't allowed inside.
Visitor – But I'm not eating anything.
Guide – No, but I am.

Why do bees have sticky hair?
Because they use honey combs!

Manager – We want you to leave on medical grounds.
Player – But I'm fully fit.
Manager – I know, but we're sick of you!

How does a sparrow land safely when it has engine failure?
By sparachute!

Which musical instrument could be used for fishing?
A cast-a-net!

Which animals on Noah's ark did not come in pairs?
Worms! They came in apples!

Garry – My nerves are so very bad that I can't close my eyes at night.
Barry – Try boxing. After my first lesson I couldn't open my eyes for days.

Customer (in store) – May I see some of your pipes?
Assistant – Gas, water, drain, or bag, sir?

Garry – I was troubled with rheumatism in school today!
Mum – Nonsense! You're too young to have rheumatism.
Garry – It wasn't that, Mum! I couldn't spell it!

Patient – I haven't slept for days!
Doctor – What's the matter?
Patient – Nothing. I sleep at nights!

Manager – So you want a job as a sardine packer? Have you had any experience in this line?
Applicant – Well, I've been a bus conductor for two years.

Smith – Hello, bought a saxophone?
Jones – No, I borrowed it from the man next door.
Smith – But you can't play it.
Jones – Neither can he while I've got it.

Mum – Did you go and see if the butcher had pigs' feet?
Dennis – Yes, but I couldn't see! He had his shoes on!

Mrs Meanie – I want you to paint my house, but I won't be able to pay you until next year. When can you start?
Painter – Next year!

Boss – What would you do with two thousand pounds?
Office boy – Gosh, I wasn't expecting a wage increase, sir!

Teacher – An epidemic is something that spreads rapidly. Now, Smiffy, can you name an epidemic?
Smiffy – Margarine?

What's worse than being with a fool?
Fooling with a bee!

When is a Scotsman like a donkey?
When he stands on the banks and brays!

Why did the burglar cut the legs off his bed?
Because he wanted to lie low for a while!

A man bought a parrot for £25 at an auction. When he went to pay for the bird he asked if it was a good talker.
The auctioneer replied: "You should know – he was the only one bidding against you!"

Charity collector – Can I have a donation for the new swimming pool?
Mrs Meanie – Certainly! Here's a bucket of water!

What runs around the forest making the other animals yawn?
A wild bore!

Man – Do you have any camouflage jackets?
Shopkeeper – Yes, we have hundreds of them, but I can't find them!

Teacher – What does the world 'asset' mean?
Charlie – It's a young donkey, sir!

Boss (to boy applying for job) – I want someone who's good at book-keeping!
Forgetful Fred – That's me! I've had six reminders from the library about the book I borrowed months ago!

Toots – Why do you wear only one glove? Lost the other?
'Erbert – No! I found this one!

Ma – There's some apple-pie left. Have you had all you want?
Tommy – No, but I've had all I can eat!

An engineering student went went to visit a factory.

"Have you any experience of working in this industry?" the foreman asked.
"Not much," the student replied.
"Well, what do you know about gas regulations?"
"I know it's mark 5 for a sponge," said the student.

Brown – I once knew a man who was so small that his shirt was only the size of a handkerchief.
Green – That's nothing!
Brown – I knew a man who was so small that when his corns hurt, he thought it was toothache!

Boy – Do you notice any change in me?
Mum – No, why?
Boy – I've just swallowed twenty-five pence!

Angry man – I'll teach you to throw stones at my greenhouse!
Boy – I wish you would! I've had ten shots and haven't hit it yet!

Customer – Is this a pedigree dog?
Dealer – Pedigree? Why, if this dog could speak, it wouldn't talk to either of us!

Patient – I keep seeing insects and creepy crawlies in front of my eyes.
Doctor – Don't worry, it's just a bug going about.

Garry – Mum, can I have fifty pence for an old man crying in the street?
Mum – Yes, of course. What's he crying about?
Garry – Toffee apples: fifty pence each.

What did the Judge say to the dentist?
"Do you swear to pull a tooth, a whole tooth, and nothing but the tooth?"

Plug – Once, I was surrounded by lions and tigers!
Toots – What did you do?
Plug – Nothing much, I just got off the roundabout at the end of the ride.

Patient – I am not feeling well.
Doctor – Well, go and stand at the window and stick your tongue out.
Patient – Why should I do that?
Doctor – Because I don't like the man on the other side of the road!

What does a monster do in the summer?
Goes on its horrordays!

Customer – Waiter, this soup is poisonous.
Waiter – Who told you?
Customer – A little swallow!

Dad – What's wrong, son?
Jamie – Tommy hurt my hand!
Dad – The big bully! How did it happen?
Jamie – I was going to punch him on the nose, but he ducked and I hurt my hand on the wall behind him!

Farmer Spriggs – I hear that you're giving your hens hot water to drink.
Farmer McKay – That's right! I want them to lay boiled eggs!

Teacher – John, your essay on your dog is word for word the same as your brother's.
John – Well, sir, it's the same dog.

Walter – Gnasher just chased an old lady on a bike.
Dennis – You must be mistaken, Gnasher hasn't got a bike.

Jo – My baby sister has been walking for four months.
Sue – Goodness, she must be tired.

A farmer had no chickens, nobody ever gave him any, he never bought, borrowed, begged or stole any, yet he had two eggs for breakfast every morning. How?
He kept ducks!

Visitor – How many people work in this office?
Office junior – Oh, about half of them!

Tim – Here's the money back that you gave me for a stamp!
Mum – Didn't you post my letter?
Tim – Yes, I posted it, but it didn't cost anything. I slipped it into the letterbox when nobody was looking.

Sailor Bob – Is that a good telescope you have?
Sailor Bill – I'll say it is. It brings that ship so close that you can hear the passengers drinking tea!

Why is a bird sitting on a fence like a penny?
Because there's a head on one side and a tail on the other!

Newsflash – A pet shop in Liverpool was broken into last night and thirty-five dogs taken. Police are looking for the culprits, but so far they haven't come up with any leads.

Collector – We are collecting for 'Save The Children Fund', can you help, madam?
Tired mother – Certainly, you can have my nine to start with!

Teacher – What do you call an American Indian's wife?
Sammy – A squaw!
Teacher – What do you call an American Indian's baby?
Sammy – A squawker!

Plumber – I'm sorry I'm late, but I just couldn't get here sooner.
Man of the house – Well, time hasn't been wasted. While we were waiting for you, I taught my wife how to swim.

Why didn't the little pig listen to his father?
He was just an old boar!

Dad – What was that noise I heard in your room last night?
Jock – That was me falling asleep!

Canoing instructor (in canoe) – Careful now, one move and the canoe will capsize!
Smiffy – Er . . . will it be all right if I move my chewing gum to the other side of my mouth?

First farmer – I had a bad time last year. My wheat was only an inch high!
Second farmer – You should worry! My wheat was so small, the sparrows had to kneel to eat it!

Teacher – I thought I told you to write an essay on "chees"?
Smiffy – Have you tried it? Your pen gets all clogged up!

In a bank, a little boy suddenly called out, "Did anyone drop a pile of money with a rubber band round it?" Several people at different tellers' windows answered, "I did."
"Well, I just found the rubber band," said the little boy.

What sort of lighting did Noah use on his Ark?
Flood lighting!

Auntie – Would you like me to give you fifty pence?
Hamish – Yes.
Auntie – Yes what?
Hamish – Yes, if you can't afford any more!

Nosey visitor – Why does that stork stand on one leg?
Zoo keeper – Because if he lifted it, he'd fall down!

Diner – If this is chicken, I'm a fool!
Waiter – Quite correct, sir. It is chicken!

Sidney – I wish Napoleon had been Russian!
Toots – Why?
Sidney – Because that's what I've written on my exam paper!

Joe – Want to buy a pen-knife?
John – What's wrong with it?
Joe – Nothing!
John – Then what are you selling it for?
Joe – Nothing!
John – Right! I'll have it at that price!

City gent – What's that noise, guide?
Country guide – That's an owl, sir!
City gent – I know that! But who's howling!

Office junior – I think you're wanted on the phone, sir.
Boss – You think? Why don't you know, boy?
Office junior – Well, the voice on the phone only said, "Is that you, you old fool?"

Henry – This watch you sold me is always slow!
Jeweller – Well, sir, you did ask for the latest type!

First camper – Isn't that drain-pipe rather hard for a pillow?
Second camper – No, I've stuffed it with straw!

Plug – It's funny how the biggest fools have the most sensible pals!
Smiffy – Stop the flattery, now!

New footman – In my last place I took things easy!
Butler – It's different here. We lock everything up!

Bookseller – This excellent book will do half your work.
Schoolboy – Good! I'll take two!

First cat – How did you get on in the milk-drinking competition?
Second cat – Oh, I won by six laps!

Quiz master – Who was the first woman in the world?
Jack – Give me a clue.

Quiz master – Apple . . .
Jack – I've got it! Granny Smith!

What can't you eat for your lunch or dinner!
Your breakfast!

Plug – I heard something this morning that opened my eyes!
Danny – What was it?
Plug – An alarm clock!

Teacher – Why are you late, Danny?
Danny – Because of a sign down the road.
Teacher – What has a sign got to do with you being late?
Danny – The sign said – "School Ahead, Go Slow".

Pharmacist (preparing lotion) – Boy, bring me a blue bottle!
New assistant – I can't see one. Will an ordinary fly do?

Smith – How do you like your new gas fire?
Jones – Great! I lit it a fortnight ago and it hasn't gone out once!

Office boy – Have you an opening for a bright young boy?
Boss – Yes, but don't slam it as you go out!

Joe – I don't like cheese with holes in it!
Mum – Stop being fussy! Eat the cheese and leave the holes at the side of your plate!

Teacher – Where does sugar come from?
Mary – From Mrs Smith next door!

Boss – That new office boy is lazy!
Clerk – Yes, slow in everything.
Boss – No – not everything! He gets tired very quickly!

What has ten legs but can't walk?
Five pairs of trousers!

Joe – I'm thirteen now!
Jim – Thirteen? But you were only six last year!
Joe – That's right! Six last year and seven this year! That makes thirteen!

Mum – Where's the sponge I told you to buy?
Smiffy – I couldn't see a good one. They all had holes in them!

Teacher – Tell me what a clean sweep is, Danny?
Danny – One that's had a bath.

Lady – Can I try on that dress that's in the window?
Assistant – Yes, but I think it would be better if you tried it on in a changing room!

Patient – Doctor, doctor, I swallowed a plank yesterday.
Doctor – How do you feel?
Patient – Board stiff.

Teacher – I hear the school fencing team lost last night.
Pupil – Yes, foiled again!

Auctioneer – Now, gentlemen, how much for this valuable cup? Someone give me a start?
Voice – Four pence!
Auctioneer (horrified) – What?
Voice – Ah, I thought that would give you a start!

Dad – What's your new teacher like?
Minnie – She's so sour-faced, that if she put face-cream on, it would curdle!

Archie – There was a burglar in our house last night!
P.C. Murdoch – What did your father do under the circumstances?
Archie – He wasn't under the circumstances – he was under the bed!

Cuddles – Do you know what Italians do with banana skins?
Dimples – No.
Cuddles – Throw them away!

Doctor – Take three tablespoons of this medicine a day.
Man – Then I'll have to borrow another tablespoon. I've only got two at home!

Teacher – What is a snail?
Sidney – A worm with a crash helmet on.

Teacher – Why do polar bears have fur coats?
Wilfrid – Well . . . er . . . oh, I suppose they'd look funny in tweed ones!

Dad – Did you break the window this morning?
Minnie – No.
Dad – Are you sure?
Minnie – Positive! I broke it last night!

The doctor stood by the bedside, and looked down at the sick man. "I cannot hide from you the fact that you are gravely ill," he said. "Is there anyone you would like to see?"

"Yes," replied the patient faintly. "Another doctor."

Girl – How much is that budgie?
Shop owner – Twenty pounds.
Girl – Fine, send me the bill.
Shop owner – Sorry, madam, but you have got to take the whole bird.

Teacher – Have you heard of Julius Caesar?
Danny – Yes, sir.
Teacher – What do you think he would be doing now if he were alive?
Danny – Drawing the old-age pension.

Teacher (explaining arithmetic problem) – Now watch the board while I run through it once more.

Terry – Where are you going?
Jerry – To collect strawberries.
Terry – In those horrible-looking trousers?
Jerry – No. In this basket.

Why did the sword-swallower start eating pins and needles?
Because he was on a diet!

Where's the best place to hold a party on a ship?
Where the funnel (fun will) be!

Teacher – Where are elephants usually found?
Danny – They're so big they aren't often lost.

Teacher – An anonymous person is one who wishes to remain unknown and . . . who is that laughing?
Pupil – Please, sir, an anonymous person.

Millionaire – I came to this country without a shirt on my back and now I've gathered two million.
Awed voice – Gosh, mister, you'll never wear them all out!

First postman – I am not going to that house again.
Second postman – Afraid on account of the dog?
First postman – Yes, my trousers are.
Second postman – Your trousers are what?
First postman – Frayed on account of the dog.

Jim – Are you superstitious?
Jack – No.
Jim – Good! You won't mind lending me thirteen pounds, then!

Diner – What kind of bird is this, waiter?
Waiter – It's a wood pigeon, sir.
Diner – I thought so. Bring me a saw!

Patient – Doctor, doctor. I keep thinking that I'm a goat.
Doctor – Have you had this feeling long?
Patient – Ever since I was a kid.

News flash – Last night a lorry carrying glue turned over on the M1. Police are asking motorists to stick to the "A" roads.

Teacher – What is the plural of hippopotamus?
Toots – The plural is . . . oh, well, er, well, who'd want more than one anyway?

Boastful man – There I was on a lonely road, miles from anywhere, with a blazing car. What do you think I did?
Bored listener – Took a deep breath and blew it out.

Dennis – Dad, what do you do at the office all day?
Dad (fed up answering questions) – Oh, nothing.
Dennis – Then how do you know when you're finished?

Customer – Have you a horse that won't jump or rear or run away, and will trot along peacefully.
Dealer – Do you want a clothes horse or a rocking horse, sir?

Lady MacDonald – Why are you cleaning the inside of the windows but not the outside?
Maid – That way, madam, you can look out, but the people outside can't look in.

Diner _ Waiter, I haven't been given a teaspoon
Waiter – There are none left, sir. But I'll tell the orchestra to play something stirring!

Tom – What goes dot, dash, croak, dot, dash, croak?
Jim – I don't know. What goes dot, dash, croak, dot, dash, croak?
Tom – Morse toad!

Customer – Waiter, I can't eat this soup!
Waiter – I'll get the manager, sir!
Customer – Manager, I can't eat this soup!
Manager – Sorry sir, I'll get the chef.
Chef – What's wrong with the soup?
Customer – Nothing. I haven't got a spoon!

Where do spacemen park their spaceships?
At space meteors!

Sam – What is white and hairy with green spots?
Tom – I don't know.
Sam – Neither do I, but there's one crawling up your leg.

Teacher – You ought to be ashamed of yourself. A boy of your age, who can only count to ten. What are you going to be when you grow up?
Micky – A boxing referee.

Mike (to an old enemy) – I'm living in a house across the river. I'd really be pleased if you'd drop in some day!

Uncle – You're awfully quiet, Tommy!
Tommy – Well, Mum gave me five pounds not to say anything about your bald head and your big red hose!

Manager – I hope you have been carefully brought up, my boy.
Office boy – Yes, sir. I came up in the lift

Have you heard of the car that runs out and in?
Out of petrol and into lamp-posts!

Charlie – Have you see a man-eating tiger?
Jimmy – No, but I've seen a man eating haddock.

Jack – Please, sir, Dad's upset a bottle of the hair-restorer over his trousers.
Barber – Then I presume he wants another bottle.
Jack – No, sir, he wants you to come and shave his trousers.

Kindly old man – Will you two boys stop fighting if I give you a pound each?
Young scamp – Make it two pounds for the winner, sir.

Why did the girl keep a loaf of bread in her comic?
She liked crummy jokes!

What is a waste of time?
Telling a hair-raising story to a bald man!

Jack – I wanted to go water skiing for my holiday, but I couldn't manage.
Jill – Oh, why not?
Jack – I couldn't find a lake with a slope!

Why did the needle start to cry?
Because it had something in its eye.

Auntie – What are you making with your chemistry set, Cuthbert?
Cuthbert – A liquid that will dissolve anything!
Auntie – How clever! What are you going to keep it in?

Footballer – This ointment makes my arm smart!
Trainer – You should rub some into your head then!

Comedian – I was insulted last night!
Friend – What happened?
Comedian – The manager put me on stage after a performing monkey act, and the audience thought it was an encore!

How do you speak to a fish?
Drop it a line!

Plug – Did you know that the most handsome person in the world was going deaf?
Teacher – Really, who is it?
Plug – Pardon?

A woman with six children was trying to get on to a crowded bus.
"You should have left half your children at home," said the conductor.
"I did," said the woman wearily.

Knock! Knock.
Who's there?
Nobel.
Nobel who?
Nobel, so I knock, knock!

Minnie and her dad are out fishing.
Minnie – Is it true that fish go about in schools, Dad?
Dad – Yes, Minnie.
Minnie – Well, these ones you've caught must have been in the infant class!

When is water musical?
When it's piping hot.

New office boy – I've added up the figures ten times, sir!
Boss – Good lad!
Office boy – Here are the ten answers!

Teacher – What is a mirror?
Smiffy – I don't know!
Teacher – You don't know? What do you look at to see if you're clean when you have washed?
Smiffy – A towel, sir.

Why is a snake clever?
Because you can't pull its leg!

Diner – Hey waiter! You've given me a wet plate!
Waiter – That's your soup, sir!

Judge – Have you anything to say?
Accused – I've plenty to say, sir if you'll just give me time to say it.
Judge – Certainly. You can have three months!

Jim – What does your father do for a living?
Joe – Chops trees down!
Jim – What does he do when he has chopped them down?
Joe – Chops them up!

Why was the 14th century known as the dark age?
Because there were so many knights!

James – I've fallen into the bad habit of talking to myself!
Jones – I wondered why you were looking so bored!

Teacher – The school orchestra played Beethoven last night.
Smiffy – Who won?

Why did the boy's granny knit him three socks for Christmas?
Because he had written to say he had grown another foot!

What do gorillas sing at Christmas?
Jungle Bells, Jungle Bells . . .

Mrs Jones to station porter – Which way to platform four, please?
Porter – Turn left and you'll be right!
Mrs Jones – I'm sure you're wrong!
Porter – Okay, turn right and you'll be left!

Patrick – I've just been out riding.
Peter – Horseback?
Patrick – Yes, the horse got back hours before me!

Landlord – I'm glad you've stopped complaining about the plaster falling!
Tenant – Yes, it's all down now!

Teacher – You'd be a good dancer if it weren't for two things.
Plug – What are they?
Teacher – Your feet!

Customer – Do you make life-size enlargements?
Chemist – Yes.
Customer – Well, here's a snapshot of Mount Everest!

Railway traveller – Congratulations! I've travelled on this railway for thirty years and this is the first time I've known the train to arrive on time. Have a cigar!
Driver – Keep your cigar! This is yesterday's train!

Mother – John, what is the cause of all that racket coming from the pantry?
John – Me! I'm busy fighting temptation, Mum!

Tom – Jack, there was a dog and a hedgehog fighting in the road a minute ago.
Jack – Who won?
Tom – The hedgehog of course, on points!

Girl – I'd like two ounces of bird seed please.
Pet shop owner – How many birds have you, dear?
Girl – None, that's why I want the seed to grow some!

Knock! Knock!
Who's there?
Felix.
Felix who?
Felix my ice cream, I'll lick his!

Patient – Doctor, doctor, I keep on dreaming I'm being followed by a snow-man!
Doctor – Just stand beside a fire and your dreams will melt away.

Teacher (to pupil) – What happens to a body when it is immersed in water?
Pupil – Please, miss, the phone rings!

Judge – Why did you steal the woman's purse?
Prisoner – I wasn't feeling well, Your Honour, and I thought the change would do me good!

Actor – I can't possibly play the three parts you've given me in the play.
Producer – Why not?
Actor – Well, in the first act I have to fight with myself and then rush in and separate the two of us!

House buyer – I want a house out in the country, at least five miles away from any other house!
Estate agent – Ah, you want to practise the simple life?
House buyer – No, I want to practise the bagpipes!

Fatty – I'm a mind reader, you know!
Smiffy – Really? Can you read my mind?
Fatty – No! I've left my magnifying glass at home!

What happened to the man who kept throwing his pudding into the street? He was held in custardy for six days!

Patient – Doctor, doctor, I feel like an ice cream.
Doctor – Here's twenty pence. Get me one too!

Jill – Why are you running?
Jack – To stop a fight.
Jill – Who's fighting?
Jack – Me and another fellow.

Lady – Could I have a bath bun, please?
Baker – Certainly, madam! Would you like a sponge to go with it?

Teacher – In Great Britain, where are kings and queens crowned?
Smiffy – On the head!

Tourist – Where does this road go to?
Local – Nowhere. It's here every day!

Bob – What's the idea of calling your dog "Swindler"?
Bill – Just for fun. You should see half the people jump when I call him in the street.

Fred – My grandfather's clock is one hundred years old.
Ted – That's nothing. My grandfa-ther's clock is so old that the shadow of the pendulum has worn a hole in the back.

I know a dog who eats garlic . . . his bark is much worse than his bite!

Son – Dad, can I have another glass of water?
Dad – Another? This is your tenth!
Son – I know, but my room's on fire!

Street hawker – Do you want any laces, studs, buckles, ribbons, ties . . .?
Mrs Jones – Go away or I'll call the police.
Street hawker – Here you are, madam: whistles, five pounds each!

How did the man feel when he was run over by a steamroller? Flattered!

Mr Jones – Excuse me, officer, I've lost my dog.
Policeman – Come back tomorrow, sir, we might have a lead on him.

Teacher – I told you to do five hundred lines for bad English, and you've only done fifteen!
Danny – Yes sir, I'm no good at maths either!

First salesman – What do you sell?
Second salesman – Salt!
First salesman – Why, I'm a salt seller too.
Second salesman – Shake!

One morning Ed saw Bob running along the road pushing his bike.
Ed – What's wrong with your bike, Bob?
Bob – It's not the bike, it's me! I got up late and haven't had time to get on it!

Diner – I've found a cuff-link in my soup!
Waiter – Thank you, sir. I've looked everywhere for it!

Dennis – Quick! Dad's being chased by a bull!
Chemist – What do you want? Bandages? Splints? Ointment?
Dennis – No! A film for my camera!

First boy – My dad's a film star.
Second boy – My dad's connected with the movies, too.
First boy – I know, I saw him driving a furniture van yesterday.

McTavish – I've been swindled! I answered an advertisement that said, "Send a pound for an instrument that will halve your bills".
McLaren – And what did you get?
McTavish – A pair of scissors.

Why is a banana like a sweater? You slip on both!

What do you call two spiders who have just got married?
Newlywebs!

Who invented the sword dance?
Someone who wanted to dance and cut his toe-nails at the same time!

What do you get if you cross a football team with some ice-cream? Aston Vanilla.

Teacher – What happens to sailors who don't eat their vegetables?
Toots – They don't get any pudding!

Two mice were sitting eating a reel of film.
First mouse – I don't think much of this film.
Second mouse – No, the book wasn't much good either.

Customer – Have you any invisible paint?
Painter – Yes. What colour would you like?

Diner – Boil my eggs for four minutes, please!
Waiter – Yes, sir. Be ready in half a second!

Servant – The doctor's here, sir!
Absent-minded professor – Tell him to go away. I'm too ill to see him!

Teacher – If I have forty apples, and eat twenty of them, what have I got?
Plug – A stomach ache!

Where do rabbits go when they marry?
On a bunnymoon!

Patient – Doctor, doctor, I feel like a ten pound note.
Doctor – Then go and buy something, the change will do you good.

Small ghost – Mum, how did you meet Dad?
Mummy ghost – Oh, it was love at first fright.

Sue – Where do tadpoles change to frogs?
Sandra – Croakrooms!

Patient – Doctor, you know those strengthening tablets you gave me?
Doctor – Yes . . .
Patient – Well, I can't get the lid off!

How does a pixie eat?
By goblin!

Mum – What are you doing, Sammy?
Sammy – I'm writing a letter to Cousin Bobby.
Mum – But you haven't learned to write yet.
Sammy – That's all right. Bobby can't read yet.

Ticket inspector – Here, you can't use this ticket. It says London to Glasgow, not Glasgow to London.
Smiffy – That's all right, I'm sitting with my back to the engine!

Mrs Gow – If you want work, Farmer McNab is looking for a right-hand man!
Lazy Len – What a pity. I'm left-handed!

What's a ghost's favourite sport?
Spooker!

What surprising things happen every day?
Day breaks, but doesn't fall – Night falls, but doesn't break!

Smiffy – These shoes you sold me don't fit.
Shoemaker – But you've got them on the wrong feet.
Smiffy – They're the only feet I've got, aren't they?

Mechanic – See how much petrol is in the tank.
Apprentice – It says 'half' on the indicator, but I don't know whether it's half-full or half-empty.

First snake – Are we supposed to be poisonous?
Second snake – Why?
First snake – Because I've just bitten my lip!

Teacher – You are fifteen minutes late for school, girl!
Toots – No, I'm actually only five minutes late. I was outside thinking of an excuse for ten minutes!

Doctor – You need new glasses!
'Erbert – How on earth do you know that?
Doctor – I could tell as soon as you walked staright through the door!

Joe – When I grow up, I'm going to be a policeman and follow in my father's footsteps.
Jack – I didn't know your father was a policeman.
Joe – He's not. He's a burglar!

Which two words have thousands of letters in them?
Post Office!

Auntie Flo – What brings you to the city, Sidney?
Sidney – I came to see the sights, so I thought I'd call on you first!

Which famous chiropodist conquered England?
William the Corn Curer!

Jack – Why is Dad singing?
Mum – He's singing baby to sleep.
Jack – If I were baby I'd pretend to be asleep.

Car dealer – This car has had one careful owner.
Customer – But it's all smashed up.
Car dealer – The other owners weren't so careful.

What do you call an elephant at the North Pole?
Lost!

Teacher – What is concrete made of?
Danny – Ooh, that's a hard question!

What swings through the jungle playing rock 'n' roll?
Guitarzan!

What can you serve, but not eat?
A tennis ball.

Terry – You say this fellow is crooked?
Jerry – Crooked? Even the wool he pulls over your eyes is half cotton.

Actor – What? You want me to jump off that cliff into the water? I won't. The water's only a foot deep.
Producer – Naturally. We don't want you to drown.

Customer – Are those eggs fresh?
Grocer (to assistant) – Feel the eggs, George, and see if they're cool enough to sell yet!

Mr Meanie – I want a cheap coat-hanger.
Shopkeeper – This one is twenty pence, sir.
Mr Meanie – Have you nothing cheaper?
Shopkeeper – Only a nail, sir.

Passenger – Does this bus stop at the Ritz Hotel?
Conductor – No we leave it in the garage at night.

Boaster – After I'd sung my encore, I heard a gentleman in the audience call out, "Fine! Fine!"
Bored friend – Dear me – and did you have to pay it?

Smiffy – There are three things I can't remember. I can't remember names. I can't remember faces and . . .
Danny – What's the third thing?
Smiffy – I can't remember.

What do you call a ghost in a doctor's surgery?
A surgical spirit!

Alan – What kind of fish can't swim?
Keith – I don't know.
Alan – Dead ones!

What is the difference between an elephant and a biscuit?
You can't dip an elephant in your tea!

Motorist – I'm terribly sorry I've just run over one of your pigs. But don't worry, I'll replace it.
Farmer – Impossible. You're not fat enough.

Boaster – I throw myself whole-heartedly into everything I undertake.
Bored listener – Have you tried digging a well?

Mum – There are two cream buns in the cupboard this morning and now there's only one. Why is that?
Fatty – It must've been so dark I didn't see the other one!

Judge – Do you mean to say such a physical wreck as the accused gave you that black eye?
Plaintiff (indignantly) – He wasn't a physical wreck till after he gave me the black eye!

Who invented the fraction?
Henry the 1/8!

Boastful Benny – I've just got back from a trip round the world.
Lenny – Did you visit Egypt?
Benny – Yeah!
Lenny – Go up the Nile?
Benny – Sure. Great view from the top.

What dance do tin-openers do?
The can-can!

Patient – Doctor, doctor, I feel like a banana.
Doctor – Come back tomorrow and I will try to slip you in.

Gentleman – Waiter, waiter! What is this fly doing in my soup?
Waiter – Well it needed a bath after falling in the flour, sir!

Why did the electrician eat electric bulbs at noon?
Because he wanted a light lunch.

How do ghosts travel?
By British scareways!

Johnny – Jimmy McDougal said his father could wipe up the floor with you.
Dad – You didn't let him get away with that, did you?
Johnny – Of course not! I asked him to bring his father round tomorrow night to prove it!

Poet – I'm going to publish a book of poems under the pen name of John Smith.
Critic – That's unfair! Think of all the innocent people who will be suspected!

Auctioneer – I am offering this splendid sofa at a bargain price. Who will take it away for twenty pounds?
Voice from the crowd – Show me the money!

Doctor – Have you been waiting long?
Patient – Well, did you know that there are 291,474 spots in your wallpaper?

Employer (to new typist) – I hope you thoroughly understand the importance of punctuation.
Typist – Don't you worry, sir. I always get to work on time.

Terry – How do you like your new gas fire?
Jerry – It's wonderful. I lit it a fortnight ago, and it hasn't gone out since!

Salesman – This car is so economical that it soon pays for itself.
McSporran – Let me know when it does and I'll take it.

Toots – What do you get if you cross soap with some toothpaste?
Sidney – I don't know, what?
Toots – A bubbling smile!

First sportsman – I've got a terrible cold. I won't be able to make the high hump.
Second sportsman – Why not?
First sportsman – I can't even clear my throat!

Teacher – Smiffy, spell weather.
Smiffy – W-E-V-V-E-R.
Teacher – That's the worst spell of weather we've had for some time.

What lies on the ground, a hundred feet up in the air?
A centipede!

How do you catch a squirrel?
Climb up a tree, and act like a nut.

What do you call Chinese spies?
Peking Toms.

Wilfrid (seeing Smiffy cutting his clothes with scissors) – What are you doing, Smiffy?
Smiffy – I'm taking all the wool labels off my clothes and putting on cotton labels.
Wilfrid – Goodness! Why?
Smiffy – I want to fool the moths!

Motorist – We've got a puncture!
Friend – You should have been more careful. You knew there was a fork in the road near here!

Landlady – I don't suppose you know what it is to starve?
Lodger – No, but I'm learning!

Smith – Jones is so conceited!
Smythe – Isn't he! On his last birthday he sent a telegram of congratulations to his mother!

Visitor – When I was here before, there were two windmills.
Farmer – We took one down to leave more wind for the other!

Jock – You're just a typical hen-pecked husband!
Jake – You wouldn't dare say that if my wife was here!

Diner – I find that I have just enough money to pay for the dinner, but I have nothing in the way of a tip for yourself.
Waiter – Let me add up that bill again, sir.

Crossword puzzle fan – I've been trying to think of a word for two weeks.
Pal – How about "fortnight"?

McBoast – I played Jones at golf the other day. He's a superb player – tremendous hitter of a ball – perfect putter.
McDonald – How much were you beaten by?
McBoast – Oh, I won.

Smith – I passed by your place yesterday!
Jones – Thanks awfully!

Olive the dinner lady – Goodness! What a noise you make when you eat! Didn't you ever learn to eat politely?
Fatty – Olive, I've had so few meals it's a wonder I've learned to eat!

Who invented fire?
Some bright spark!

What time is it when an elephant sits on your fence?
Time to get a new one!

Teacher – Order, children, order!
Pupil – I'll have an ice-cream and jelly, please.

Cuddles – What is the opposite of "cock-a-doodle-do"?
Dimples – Cock-a-doodle-don't!

Sidney – What's the similarity between a pork chop and an old radio?
Fatty – Don't know.
Sidney – You get crackling off both!

Boy – If there's a referee in football, and an umpire in cricket, what is there in bowls?
Teacher – I don't know.
Boy – Goldfish.

Uncle Jim – Don't give in to bullies Johnny. I always believe in fighting an enemy with his own weapons!
Johnny – But, Uncle Jim, have you ever tried stinging a wasp?

Guest – This is a boring party! I'm going to leave right now!
Mrs Green – I would, too, but I've got to stay. I'm the hostess.

First man – I'm a man of few words.
Second man – I know what it's like – I'm married too.

Mr Green – Mr Brown, this is Mr White!
Mr Brown – Ah, Mr White! I've heard a great deal about you!
Mr White – You'll never prove it!

Old lady (seeing tug-of-war for the first time) – Why don't they take a knife, and cut it?

Boss – Why didn't you deliver that message as I instructed?
Terry – I did the best I could, sir!
Boss – The best you could? Why, if I had known I was going to send a fool, I would have gone myself!

Jack – How do you make a skeleton laugh?
Jill – I don't know.
Jack – You tickle its funny-bone!

Here's the bad news! My friend swallowed twenty five pence.
Here's the good news! It's all right, because it was his dinner money!

Customer – If I go on holiday to the Isle of Man, can I swim there?
Travel agent – Certainly, sir, but it's easier to take the ferry.

Why did the bird sleep on the chandelier?
Because he was a light sleeper.

Dennis – You must be an awfully clean lady, Mrs Jones!
Mrs Jones – Thank you, Dennis!
Dennis – Yes, my Dad says you're always sponging!

Cuthbert – Here, Toots, I've been told you've been calling me a bookworm!
Toots – Who said anything about books?

Jack – How is your father getting on with his diet?
John – Fine! The battleship he had tattooed on his chest is now a rowing boat!

Lady – No, thank you, I never buy anything at the door.
Salesman – Then I've just the thing for you, madam: "No Salesman" notices.

Nice old lady – And what are you going to do when you get as big as your father?
Little boy – Go on a diet!

Doctor – Did you follow my advice and count sheep till you fell asleep?
Patient – I counted up to 18,000.
Doctor – And then you fell asleep!
Patient – No, then it was time to get up.

First man – I don't think anyone will ever give us work!
Second man – Oh, I could work for anyone I please!
First man – Why don't you, then?
Second man – I don't seem to please anyone!

Smart – What are you doing with that bandage around your arm?
Simple – I fell on my face.
Smart – Then why bandage your arm?
Simple – I wouldn't be able to see where I was gong if I bandaged my face.

A little centipede came home crying. "Mummy, mummy, I've sprained my foot."
"Which foot have you sprained, dear?" said the mum.
"I can't tell you, I can only count to ten," replied the baby.

What is a meatball?
A dance in a butcher's shop!

Teacher – What is the capital of Iceland?
Pupil – "I" sir.

Peter – Would you like two fifty pence tickets?
Sandy – What for?
Pete – A pound!

Boy – How do you keep a boy in suspense?
Friend – I don't know. How?
Boy – I'll tell you tomorrow!

Traveller – Can I catch the express for London?
Porter – That depends on how fast you can run, sir. It left five minutes ago!

How does a bear forecast the weather?
With a bearometer!

Customer – A mousetrap! Quickly! I want to catch a bus!
Assistant – I don't think we've got one big enough for that!

Sergeant – Now then, I want some volunteers for railway work.
Private – Put me down as a sleeper, sir!

Pat – That barber's the meanest man I know!
Mike – Why?
Pat – He puts hair-restorer in the shaving-cream!

First diner – Don't you find eating rather difficult with that large moustache hanging over your lips?
Second diner – Yes, it's rather a strain!

Patient – Doctor, doctor, I've just swallowed a sheep!
Doctor – How do you feel?
Patient – Very ba-a-a-ad!

Dodgy Dan – I always admire people who sleep with their windows open.
Crafty Ken – Why, are you a doctor?
Dodgy Dan – No, a burglar!

Mary – Mum, please may I play the piano?
Mum – No, you can't. Your hands are dirty.
Mary – I will only play the black notes.

Garry – Your dad's car is like a baby!
Barry – Why do you say that?
Garry – 'Cause it doesn't go anywhere without a rattle!

Judge – Thirty days!
Cheerful prisoner – Hath September, April, June and November . . .

Bill – What do you call a hippy's wife?
Ben – Mississippi.

Mrs McTavish – When does the nine o'clock train leave?
Porter – Sixty minutes past eight, ma'am.

Car driver – It's great speeding along like this. Don't you feel glad to be alive?
Passenger – Glad isn't the word. I'm amazed!

Boss – What made you so late?
Lorry driver – I ran into a garage on the way!
Boss – Did you need repairs?
Driver – No, but the garage will!

Diner – Call the manager! I've never seen anything so tough as this stead.
Waiter – Wait till you see the manager!

Horse owner – Why didn't you keep up with the others?
Jockey – What? And leave the horse behind?

Diner – Waiter, there's a funny film in my soup.
Waiter – Well, what do you expect for two pounds? Star Wars?

What do you call a musical insect?
A humbug!

How do you make a poisonous snake cry?
Take away its rattle!

What do you get if you cross a turkey with an octopus?
Something with a leg for everyone at Christmas!

Manager – Look at the dust on my desk! Why can't you keep it polished like the banister rails?
Office boy – I can't slide down your desk!

How do you find out if a flea has bitten you?
Start from scratch!

Beryl – You know Fatty Johnson, the butcher? What do you suppose he weighs?
Cynthia – I don't know. What does he weigh?
Beryl – Meat!

Jack – A big beer keg fell on my head yesterday.
Bill – I bet it hurt.
Jack – No, it was light ale!

What do monkeys clean their bikes with?
Gorilo pads!

What happens when you throw a green rock into the red sea?
It gets wet!

Did you hear about the teenage boy who ran away with the circus?
The police made him bring it back!

What do you get if you cross a sheepdog with a jelly?
The collie wobbles?

American – The ceiling in my house is so high that I have to go up in a balloon to whitewash it.
Scotsman – That's nothing. In my house, the ceiling is so low that all we can eat is flat fish and pancakes.

Johnny – I'm going to be a teacher when I grow up, Dad.
Dad – But you don't know enough to be a teacher, my boy.
Johnny – Oh, that doesn't matter. You only have to ask questions.

Diner – Waiter, I have only one piece of steak today instead of the usual two.
Waiter – Sorry, sir. The cook must have forgotten to cut it in half.

Why was Goliath surprised when David hit him with a stone?
Because such a thing had never entered his head before!

Kevin – How are you doing these days?
Terry – Oh, I'm just managing to keep my head above water.
Kevin – I can see that by the colour of your neck!

Teacher – Can you tell me what happened in 1066, Smiffy?
Smiffy – Me? No. I can't even remember what happened last week!

Why is it cheap to feed a giraffe?
Because a little goes a long way!

Why do dragons sleep in the daytime?
Because they like to hunt knights!

Where do wasps come from?
Stingapore!

Jack – Your face is like a million dollars.
Jill – Why, thank you, Jack.
Jack – It's all green and wrinkled!

Mad scientist – I've just crossed a kookaburra with a man-eating tiger.
Assistant – What did you get?
Mad scientist – I don't know, but when it laughs, you'd better join in.

Teacher – Any more questions?
Smiffy – Please, sir, how many crumbs are there in a loaf of bread?

Mother – And do you really feel ill, Bobby?
Bobby – Well, Mum, I'm too ill to go to school, but I'm not ill enough for that yucky medicine.

Newsflash – There has been a theft in Disneyland. A crook was charged with taking the Mickey?

When does a bed change its size?
At night, when two feet are added to it!

Small boy – If I wash my face, will I be clean?
Mother – Let's soap for the best!

A doctor had just given a boy a vaccination, and was about to put a bandage on his arm.

"Would you put it on the other arm, please, doctor?" asked the boy.

"What's the point of that?" said the doctor. "I'll put it over your vaccination so that the other boys will know not to bang into it."

"You don't know the boys at my school!" said the boy sadly.

Doctor – You need glasses.
'Erbert – But I'm already wearing glasses!
Doctor – In that case, I need glasses!

How can you tell which end of a worm is it's head?
Tickle his tummy, and see which end smiles!

Teacher – If you had five apples on your desk, and the boy next to you took three, what would you have?
Boy – A fight, miss!

Little boy – Mister, why is your dog wearing black boots?
Old man – Because his brown ones are in the cobblers.

Manager – You let in thirteen goals, today.
Goalie – That's all right, I'm not superstitious!

Smiffy's dad – You know that music stool you sold me?
Shopkeeper – Yes.
Smiffy's dad – Well, I've twisted and turned it in all directions, and I can't get a single tune out of it.

When is it dangerous to enter a flower shop?
When the bulbs are shooting!

What do you call an interfering pig?
A nosy porker!

Diner – Waiter, there are two flies fighting my soup.
Waiter – Well, what do you expect for three pounds, a bull-fight?

Old lady – You say you were sent to prison for telling the truth?
Convict – Yes, lady. The judge asked me if I was guilty and I said "yes".

Mum – Come along, Danny, it's past time to get up.
Danny – Huh! It's no pastime for me – it's very hard work.

Teacher – How is it that you can never answer any of my questions?
Smiffy – Well, if I could, what would be the use of coming here?

First scout – I failed my first aid test.
Second scout – Why?
First scout – I tried to put a plaster on a hiccup!

Patient – Doctor, doctor, I feel like a pound note!
Doctor – Go shopping. The change will do you good.

What has feathers, fangs and goes quack-quack?
Count Duckula!

Dad – Didn't you promise not be naughty again?
Tommy – Yes, Dad!
Dad – Well, didn't I promise to punish you if you were?
Tommy – Yes, Dad, but since I didn't keep my part of the bargain you needn't keep yours!

Diner – Waiter, why are the flies so thick around here?
Waiter – Well, sir, we just can't keep them thin. The food is too good.

Teacher – What is memory?
Smiffy – The thing you forget with.

Uncle – You look rather puzzled, Freddie.
Freddie – Yes, uncle, I was just wondering if a wasp settled on a nettle, would the wasp sting the nettle or would the nettle sting the wasp?

Teacher – Make a sentence, using the word "politics" in it.
Jack – Our parrot swallowed a wrist watch, and now Polly ticks!

Friend – Why are you putting up your wallpaper with tacks?
Miser – You don't think I'm staying here all my life, do you?

Sandy – May I have an extra day's pay this week, sir?
Boss – Whatever for?
Sandy – I dreamt about my work all last night!

First workman – Does the foreman know that the trench has fallen in?
Second workman – No, but we're just digging him out to tell him!

Teacher – Can you give me an example of a collective noun?
Sidney – A vacuum cleaner, sir.

Teacher – Now Bobby, if your father could save thirty pounds a week for two years, what would he have?
Bobby – A new car, miss!

Did you hear about the cat who joined the Red Cross?
He wanted to be a first aid kit!

Jo – Flo, if a red house is made of red bricks, a blue house made of blue bricks and a yellow house made of yellow bricks, what's a green house made of?
Flo – Green bricks!
Jo – No, glass, stupid!

What did one ear say to the other?
"I didn't know we lived in the same block!"

Man to friend – How do you know I live in a small flat?
Friend – Your dog is wagging his tail up and down!

Why do people laugh up their sleeves? Because that's where their funny bones are!

Bert – That's a fine dog you've got. Is he faithful?
Bob – He is that! I've sold him five times and he always comes back!

Teacher – What is an optimist?
Danny – An optimist is someone who doesn't care what happens as long as it happens to somebody else!

Boss – So you want a job, eh? Do you ever tell lies?
Applicant – No, sir – but I could learn if I had to.

Terry – My brother has a new job.
Jerry – He's connected with the police department.
Terry – Police department. How?
Jerry – By a pair of handcuffs.

Boy – Why did the hedgehog cross the road?
Girl – Don't know.
Boy – To get a chocolate bar. Did you get it?
Girl – No.
Boy – Neither did he, he only had twelve pence!

Why is it against the law to whisper? Because it isn't aloud.

What do you put in a currant cake?
Your teeth!

George – The lion-tamer at the circus was attacked by his lions last night.
Dave – Was he clawed?
George – I don't know what his name was.

Where do flies go in the winter time?
To the glassworks to make bluebottles!

**Lord Posh – My last butler left me
without any warning.
Lord Posher – You're lucky, mine left
me without any silver!**

*Freddie – Mum, what happens to a car
when it's too old to go any more?
Mother – Somebody sells it to your dad!*

Hector – I've seen ants so big that they
could uproot a tree.
Hamish – What kind of ants.
Hector – Elephants!

**Sandy – Mum, I dreamed last night
that I fell into the sea.
Mum – Well?
Sandy – Well . . . er . . . I won't need to
wash my face this morning, will I?**

*What exams do farmers have to take?
Hay levels!*

Jean – Why did Cinderella get put out of
the football team?
Joan – She ran away from the ball!

**What do you call a Roman Emperor
with hay-fever?
Julius Sneezer.**

*Why did the biscuit cry?
Because its mother was a wafer too long!*

Who did Dracula marry?
His necks door neighbour!

**What do you do at a clock factory?
Sit down and make faces.**

*Patient – Doctor, doctor, I've lost my
memory.*

Hugh – You don't mean to tell me that
fish are musicians?
Charlie – Certainly. Have you never
heard of the piano tuna?

**Doctor – When did this happen?
Patient – When did what happen?**

*One mouse collapsed. What did the other
mouse do?
He used mouse-to-mouse resuscitation!*

What do misers do in cold weather?
Sit around a candle!
What do misers do in exceptionally cold
weather?
Light the candle!

**What's grey and flies out of a burrow
at 200 mph?
A hareoplane.**

*What is white and furry, and smells of
peppermints?
A polo bear!*

What's the difference between a mouldy
lettuce and a dismal song.
One's a bad salad, and the other's a sad
ballad!

**Terry – This neighbourhood seems a
bit noisy.
Jerry – Yes, the only time it's quiet
here is when a train goes by and
drowns outthe noise.**

*Boastful singer – I just can't help break-
ing into song.
Bored listener – If you got the right key,
you wouldn't have to break in.*

Joe – So you're good at conundrums, eh?
Well, try this one. Take away my first let-
ter, then my second, then all my letters,
and I'm still the same. What am I?
Moe – I give in.
Joe – A postman.

**Fatty – I'm putting on weight, doctor.
What can I do about it?
Doctor – Take regular exercise.
Fatty – What kind of exercise?
Doctor – Push yourself away from the
table three times a day!**

What's it called when a policeman goes to bed?
Laying down the law!

Penny – Do you know what the dragon said when he saw St George, in shining armour, bearing down on him?
Jenny – What?
Penny – Oh, no, not more tinned food!

What would you do if you saw two skeletons crossing the road?
Jump out of your skin and join them!

What is the opposite of minimum?
Minidad!

What is green and sings in the garden.
Elvis Parsley.

Teacher – Name four animals that live in the jungle.
Smiffy – Three lions and a tiger!

Syd – Does the giraffe get a sore throat if it gets its feet wet?
Fred – Yes, but not until the following week.

Teacher – How many ribs have you got, Jenny?
Jenny – I don't know, miss. I'm so tickly I can never finish counting them.

Diner – Waiter! This soup is cold. Bring me some that's hot.
Waiter – What? And scald my thumb?

Teacher – What was the former ruler of Russia called?
Toots – Tsar.
Teacher – Correct. And what was his wife called?
Toots – Tsarina.
Teacher – Right. What were the Tsar's children called?
Toots – Tsardines!

What are dog biscuits made of?
Collie-flour!

Erbert – I didn't know they played tennis in biblical times.
Teacher – They didn't, why?
'Erbert – Well, it says here that Joseph served in Pharaoh's Court!

Patient – Doctor, doctor what's that axe in the wall for?
Doctor – That's for splitting headaches!

What kind of fish do you find in a bird's cage?
A perch!

What birds fly in formation, and let off red, white and blue smoke?
The Red Sparrows!

Gent – Do you have any trouble in selling parrots?
Pet shop owner – Oh, no! They do their own sales talk!

Waiter – How did you find the steak, sir?
Diner – Quite easily. I just looked under a pea.

Foreman – You're not one of those men who drop their tools as soon as the whistle goes, are you!
New hand – No. I sometimes have to wait about five minutes after I've put my tools away before the whistle goes.

Hamish – What's the difference between a barber in Rome and an angry circus owner?
Donald – One is a shaving Roman and the other is a raving showman!

Donald – You couldn't lend me fifty pence, could you?
John – No, but how did you know?

Aunt – Is you mother in, Donald?
Donald – Of course she's in. Do you think I'd be standing here cleaning windows on a Saturday afternoon if she was out?

Dad – You get more pocket money in a week than I used to get in a month!
Minnie – Well, don't grumble at me about it, go and complain to Grandpa!

What do you call a gentle, kind, loving, careful, shy monster?
A failure!

Why did the boy clean up the spilt coffee with cake?
Because it was sponge cake!

Who are the strongest people in the world, men or women?
Women, because they can carry ladders in their tights!

What do you all an unmarried mermaid?
A single fish!

Why don't elephants ride bicycles?
They haven't got a thumb to ring the bell!

What do you call a flying policeman?
A heli-copper!

Danny – Did your father punish you when you went home last night?
Sidney – Yes, he made me stay in the room where my sister was doing her singing practice.

Johnny – What's up, Davie? Been fighting again?
Davie (face covered in plasters) – No. We've been moving house, and I had to carry the cactus plants!

Chairman – When you have finished your lecture, sir, bow gracefully and leave the platform on tiptoe!
Lecturer – Why on tiptoe?
Chairman – So as not to wake the audience!

What do you call Dracula?
A pain in the neck!

Athlete – What's my temperature, doctor?
Doctor – A hundred and one.
Athlete – What's the world record?

Small car owner – Half a pint of petrol, please and two spoonfuls of oil.
Garage attendant – Would you like me to sneeze into the tyres, too?

Customer – I haven't come to any ham in this sandwich yet.
Waiter – Try another bite.
Customer – (taking a mouthful) – Nope, none yet.
Waiter – Hmm! You must have gone right past it.

What do you call a vampire's favourite dance?
A fang-dango!

Knock! Knock!
Who's there?
Butcher.
Butcher who?
You butcher left leg in, you butcher left leg out.

Newsflash – A thousand mattresses have been stolen from a warehouse in the city. Police are springing into action.

Cinema attendant – That's the sixth ticket you've bought, sir.
Customer – Yes, I know. There's a girl in there who keeps ripping them up.

Sandy – Did you hear about the man who was listening to the match?
Andy – No, what about him?
Sandy – He burnt his ear!

Teacher – Did you have much trouble with your French when you were in Paris?
Dennis – No, but the Parisians did!

Why is a railway line like a blanket?
Because it lies on sleepers.

Diner – Hey, waiter! This steak's so tough, I can't get my fork into it.
Waiter – That's not so bad, sir. At the place across the road, you can't get your fork into the gravy!

Alf – What's the difference between a jeweller and jailer?
Dick – I don't know. What is the difference?
Alf – One sells watches and one watches cells?

Bob – I never wear a coat or a hat when it rains.
Bert – You must get soaked.
Bob – No. I just don't go out when it rains.

Uncle Jack – How are you getting on at school, Tommy?
Tommy – Oh, fine! The teacher said that if all the boys were like me, he would shut the school tomorrow.

Patient – Doctor, doctor! I feel like a pop star!
Doctor – Nurse, get his records.

What did the mouse say when he chipped his tooth?
Hard cheese!

First candle – What shall we do tonight then?
Second candle – Well, I was thinking of going out!

Bill – Did you hear about the man who got employed as a dustman?
Bob – No.
Bill – He said he would pick it up as he went along.

Why did the scout feel dizzy?
Because he did so many good turns!

What do you call a seven-foot gorilla with a machine gun?
Sir.

What do you get if you cross an owl with a skunk?
A bird that smells horrible but doesn't give a hoot!

When is an operation funny?
When it leaves the patient in stitches!

Teacher – What is a yokel?
Pupil – The centre of an eggle!

Bill – Why did the Manx cat cross the road?
Ben – To get to the tail-ors!

Hamish – I went horseback riding today.
Duncan – Well, sit down and tell me about it.
Hamish – I can't.
Duncan – You mean you can't tell me about it?
Hamish – No, I can't sit down.

John – Did you hear about the silly photographer?
Peter – No.
John – He saved burnt-out light bulbs to use in his darkroom!

What do you get if you put duck eggs in a cement mixer?
Quacks in the wall!

What do you get if you cross a palm tree with a toad?
A croakanut.

How did Luke Skywalker shave his beard?
With a laser blade!

Old man – When does the last train leave for Auchentogle.
Porter – Ten-thirty, sir.
Old man – All the clocks in the station are at different times, so which one am I going to go by?
Porter – Well, sir, you can go by any clock you like, but you can't go by the last train. It has already gone!

WHY DID TOMMY THROW THE CLOCK OUT OF THE WINDOW?
BECAUSE HE WANTED TO SEE TIME FLY!
CHUCKLE CHUCKLE!
THREE PEOPLE WERE STANDING UNDER AN UMBRELLA . . . WHICH ONE GOT WET?
NONE OF THEM, IT WASN'T RAINING!

McKenzie – My wife dreamed last night she was married to a millionaire.
Campbell – You're lucky! My wife dreams that in the daytime.

Harry – You know, the other night at the theatre a man fell out of the balcony, and everybody laughed but me.
Larry – Why didn't you laugh?
Harry – I was the man.

Customer – I want a pair of spec-rimmed hornicles . . . I mean sporn-rimmed hectacles . . . confound it . . . I mean heck-rimmed spornacles . . . I . . .
Optician – I know what you mean, sir. Mr Peck, show this gentleman a pair of rim-sporned hectacles. Oh, no! Now you've got me doing it!
Customer – Never mind, fit me with some contact lenses.

Harry – What do you think of your new teacher?
Tom – He's the kind of a fellow who, when you first meet him, you don't like him. But when you get to know him, you hate him.

Where do frogs borrow money?
From the river bank!

Why did the man go up the mountain with only one wellington boot on?
Because the forecast had said there was only one foot of snow!

Where does Tarzan buy his clothes?
At the Jungle Sale!

Which tree would you make a deck chair from?
A beech tree!

Terry – Have you had an accident?
Jerry – No.
Terry – Then why are you limping?
Jerry – A bull pitched me over a fence.
Terry – Well, wasn't that an accident?
Jerry – No, that bull did it on purpose.

Waiter – How would you like your steak, sir?
Diner (tired of waiting) – Very much.

Mother – What are you looking for?
Tommy – A fifty pence piece.
Mother – Where did you lose it?
Tommy – I didn't lose it, I'm just looking for one!

Teacher – I asked for a two-page composition about milk. Your paper is only half a page long.
Tommy – That's right. I wrote about condensed milk!

Mum – I think Dad's going to take us to the pictures, Danny. You'd better wash your face and hands.
Danny – I'd rather make sure he's going to take us before I do that, Mum.

Ian – Auntie, what do caterpillars taste like?
Auntie – How should I know, Ian?
Ian – Well, there was one in that piece of lettuce you just ate!

Sam – I know everything about football.
Geordie – Is that so?
Sam – Yes.
Geordie – Well, how many holes are there in a goal net?

How do you make an apple puff?
Chase it around the garden!

Patient – Doctor, will I be able to play the piano when my fingers get better?
Doctor – Yes, certainly!
Patient – That's good! I never could play it before!

Man – Doctor, doctor I keep seeing the future!
Doctor – When did this happen?
Man – Next Wednesday!

Why is it crazy to break into a bank?
'Cos it's full of coppers!

What do policemen have in their sandwiches?
Truncheon meat!

Why do they put telephone wires so high?
To keep up the conversation!

Daisy – Dad, Jack's just broken my new doll.
Dad – How did he do that?
Daisy – I hit him with it.

Mad scientist – I have just successfully crossed a giraffe with a hedgehog?
Assistant – Brilliant, master. What have you created?
Mad scientist – An eight-foot toothbrush.

Where do nomads of the desert get married?
At a mirage bureau!

Why did the man fail his driving test?
He opened the door to let the clutch out!

What is caught but never thrown?
A cold.

Why did the boy take a car to school?
Because he wanted to drive the teacher round the bend!

Man – Can I cut your grass for my dinner?
Lady – Certainly, and I hope you enjoy eating it!

Margaret – You said you wouldn't give away that secret I told you.
Jean – I didn't give it away! I exchanged it for another!

Boss – What do you mean by going for a haircut in the firm's time?
Office boy – Well, it grows in the firm's time, doesn't it?

Why is it fun to work in a clock factory?
Because you're making faces all day!

Jimmy – Dad, was Robinson Crusoe a contortionist?
Dad – No, why?
Jimmy – Well, it says here he sat down on his chest!

Chef – How would you make a sausage roll?
Apprentice – Push it!

Post Office assistant – There we are, miss, one first class stamp.
Young girl – Do I have to stick it on myself?
Post Office assistant – No, miss, on the envelope.

Biology teacher – Name two crustaceans.
Mike – Kings crustacean and Charing crustacean.

Teacher – To do anything in life, you must start at the bottom and work up.
Danny – What about learning to swim, sir?

Patient – Doctor, doctor, I keep seeing spotted horses.
Doctor – Have you seen a psychiatrist?
Patient – No, I just keep seeing spotted horses.

Teacher – Name a collective noun.
Eric – Dustman.

Commuter – I want to catch a late train to London.
Porter – Take the 9.30 train – it's usually as late as any!

Charlie – Why does this radio whistle when I turn the dials?
Mick – That means you're coming to the station!

Smith – I've certainly outfoxed the railway company this time.
Jones – How?
Smith – I've bought this return ticket and I'm not going back!

Teacher – What is a distant relative?
Sandy – My brother Andy is one.
Teacher – How can your brother be a distant relative?
Sandy – Because he lives in New Zealand.

Terry – I'm looking for someone to lend me five pounds.
Jerry – Let me know if you find anyone. Perhaps he'll lend me some money, too.

Why did the computer cross the road?
Because it was programmed by a chicken!

Why was the sheep arrested on the M1?
It made a ewe turn!

Patient – Doctor, doctor, my wife keeps thinking she's a hen.
Doctor – Why didn't you tell me earlier?
Patient – We needed the eggs.

Why do leopards never escape from the zoo?
Because they are always spotted.

Bill – How do you make antifreeze?
Ben – Don't know.
Bill – Hide her woolly socks!

Old man – Why are you crying, my boy?
Boy – Harry hit me!
Old man – Why don't you hit him back?
Boy – Because then it would be his turn again.

Crook – Look at that car. Let's pinch it.
Mate – We can't do that, we don't have driving licences!

Patient – Doctor, doctor can you help me out?
Doctor – Yes, which way did you come in?

Holiday maker – What are your weekly rates?
Receptionist – Well, that's rather difficult, I don't know anyone who's stayed for a week!

Speaker – There are so many interruptions I can't hear myself speak.
Voice – Don't worry, mate! You're not missing much.

Customer – I'd like some buttered bop corn . . . that is . . . poppered butt corn . . . I mean corn buttered pop . . . or rather cuttered pot born . . . I mean – oh, give me a hot dog.

Fortune-teller – I'll tell you your fortune for two pounds!
McTavish – If you were a real fortune-teller you'd know I don't have two pounds.

Golfer – How do you like my game?
Caddy – I suppose it's okay, but I still prefer golf!

Danny – Mum, does an apple a day keep the doctor away?
Mum – Yes.
Danny – Well, you'd better give me one now. I've broken the doctor's window with a cricket ball.

What's green, covered in custard, and miserable?
Apple grumble!

What monster only rings the doorbell when he comes to visit?
The knock-less monster!

What do you get if you cross a centipede with a parrot?
A walkie-talkie!

Old man – What is you dog's name?
Boy – Ginger, sir.
Old man – Does Ginger bite?
Boy – No, sir, but Ginger snaps.

Actor (playing a detective) – There has been foul play. What shall I do?
Voice from the audience – Give yourself a free kick.

Visitor to Wild West – How can you tell a poisonous snake from a non-poisonous one?
Bronco Bill – Just let it bite you. If you die, it's poisonous. If you live, it ain't!

Mum – Keep that dog out of the house, it's full of fleas.
Son – Rover, don't go in the house. Mum says it's full of fleas!

What do you call a magician from outer space?
A flying sorcerer!

Girl – Mum, what do you think I should wear with my pink and green spotted ankle socks?
Mum – Knee length boots!

Which two animals keep you company wherever you go?
Your calves, of course!

What is round, yellow, flies, and is made of egg?
An unidentified flying omelette!

Archie – Have you forgotten about the five pounds you owe me?
Alistair – Not yet. Give me time

Mum – Now, lads, stop quarrelling. Can't you ever agree?
Dave – We've agreed this time, Mum. Andy and I both want the biggest piece of cake.

Teacher – Any questions?
Smart Alec – Yes. How many full stops are there in a bottle of ink?

Did you hear about the Scotsman who washed his kilt?
He couldn't do a "fling" with it!

Donald – Well, Dad, I've got better news from school this time.
Dad – Have you passed your exams at last?
Donald – Well, I didn't exactly pass, but I was top of those who failed.

Ian – What sort of a boat would you use to shoot the rapids?
Charlie – A gunboat.

Jones – Were you relieved when the thief went away?
Smith – I'll say! He relieved me of fifty pounds!

Jimmy – Dad, can I ask you something?
Dad – Sure son, go ahead.
Jimmy – I've just asked it!

What did the hungry lion do?
Kept walking until he was fed up!

Bill – What travels around the world, but stays in a corner?
Ben – I don't know.
Bill – A stamp!

What does a monster eat after he's had a tooth out?
The dentist!

Describe, in one word, 962 little cakes dancing.
Abundance!

Auntie Jean – Danny, why is your baby brother crying?
Danny – He doesn't want to learn anything, Auntie. I took his piece of cake and showed him how to eat it.

Terry – Did you hear of the man who invented something for looking through brick walls?
Jerry – No, what did he call it?
Terry – A window.

What's green and miles and miles long!
The Grape Wall of China!

What do you get if you cross a policeman with a dog?
A copper spaniel.

What do you do if you find an eight-foot ape in your bed?
Sleep somewhere else!

Actor – I once acted in a play called Breakfast in Bed!
Interviewer – Did you have a big role?
Actor – No, just toast and marmalade!

First artist – Why have you got your face bandaged?
Second artist – I drew a pop bottle yesterday, and it was so real that the cork flew out and hit me in the eye!

Cinema manager – Hello! Where's the queue tonight?
Door attendant – It started fighting, and a policeman came round and arrested both of them, sir.

Policeman – What's the matter, laddie?
Little boy – Please sir, have you seen a lady without a little boy that looks like me?

Dad – I hear you and Garry nearly had a fight yesterday.
Andy – Yes, we were going to fight, but there was nobody there to hold us back.

Diner – Waiter, bring me a jug of water.
Waiter – For drinking, sir?
Diner – No, I'm going to give a high-diving display!

Tommy – Mum sent me back with this steak. She says it's so tough she could almost sole her shoes with it.
Butcher – Why didn't she?
Tommy – The nails wouldn't go through it.

What do sea-monsters live on?
Fish and ships!

What do you call a parrot with a machine gun?
A parrot trooper!

What is a ghost's favourite music?
Haunting melodies!

What does a mouse eat for breakfast?
Mice Krispies.

Kevin – Garry Thomson told me that I'm like you.
Ashley – And what did you say to that?
Kevin – Nothing. He's bigger than me!

Impatient customer – Haven't you finished mending those boots yet?
Cobbler – Not quite. I'm doing the second one now!
Impatient customer – Well, where's the first one?
Cobbler – I'll do it when I've finished the second.

McKay – This cornflour is no good.
Grocer – What's wrong with it?
McKay – Well, I've used it on my corns for a fortnight now, and they're just as bad as ever.

Dennis – A bottle of cod liver oil.
Chemist – Wouldn't you prefer the tasteless capsules?
Dennis – Nah! It's for my Dad!

Smith – Do you think you could lend me your CD player for tonight?
Jones (his neighbour) – Certainly. Are you giving a party?
Smith – Oh, no. We just want to get some sleep.

What's small, round, white and giggles?
A tickled onion!

Peter – Would you rather a crocodile attacked you or an elephant?
Tom – I'd rather he attacked the elephant!

What is the difference between China and Japan?
You can't eat off Japan!

Tim – They're not going to grow bananas any longer.
Tom – Really, why not?
Tim – Because they're long enough already!

Why do devils and ghosts get on so well together?
Because demon's are a ghoul's best friend!

Lady – I would like a pair of crocodile shoes, please.
Assistant – Certainly, madam. What size is your crocodile?

Inventor – I've only two more difficulties to overcome and my new aeroplane will be a great success.
Friend – What are they?
Inventor – Getting it into the air and making it say there.

Dad – You've taken a long time to blacken these boots.
Smiffy – Yes, but some of them were brown when I started.

What sits in the garden and rings?
A telegnome!

What question can never be answered "yes"?
Are you asleep?

What do elephants have that other animals don't?
Baby elephants!

May – Is this hand-knitted?
Jay – No, it came with the arm!

Alistair – Why does a giraffe have such a long neck?
Archie – Because its head is so far from its body.

How do you tell that a kangaroo is annoyed?
He goes hopping mad!

What looks after a haunted stretch of beach?
The ghost guard!

Did you hear about the man who was told to dress in white when going out at night, so he could be seen in the dark?
He was run over by a snowplough!

Baker – Try these cakes, sir. You can't get better.
Customer – I know. I had one last week, and I don't feel well yet.

Why did the taxi driver give up his job?
Because people kept talking behind his back.

What do you find in a haunted cellar?
Whines and spirits!

First farmer – What did the baby ear of corn say to the mummy ear of corn?
Second farmer – I don't know, what did the baby ear of corn say to the mummy ear of corn?
First farmer – Where's pop corn?

Where is Felixstowe?
On the end of Felix's foot!

Policeman – How did you get up that tree?
Sarcastic young man – I sat on it when it was an acorn.

What would you have if you owned a cow and two ducks?
Milk and quackers.

Grandpa – Well, Jimmy, and what do you want to be when you grow up?
Jimmy – I want to be an old man like you, with nothing to do all day but sit about and ask questions.

Doctor (to stuntman in hospital) – How did you get these injuries?
Stuntman – I tried to jump over twenty-five cars in a bus.
Doctor – What happened?
Stuntman – Someone rang the bell!

Why will television never take the place of a newspaper?
Have you ever tried swatting a fly with a television?

What do ghosts watch at the theatre?
A phantomime.

If you were surrounded by Dracula, Frankenstein's monster, a ghost and a werewolf, what would you be hoping?
That it was at a fancy dress party!

Cuthbert – Can you telephone from an aeroplane?
Fed-up airman – Of course I can tell a phone from an aeroplane!

Policeman – What are you crying for, sonny?
Bobby – Ma's giving me a party today.
Policeman – Well, that's nothing to cry about.
Bobby – Aye, it is. I can't find my way home.

What do you call a Scottish kangaroo locked in a cage?
A kana gar oot!

Jack – Yesterday my dog started chewing up my dictionary.
Jill – What did you do?
Jack – I took the words right out of his mouth!

What do you call an egg that loves playing tricks?
A practical yolker!

What do sheiks use to hide from their enemies?
Camelflage!

First fortune teller – Lovely weather we're having at the moment.
First fortune teller – Yes, reminds me of the summer of 2040!

First boaster – Where I come from we had rain one year that flooded the streets to the height of the lamp-posts.
Second boaster – Huh! When we had our last rainstorm we had to go down in submarines to milk the cows!

Moe – What side of a chicken has the most feathers?
Joe – I don't know.
Moe – The outside!

What did the pencil say to the sharpener?
"Stop going round in circles and get to the point!"

Did you hear about the man who gave a party for his chickens?
He had to cancel it because he couldn't make hens meet!

Teacher – Name of famous designer of coats.
Pupil – Anna Rack.

Teacher – If you had three eyes, where would you like the third one to be?
Jock – On the point of my finger.
Teacher – Why?
Jock – So that I could stick it through a hole in the fence to see the football match every week!

Jimmy – Please, may I have a pair of rubber gloves?
Auntie Jean – What for?
Jimmy – So I can wash my hands without getting them wet!

Hector – Have you ever seen an elephant's skin?
Hamish – Yes.
Hector – Where?
Hamish – On an elephant of course.

Landlady – How do you like your eggs boiled?
Lodger – Three at a time.

Jack – What's wrong with your head, Jock?
Jock – Some water fell on it.
Jack – But surely that wouldn't hurt it?
Jock – Yes, but the water was in a jug!

Jim – I've got a terrible cold. I won't be able to do the high jump.
PE Teacher – Why not?
Jim – I can't even clear my throat!

Lodger – I don't like all these mice in my room.
Landlord – Point out those you do like and I'll get rid of the rest!

What makes a chess player happy?
Taking a knight off!

Why are sardines stupid?
They lock themselves inside the tin and leave the key outside!

Boy – Mum, my torch is not working.
Mum – Maybe the batteries have run out.
Boy – No, they're still inside it!

How do you keep cool at a football match?
Sit next to a fan!

Henry – My cat took first prize at the bird show.
Harry – How was that?
Henry – He ate the prize canary.

Lord Toff – You know that horse you sold me yesterday? He died this morning.
Stable man – That's funny. He never did that before.

McNab – Do you think it's unlucky to have thirteen people at the table?
McKay – No – unless there's only food for twelve.

Boss – Stop whistling while you're working.
Office boy – Who's working?

Yes, this is the lost property office.
Well, I'm lost!

What's black, furry and knocks down buildings?
A de-mole-ition gang!

When is a pound note like a bridge?
When it goes from bank to bank!

What did the artist do when he was stopped by a robber?
He drew a gun!

What does a ball do when it stops rolling?
Looks round!

Frank – I am glad my parents named me Frank.
Jack – Why?
Frank – Because that's what everyone calls me!

Shop manager – Smith! Fetch in those waterproof overcoats. It's raining!

Waiter – Excuse me, sir, but I think I've seen you before. Are you a brother or relative of Major Brown?
Major Brown – No, I am Major Brown.
Waiter – Ah, then that accounts for the remarkable resemblance, sir.

Alan – Hello, Pat! Seen Mike lately?
Pat – Well, I thought I saw him across the street the other day, and he thought he saw me, but when we got up close to each other, it was neither of us!

Jim – My brother is a cashier in a police station.
Tim – What does he do?
Jim – He counts the coppers as they come in.

Optician – Here are your new glasses. Remember, you will only wear them when you are working.
Patient – That might be difficult.
Optician – Why, what do you do for a living?
Patient – I'm a boxer.

Diner – Waiter, waiter, this soup tastes funny!
Waiter – Then why aren't you laughing, sir?

What did one rock pool say to another rock pool?
"Show us your mussels!"

Two flies were on a cornflakes packet. "Why are we running so fast?" asked one. "Because," said the second, "it says 'tear along dotted line'!"

Servant – Your bath is ready, sir!
Absent-minded professor – Oh! I'm too busy. You take it for me.

Lady – What is the best way to cover a cushion?
Fed-up assistant – Sit on it!

Andy – How long have you been working for the boss you have now?
Barry – Ever since he threatened to fire me.

Customer – I won't buy this hat. It makes me look like an idiot.
Salesman – But that's the one you were wearing when you came in, sir.

Green – Have you heard of the tragedy that happened in the library last week?
Brown – No, what was it?
Green – A man was found buried in a book.

How did the glow-worm feel when it wouldn't glow.
De-lighted!

Why did the boy go to night school?
To learn to read in the dark!

Stranger – Do these steps take you to the station?
Local – Course not! Steps can't walk!

What is the best thing to take to the desert?
A thirst-aid kit!

What do you get if you cross a zebra with a pig?
Striped sausages!

Where are there no fat people?
In Finland!

Teacher – How do you spell "inconsequentially"?
Smiffy – Always wrong!

What do you get if you cross grass seeds with a cow?
A lawnmooer!

Moe – Hey, Jock, what's a black pudding?
Joe – A sausage in mourning.

Teacher – What grows on palms?
Sidney – Four fingers and a thumb!

Who was the first underwater spy?
James pond!

What are chiropodists' favourite crisps?
Cheese and bunion!

What can cut waves?
A sea-saw!

First-aid teacher – What would you do if you broke your arm in two places?
Boy – I'd never go to either place again!

How can you avoid starving on a desert island?
Eat the sand-which is there!

Teacher – You all know, I suppose, that it is the law of gravity that keeps us from falling off the earth.
Smiffy – Please, sir, what kept people on the earth before the law was passed?

Mother – Dennis, how many more times will I have to tell you to leave the chocolate spread alone?
Dennis – No more, Mum, the jar's empty now!

Mother – I hope the boys at school don't give you nasty nicknames?
Sammy – They call me "Toe Nails" because I'm at the foot of the class.

Diner – Waiter, there's a button in my lunch!
Waiter – Well, sir, you did ask for a jacket potato!

Where does a gardener play snooker? The potting shed!

Why are giraffes slow to apologise? Because it takes a long time for them to swallow their pride!

Boy – Doctor, doctor, my knees won't stop shaking! What can I do about it?
Doctor – Tie a pair of cymbals to them and join the school band!

**What does a vicar fly in?
A holycopter!**

*How do you post a rabbit?
Hare mail!*

What goes whistling up the aisle at a wedding?
The bride's train!

**Why was the envelope on the roof?
Because it wanted ceiling!**

Did you hear about the man with five legs? – His trousers fitted him like a glove!

Dad (pointing to a statue) – That is Sir Thomas Rich, my boy. He gave big sums to the school.
Jimmy – Is that so? Couldn't he do them himself?

Michael – You don't seem to be growing any taller.
Bobby – I know. It's all my mother's fault. She washes me so often that I shrink.

Teacher – A fool can ask questions that a wise man can't answer.
Plug – No wonder we didn't pass our exam.

Actor – When I played my last part on the stage, the audience were glued to their seats.
Critic – Well, that was certainly a good way to keep them there.

Teacher – Dear me, Jack, how dirty you are! What would you say if I came to school as dirty as that?
Jack – Please, sir, I'd be too polite to mention it.

Drowning man – Help, help! I can't swim!
Passer-by – I can't play the piano, but I don't shout about it!

Girl – My teacher does bird impressions.
Mother – Really?
Girl – Yes, she watches me like a hawk!

Teacher – Tommy, can you tell me how iron was discovered?
Tommy – Yes, sir, I heard Dad say the other day that they smelt it!

*What do you get if you cross a cocker spaniel, a poodle and a rooster?
A cockapoodledoo!*

Music teacher – Is there anything special you'd like to be able to play?
Pupil – Yes, miss, truant!

Father – Why didn't you tell me the truth when I asked you who broke the window?
Son – I thought my story was more interesting.

Customer – Waiter! Waiter! There's a fly in my soup!
Waiter – Don't worry, sir. There's a spider on your bread!

Patient – Doctor, doctor, I keep thinking I'm a needle!
Doctor – Yes, I can see your point!

Why did the boy want to become a chimney sweep?
Because he thought it would soot him!

Why did the man have to repair the horn of his car?
Because it didn't give a hoot!

Sam – Why are you going upstairs with the piano, Bill?
Bill – I'm going to mend it.
Sam – But why take it upstairs?
Bill – Well, the hammer's up there.

Town boy (in country for first time) – Why doesn't that cow have horns?
Country friend – Well, the chief reason is that it's a horse, not a cow.

Teacher – Now, children, I hope you have a nice weekend, and come back to school with a little sense in your heads.
Class (in unison) – Same to you, sir!

Judge – Didn't I say when you were here before that I never wanted to see you again?
Prisoner – Yes, but I couldn't make the policeman believe me.

Why do birds in a nest always agree?
Because they don't want to fall out!

What do computers eat?
Fish and microchips!

What do you do when a kangaroo has appendicitis?
You hoperate on him!

Jones – Smith wants to borrow five pounds. Do you think I should give it to him?
Brown – Yes, of course.
Jones – Why?
Brown – Well, if you don't let him have it, he'll come to me for it.

Why couldn't the sailors play cards?
The captain was standing on the deck!

Teacher – Why did Robin Hood only rob the rich?
Wilfrid – Because the poor people didn't have any money?

Moe – My big sister uses lemon juice for her complexion.
Joe – No wonder she always looks so sour!

"This is the worst essay I've ever read," complained teacher. "I shall tell your father about it."
"I wouldn't if I were you," grinned Sammy. "He wrote it for me!"

Bill – Why have you put that bit of looking-glass in the foot of your dog's dish, Sandy?
Sandy – Don't you see that Rover thinks he's getting two bones instead of one?

Mum – I don't like the boy next door, so I want you to keep away from him as much as possible at school.
Pete – Oh, that's easy. He's usually at the top of the class!

Teacher – Can anyone tell me something of great importance that didn't exist one hundred years ago?
Small girl – Yes, miss, me!

Judge – Did you get hurt in the riot?
Witness – No, in the eye.

Postman – Is this letter for you? The name is illegible.
Man – No, it can't be mine. My name is Brown.

Canvasser (to little boy standing by house door) – Is your mother in?
Boy – Yes.
Canvasser (after knocking about a dozen times) – I thought you told me your mother was in.
Boy – So she is, but we don't live here.

Harry – Give me fifty pence to go to the zoo to see the snakes, Dad.
Dad – What a waste of money! Take this magnifying glass and go and look at the worms in the garden.

Don – Why are you putting your hand in the dog's mouth?
John – Putting it in? I'm trying to get it out!

Bobby – I can fight anybody.
Henry – You can't fight my brother!
Bobby – Yes, I can.
Henry – No, you can't – 'cause I don't have a brother!

What do you get if you cross a cow with a duck?
A milk float!

Mum – Why did you not do your decimals homework?
Son – I couldn't see the point!

Son – How much am I worth, Mum?
Mum – To me, you're worth a million pounds, son.
Son – Well, could you lend me five of them?

What do you get if you cross an elephant with a swallow?
A lot of broken telephone wires!

Teacher – What do we make from horns?
Dunce – Please, sir, hornaments!

Patient – Doctor, doctor, for ages now, I've thought I'm a bit of string.
Doctor – Why didn't you come to me earlier?
Patient – Because I was tied up for a while.

Daisy (sobbing) – A man ran over my hula hoop with his motor cycle.
Dad – The scoundrel! I'll teach him! Where is he?
Daisy – In the infirmary.

Brainy – Why are you putting all those patches on your inner tube?
Dopey – Well, it's like this, if I get a puncture it will be mended already!

Patient – I keep thinking I'm covered in gold paint.
Doctor – Don't worry, it's just a gilt complex!

Where does a dog go when he loses his tail?
To a retailer!

Why was the tennis ball deaf?
Because it put up with too much racket!

Zoo keeper – We've lost a giraffe and a mouse.
Visitor – What are you going to do about it?
Zoo keeper – Search high and low!

Mother – No, Fatty, no more cake tonight. Don't you know you can't sleep on a full stomach?
Fatty – Well, I can sleep on my back.

Copper – Well, sonny, are you lost?
Ken (tearfully) – No, but I've found a street I don't know!

James – They tell me they have buildings more than eighty storeys high in New York.
John – Oh, boy! What a time we could have sliding down the banisters!

GNOCK! GNOCK!
Who's there?
Howard.
Howard who?
Howard is it raining out here?

Variety agent – You say you are a magician?
Applicant – Yes.
Variety agent – Well, vanish!

Joe – Ever seen sausages hanging up in the shop?
Len – Course I have.
Joe – That's funny. I always thought they hung down!

Mum – You mustn't play the piano when Dad is sleeping.
Jess – But, Mum, I can put thick gloves on.

Lou – How many seconds are there in a year?
Sue – I don't know.
Lou – There are twelve seconds in a year!
Sue – How do you make that out?
Lou – For example, January 2nd, February 2nd . . .!?

What did the dog say to the bone?
It was nice gnawing you!

What always weighs the same, no matter how big it gets?
A hole!

Son – Do you remember you said that if I got a good report you would give me five pounds?
Dad – Yes, why do you ask?
Son – Well, I've just saved you the expense!

General (to sergeant) – You idiot! Instead of addressing this despatch to the "Intelligence Office" you've addressed it to the "Intelligent Officer". Don't you know there's no such officer in the Army?

Diner – Waiter, there's a dead fly swimming in my soup.
Waiter – That's impossible, sir, dead flies can't swim.

Inquisitive boy – Have you ever had any narrow escapes all the time you've been a sailor?
Old sailor – Yes, I was nearly drowned once.
Boy – How did it happen? Did your ship hit a rock?
Old sailor – No, no! I went to sleep in my bath and left the water running!

Passenger – Here, driver, why is the taxi jumping about like this? Have you lost your head?
Driver – No, sir. I've lost the steering wheel.

Shopkeeper (to assistant) – How many new-laid eggs have we in stock?
Assistant – Oh, about enough to last us six weeks.

Why is your nose in the middle of your face?
Because it is the scenter!

Mother – Billy, why did you put this frog in your aunt's bed?
Billy – Because I couldn't find a mouse!

What did the wig say when it was blowing along the street?
"I'm off my head!"

Teacher – Johnny, why are you doing your sums on the floor?
Johnny – But miss, you told me to try them without using tables!

Boy to dentist – How much would it be to have three teeth out?
Dentist – Ten pounds.
Boy – Huh, forget it! I'll pick a fight on the way home!

Master – You might get my bath ready for me.
Butler – I'm sorry, sir, it's being used by the goldfish. The mistress said it was to have a treat on its birthday.

Knock! Knock!
Who's there?
Mavis.
Mavis who?
Mavis be the last time I knock on this door!

Car salesman – Our cars no good? Why, we're selling them by the dozen. Prospective buyer – I'm not surprised. How much are they a dozen?

Teacher – Dear me, you haven't put any answers to these sums.
Smiffy – No, sir, I left those out. I always get that part wrong.

Jamie – Is it true, Ma, that you shouldn't put off until tomorrow what can be done today?
Ma – Yes, James.
Jamie – Well, in that case I'd better finish off that cake in the cupboard.

Teacher – Would it be correct to say, "You can learn me nothing"?
Danny – Yes, sir.
Teacher – Why?
Danny – 'Cos you can't.

First golfer – That fool Brown crossed my tee as I drove off.
Second golfer – Well, if he crossed your tee, you should have dotted his eye.

How do you spell "dried grass" in three letters?
H-A-Y!

What happened to the cricketer who opened Dracula's coffin?
He got a bat in the mouth!

Tom – I've just got a job at the Eagle Laundry.
Tim – That sounds dangerous!

Boy – Farmer, do you like baked apples?
Farmer – Yes, why?
Boy – Because your orchard is on fire!

Benny – What time is it, please?
Kenny – Three o'clock.
Benny – Oh, no, not again!
Kenny – Why, what's the matter?
Benny – I've been asking people the time all day, and everyone tells me something different!

Who rides a camel and carries a lamp?
Florence of Arabia!

Teacher – Have you learned anything today, Sidney?
Sidney – No, sir! I've been listening to you all the time.

Golfer – I'll stay here until I hit his ball!
Caddie – You'll need a new caddie, then. I'm going on holiday next week.

"Just think of it," said Johnny. "My mum was born in Iceland, and my dad was born in Cuba. I must be an ice-cube!"

How can you tell a miser's house? There's a padlock on the dustbin, a fork in the sugar bowl and tea bags on the washing line.

Smiffy – What do you mean, telling everybody I'm an idiot?
Toots – Oh, I'm sorry. I didn't know it was meant to be a secret.

Doctor – Nurse, where's the next patient?
Nurse – She didn't look very well, so I sent her home.

What goes black, white, green, black, white, green, black, white, green? A zebra rolling down a hill!

Brown – What's an optimist?
Green – A man who looks in a cuckoo clock for an egg!

What would you do if you saw two snails fighting?
Let them "slug" it out!

Chemist – The meat you sold me yesterday didn't taste very good.
Butcher – Then we're quits. The medicine you sold me last week tasted awful.

Dad – I promised you a bicycle if you passed your exams, but you've failed in everything. What have you been doing with your time?
Sidney – Learning to ride a bicycle!

How do you make gold soup?
Put 14 carats in it!

Patient – Doctor, doctor, everyone thinks I'm a liar.
Doctor – Come now, I don't believe that for a minute!

What did one ear say to the other ear?
Between you and me we need a haircut.

Why is it unwise to buy a cheap violin?
Because it might be a fiddle!

What party game did Doctor Jekyll like best?
Hyde and seek.

Where do ghosts like to swim?
The Dead Sea!

Patient – Doctor, there's a mist before my eyes. What can it be?
Doctor – I haven't the foggiest idea!

Teacher – Now, Plug, what do you know about the Dead Sea?
Plug – I never even knew it was ill, sir!

Young singer – And now that you've tested my voice, Professor, what do you think it is best suited for?
Professor – Selling papers.

Patient – Will my measles be better next week, doctor?
Doctor – Well, I hate to make rash promises!

Judge (to prisoner) – How did you manage to pick the lock after it was fitted with a safety catch?
Prisoner – Sorry, guv'nor, but it's a pound a lesson!

Nephew – That 20p you gave me dropped through a hole in my pocket.
Uncle – Well, here's another.
Nephew – Wouldn't a bigger coin be safer?
Uncle – Quite right – here's 2p!

Slow barber – Your hair is getting grey, sir.
Customer – No wonder. Hurry up!

When does an astronaut have his main meal of the day?
At launch time!

Why are mother cats tidy?
Because they always pick up their litter!

What has the teacher got that we haven't got?
The answers!

How do you cut the material for a Roman toga?
With a pair of Caesars!

Baker (in shop) – What is the best thing to put in pies?
Fatty – Teeth!

Gent (to policeman directing traffic) – Where shall I get the bus for King's Cross?
Policeman – Right in the back, sir, if you stand there much longer.

What's the cheapest way to see the world?
Buy an atlas!

What do you call a happy can that lives in the United States?
A-merry-can!

Maid (to absent-minded professor) – What are you looking for?
Professor – My hat.
Maid – Why, it's on your head.
Professor – It's a good job you told me or I'd have gone away without it.

Why did the Cyclops have to close his school?
Because he only had one pupil!

Who chews gum and chases spies?
Bubble-oh-seven!

How does a flea get from one place to another?
By itch-hiking!

What do cats read every morning?
Mewspapers!

Why is it hot in a beehive?
Because the bees make it s'warm!

Patient – Doctor, doctor, I'm at death's door!
Doctor – Don't worry, I'll pull you through!

Freddie – My brother has taken up French, Italian, German, Spanish and Greek.
Old man – Goodness! What does he do?
Freddie – He's a lift boy.

Friend (to farming student) – What's the hardest thing to learn about farming?
Student – Getting up at four o'clock in the morning!

Teacher – Robert, I told you to do 1,000 lines on this paper!
Robert – Well, sir, I didn't bother, because there were already a lot of lines on the paper.

Why did the composer stay all day in bed?
He wrote sheet music!

How are dog catchers paid?
By the pound!

Patient – Doctor, doctor, I feel like a dishcloth!
Doctor – Take these tablets, and I'll give you a wring in the morning!

Patient – Doctor, doctor, I keep seeing double!
Doctor – Sit on the couch, please.
Patient – Which one?

Why did the bald man put his head out of the window?
To get some fresh (h)air!

Gent – Goodness, why are you putting that muzzle on your brother?
Jimmy – I'm sending him to get some sweets and I'm taking no risks!

Mother (to small son who is going to party) – Now, dear, what are you going to do when you've had enough to eat?
Small son – Come home.

Teacher – Why weren't you at school this morning?
John – I was coming, sir, but I saw a road-roller, and a policeman said to me, 'Mind that roller' and I stayed and minded it all morning.

First lady – Our Jack slept in a field of cows last night.
Second lady – Wasn't he cold?
First lady – No, it was a field of Jerseys!

What do you call electric bulbs made in Israel?
Israel-lites!

What would you say to a German barber?
Good morning, Herr Dresser!

Sue – What do you call a boomerang that doesn't come back?
Lou – A stick!

John – My grandad was still alive at the age of 102!
Jim – That's nothing! My grandad is still living at 133!
John – What? 133?
Jim – Yes – 133 High Street!

Teacher – In Greek mythology, what was half man and half animal?
Smiffy – Buffalo Bill?

Why did the bee go to the bank?
Because it wanted some 'oney.

Patient – Doctor, doctor, I feel like a tub of butter.
Doctor – Well, spread yourself out on the couch!

Why was the ghost arrested?
Because he hadn't got a haunting licence!

What do scientists' children swim in?
Microwaves!

Hard-up householder – Hey, what are you looking for?
Burglar – Money!
Householder – Wait a minute. I'll put on the light and we'll both look!

Joe (from top of a high tree) – How do I get down?
Bill – Same way as you got up.
Joe – No fear! I came up head first.

Teacher (to latecomer) – Where have you been, Tom?
Tom – I slept late, dreaming I was going to America.
Teacher (to another latecomer) – And where have you been, Sam?
Sam – I was seeing him off, miss.

Joe – I've had my nose broken in three places!
Pete – Oh, really?
Joe – Yes, in London, in Liverpool and in Manchester!

Teacher – Boy, when I was your age I could do problems twice as hard as that.
Fatty – Yes, sir, but perhaps you had a better teacher.

What do you say to a flying dog that thinks it's a vehicle?
"Land Rover!"

Patient – Doctor, doctor, one minute I think I'm a wigwam, the next minute I think I'm a teepee.
Doctor – You're too tense (two tents)!

What tools de we use in arithmetic?
Multipliers!

Sally – You certainly hammer those nails in like lightning!
Paul – You mean I'm fast?
Sally – No, you never strike in the same place twice!

Stranger – Will this road take me to the village?
Farmer – No, sir. You'll have to walk.

Old lady – And what are you in prison for, my good man?
Prisoner – Well, the Government and me had a competition to see who could make the best pound notes, and the Government won.

Singer's mother – What a good singer. His voice really filled the hall.
Critic – Yes, I noticed several people had to leave to make room for it!

Which animal needs oil?
A mouse, because it squeaks!

Teacher – If you had £4 in one pocket, and £3 in the other pocket, what would you have?
Pupil – The wrong trousers!

Barber – Do you want a haircut?
Customer – I want them all cut.

What do you get if you cross a camel with a cow?
Lumpy milk!

What did one lift say to the other lift? "I think I'm going down with something!"

Teacher – Do you like Beethoven's works, William?
William – I've never visited them. What does he make?

What does the Statue of Liberty stand for?
Because it would look funny lying down!

Mean boss – No, I don't need an office boy. I do all the work round here myself.
Applicant for job – Gosh, sir, that would suit me fine.

Patient – Doctor, doctor, skin trouble has given me a broken arm.
Doctor – How could skin trouble give you a broken arm?
Patient – It was a banana skin.

How does a frog cross the English Channel?
By Hoppercraft!

Boy – Dad, what did Tarzan say when he saw five elephants coming over the hill wearing dark sunglasses?
Dad – I don't know. What did Tarzan say?
Boy – Nothing! He didn't recognise them!

What doesn't get any wetter no matter how much it rains?
The xcean!

Teacher – Tony, point to America on the map. (Tony does it). That's right, well done. Now then, children, who found America?
John – Tony, sir!

What do you call an area where ghosts live?
A terrortory!

Diana – Did you hear about the silly girl who goes around saying "no" to everything she hears?
Jane – No.
Diana – Oh, it's you, is it?

What do cannibals have for breakfast?
Beings on toast!

Customer – Waiter, do you have frogs' legs?
Waiter – Of course, sir.
Customer – Then leap over the counter and get me a drink!

Customer – Could I please have an old television set?
Assistant – Why an old one?
Customer – I want to see a programme I missed.

What do you call a plastic king?
A ruler!

Nan – How did you make this cake?
Jan – Here's the recipe. I cut it from a magazine.
Nan – Are you sure you read the right side? The other side tells you how to make a rock garden!

What kind of shoes do frogs wear?
Open-toad!

Mum – Where do you think you're going?
Minnie – To school.
Mum – What with dirt all over your face?
Minnie – No, with Sue from next door!

John – I am going to fail my English exam through illness.
David – Why, what's wrong with you?
John – The boy I copy from is off with the mumps!

Why did the wasp dance on top of the jam jar lid?
Because it said "twist to open"!

Nurse – Can I take your pulse now?
Patient – Why, haven't you got one of your own?

Teacher – Here is a biblical question. What was Noah's profession?
Pupil – Please, sir, he was an arkitect!

Why did the dragon enter the Grand National?
Because he was a hot favourite!

Teacher – And what are you going to be when you leave school?
George – Sixteen, sir!

Who wrote music for feet?
Shoe Burt!

Why did the boy wear his shirt in his bath?
Because the label said wash and wear!

Why do men get paid extra for working on top of Big Ben?
Because they are working overtime!

When do elephants have sixteen feet?
When there are four of them!

Who always goes to bed wearing shoes?
A horse!

Jean – Did you hear about the leek in the Clyde Tunnel?
Betty – No.
Jean – It fell off the back of a vegetable cart!

Willie – What is the best way to prevent infections caused by biting insects?
Millie – Don't bite any insects!

What is the most important part of a horse?
The mane part!

Why is a football park cold?
Because it has so many fans!

Roger – Dad, will you play at zoos with me?
Dad – All right, lad, but how do you play it?
Roger – I'll be a bear and you'll be the kind gentleman who feeds me with buns and sweets.

Bob – I suppose you were relieved when you found that the ghost had stopped following you?
Norman – I'll say! I was so relieved, I slowed down to a sprint.

Girl – What do you get if you cross an Alsatian with a giraffe?
Mum – I don't know.
Girl – A dog who barks at aeroplanes!

Patient – Doctor, doctor, my brother thinks he's an orange.
Doctor – Tell him to come in and see me.
Patient – Oh, that's all right, I've got him here in my pocket!

What's the cure for water on the knee?
Drainpipe trousers!

Billy – What's blue and swings through the trees?
Fred – I don't know!
Billy – Tarzan with the cold!

Teacher – I asked you to draw a horse and cart, John, and you've only drawn the horse. Why?
John – I thought the horse would draw the cart itself, sir.

Uncle – Are you saving 20p pieces?
Nephew – Yes.
Uncle – There's one for you. How many have you got now?
Nephew – One!

What grows up as it grows down?
A baby duckling!

Diner – Waiter, there's a twig in my soup.
Waiter – Wait a moment, sir, while I fetch the branch manager!

What trees do fingers and thumbs grow on?
Palm trees!

Patient – Doctor, doctor, I feel like a pin!
Doctor – I see your point!

Why is a paper boy never cold?
Because selling papers increases circulation!

What do you get if you cross bubble bath with a famous detective?
Sherlock Foams!

Optician – What made you need glasses?
Customer – I strained my eyes reading your book on how to avoid eye strain and strengthen the eyes.

Boxing promoter – How good is this new heavyweight you're training?
Manager – Why, he's so good that when he's shadow-boxing, his own shadow gets scared and runs away.

Diner – This pea soup is full of sugar.
Waiter – It must have been made with sweet peas.

Terry – I've had to ask you five times for that money you owe me.
Jerry – What if you have? I had to ask you eight times before you'd lend it to me.

Billy – How much are those guinea pigs?
Pet shop owner – A pound apiece.
Billy – How much for a whole one?

Doctor (to patient who has just rushed in) – Don't you know my hours are between two and five?
Patient – Yes, but the dog that bit me didn't.

Schoolmaster – Can anyone tell me the name of something that shrinks when it is washed?
Bright pupil – A piece of soap!

Gardener – Is that your ball in my garden?
Sandy – Are there any windows broken, or anything that the lad who owns the ball will have to pay for?
Gardener – No.
Sandy – Well, it's my ball, then!

Doctor – Did you drink that water an hour before breakfast, as I told you to?
Patient – I tried, Doctor, but I couldn't keep it up for more than five minutes.

Mrs Brown (at party) – Have another piece of cake, Fatty.
Fatty – I'm full up!
Mrs Brown – Well, put some in your pockets.
Fatty – They're full up, too, Mrs Brown!

Bald boss (to the office boy) – What untidy hair you have! When I was a boy, I used to brush my hair every morning.
Office boy – And look what you've done. You've swept it all away.

Theatre doorkeeper – You're too late, sir. The show has begun.
Gent – But I can slip in without making a sound.
Doorkeeper – It ain't that, sir. If I open the door, the audience will slip out!

Patient – Doctor, doctor, I keep thinking I'm a packet of biscuits!
Doctor – Are they square ones? Have they got writing on them?
Patient – Yes!
Doctor – You must be crackers!

Why do goldfish always seem so well travelled?
Because they go round and round the globe!

First little girl – I want to marry a Dutchman.
Second little girl – Why?
First little girl – I want to be a Duchess!

Jane – Why do bears have fur coats?
John – I don't know!
Jane – Because they would look stupid in plastic macs!

Kay – Do you know what happened to the lady who turned up her nose at everything?
Fay – No, what happened?
Kay – She sneezed and blew her hat off!

Bore – Below us yawned the chasm.
Listener – Why, were you talking to it?

Bobby – Dad, I've got a pain today.
Dad – Where do you feel it worst?
Bobby – At school!

McTavish – I want to buy a hundred tons of sand.
McDonald – Whatever for?
McTavish – I won a camel in a raffle!

Teacher – Smiffy, what comes after G?
Smiffy – Whizz!
Teacher – Let's try again. What comes after U?
Smiffy – The bogey-man!
Teacher – Last chance. What comes after T?
Smiffy – Supper!

Why did the ball become deaf!
Because of the racket!

Why was the banker bored?
Because he lost interest in everything!

What's a frog's favourite sweet?
A lollihop!

Arab – This palm tree is over 3,000 years old.
Tourist – How do you know?
Arab – It's got a date on it!

Doctor, doctor, I feel like a crystal ball!
Sit down and I'll look into this!

Why are robots never afraid?
Because they have nerves of steel!

I've lost my budgie!
Well, notify the flying squad!

First builder (on tall building) – There's an ambulance and a big crowd down below.
Second builder – That's quick work. It's only five seconds since I dropped my hammer.

Johnny – You know, Dad, you're a very lucky man.
Father – Why?
Johnny – Well, you won't need to buy me any new school books next year because I'm going to be kept in the same class!

First plumber – You remind me of Henry the Eighth!
Second plumber – But he didn't know anything about plumbing.
First plumber – That's why!

Uncle – Do you have much trouble when you are doing your lessons in school?
Harold – Yes, Uncle!
Uncle – What troubles you most?
Harold – The teacher.

Diner – Waiter, is this a lamb or pork chop?
Waiter – Can't you tell by the taste?
Diner – No, I can't.
Waiter – Then what does it matter?

Why is a retired carpenter like a lecturer?
He is an ex-planer.

Black – Every man should sing at his work.
Brown – I can't.
Black – Why?
Brown – I'm a trombone player.

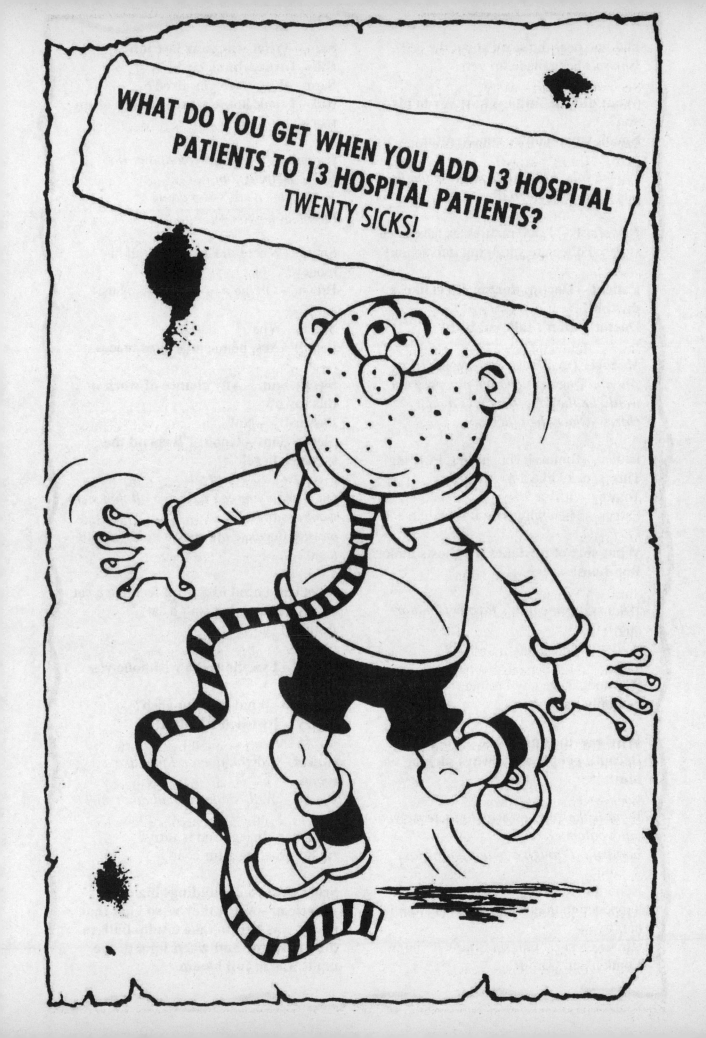

Did you hear the story about the bed?
It hasn't been made up yet!

What did the father ghost say to his son?
Spook when you're spooken to!

Why did the lady put her bed in the fire?
She wanted to sleep like a log!

Newsflash – 1,000 mattresses have been stolen. Police are springing into action!

Patient – Doctor, doctor, I feel like a dustbin!
Doctor – Don't talk rubbish!

Manager (to office boy) – Now, Harry, if you and I were to change places, what would be the first thing you'd do?
Harry – Sack the office boy.

Father – Tommy! This is awful writing!
This 3 looks like a 5.
Tommy – It is a 5.
Father – Then why does it look like a 3?

What sort of mistakes do ghosts make?
Boo-boos!

What is a comedian's favourite motor-bike?
A Yama-ha-ha!

Do robots have any brothers?
No, only tran-sisters!

Why was the apple tree crying?
Because people are always picking on him!

What is the simplest way to increase your bank balance?
Look at it through a magnifying glass!

Reporter (to circus owner) – Whatever happened to the lady you used to saw in half?
Circus owner – Oh, she's now living in London and Cardiff!

Sam – What was your last job?
Bill – I was a bank cashier.
Sam – Why were you fired?
Bill – I took home some samples of my work!

Foreman – What are you doing, Bob?
Bob – Helping Jim.
Foreman – What's Jim doing?
Bob – Nothing.

Smith – Where did James get all his money?
Brown – Oh, he's in the hold-up business.
Smith – What!?
Brown – Yes, he manufactures braces.

Sleepy Sam – Any chance of work in this town?
Passer-by – No!
Sleepy Sam – Good! I'll spend the summer here!

Pete – Why are you carrying all that steel wool around?
Steve – Because my mum's going to knit me a car!

What has a head like a cat, feet like a cat, a tail like a cat, but isn't a cat?
A kitten!

Harry – I swallowed a wishbone yesterday.
Horace – What did you wish?
Harry – I wished I hadn't!

Patient – Doctor, doctor, I feel like a spoon.
Doctor – Well, sit down, and don't stir!

What has six legs and is furry?
An ant wearing a fur coat!

Scot – Are your buildings high?
American – Why, they're so high that once I was told to take a tulip bulb to the top storey and when I got to the top it was in full bloom.

Jack – I like to read something with a punch in it.
Bill – Well, here's a train ticket.

Dad – Why didn't you cry as you fell downstairs, Kevin?
Kevin – Well, every time I opened my mouth to cry, another step shut it.

Gent – These aren't very good bananas. I can hardly peel them.
Fruiterer – What do you expect for 15p each? Bananas with zip fasteners?

Knock! Knock!
Who's there?
Mr.
Mr Who?
Mr Bus Home. That's why I'm late!

Who are the two smallest ladies in the world?
Molly Cule and Milli Metre!

Patient – Doctor, doctor, I feel like an apple.
Doctor – Sit down, I won't eat you!

Ben – What do raisins do at school?
Jen – I don't know. What do raisins do at school?
Ben – Currant affairs!

Carla – I keep thinking that it's Sunday.
Lisa – But it is Sunday.
Carla – I know, that's why I keep thinking it!

Mike – Do you like tripe, Pat?
Pat – I don't, and I'm glad of it, for if I did I'd be eating it all the time and I hate the rotten stuff.

Peter – What goes ABCDE-FGHIJKLMNOPQRSTUVWXYZ slurp?
Kay – Someone eating alphabet soup!

What stops the moon falling down?
Moonbeams.

Newsflash – A large hole has appeared in the fence of a nudist centre. The police are looking into it!

Why did the baker stop baking dough-nuts?
Because he was tired of the "hole" busi-ness!

Why do white sheep eat more grass than black sheep?
Because there are more of them!

Patient – Doctor, doctor, I feel like a tree!
Doctor – We must get to the root of the matter!

Which fruit do vampires like best?
Neck-tarines!

What is black and yellow and always moans?
A grumble bee!

What is big, purple and near to France?
Grape Britain!

George – Do you like my new swimming pool?
Rose – There's no water in it!
George – I know! I can't swim!

What bird can't get through customs?
An ill-eagle!

What lives under the water and goes dit, dit, da, dit?
A morse cod!

Plug – I'd like a suit to make me look slim, debonair and handsome.
Tailor – I'm a tailor, sir, not a magician.

Jones – I know a man who's so mean he stops his clock at night so that the cogs won't wear out.
Smith – That's nothing. My neighbour is so mean, that when he found a French coin he swam across the Channel to spend it!

Wife – You're always complaining. I wish you would make allowances for my mother's little shortcomings.
Husband – I'm not complaining about her shortcomings, it's her long stayings I object to.

First clerk – Well, and how are you getting on with your requests for a rise?
Second clerk – Not so bad. I'm getting some encouragement now.
First clerk – Really, has the boss said yes?
Second clerk – Not exactly, but today he told me he's said no for the last time.

New shop assistant – Ah, good morning, Mr Right.
Customer – My name's Brown.
Assistant – That's funny. I've just been told the customer's always right.

Ringmaster – What's become of the contortionist?
Clown – Oh, he's doing a stretch in prison.

What language do twins speak in Holland?
Double Dutch!

Customer – Are you sure this fish was fully cooked?
Chip shop manager – Yes, why?
Customer – Because it ate all my chips!

What kind of warmth do sheep like in cold weather?
Central bleating!

Doctor to man – You've broken your arm in three different places.
Man – But that's impossible! I've only been in one place!

Dick – So you're a golfer, eh? What's your favourite course?
Harry – Soup!

Bobby – Are you ready for the fancy dress party?
Tommy – Yes.
Bobby – Why are you wearing two suits?
Tommy – I'm going as twins!

Sammy – Hey, Sandy, where are you going?
Sandy – Can't you see? The dog's taking me for a walk!

Jack – Have you seen a chap with one leg named Johnson about here?
Jim – What was the name of the other leg?

Brown – I say, didn't you say your dog's bark was worse than his bite?
Smith – Yes.
Brown – Then please don't let him bark. He's just bit me.

Maid – You know, ma'am, how you've been trying to get a vase to match that one in the living room?
Lady – Yes.
Maid – Well, madam, I've solved your problem – I've broken it.

Boss – Why are you late for work?
McLaren – When I got up this morning I looked in the mirror and I couldn't see myself, so I thought I'd gone to work. Two hours later I found that the mirror glass had fallen out of the frame.

Diner – Waiter, the tea has a soupy taste.
Waiter – Yes, sir, that's to wash your meal down.

Teacher – Now, Benny, what letter in the alphabet comes before "J"?
Benny – I don't know, sir.
Teacher – Think, boy, think! What have I got on both sides of my nose?
Benny – Freckles.

Guest – Is this a quiet room?
Hotel manager – It's never been known to make a sound, sir!

Teacher – Now, Sandy, what happened in 1759?
Sandy – Rabbie Burns was born.
Teacher – Quite correct. And in 1765?
Sandy (after pause) – Burns was six years old.

Diner – This water is cloudy.
Waiter – No, no, sir, our water is always fresh. It's only the glass that's dirty.

What's yellow and always points north?
A magnetic banana.

What speeds along the bottom of the sea at 100 mph?
A motor pike and side carp!

What do you do if someone offers you a rock cake?
Take your pick!

How do you start a book about ducks?
With an intro-duck-tion!

What kind of car would a sausage-maker buy?
An old banger!

What's French, very wobbly, tall and tasty?
The Trifle Tower!

Office boy – Well, here I am – bright and early.
Boss – You're early anyway.

Actor – What part do I take in this play?
Producer – The part of the heroine's uncle.
Actor – Well, what does he do?
Producer – He dies ten years before the curtain rises.

Boss – Well, why are you late? Didn't your alarm clock go off?
Mike – Yes, sir, it went off all right, but the trouble was that it went off while I was asleep.

Dennis – How do they get the water into water melons?
Dad – Oh, they plant the seeds in the spring.

Waiter – How did you know we had a new person washing the dishes?
Diner – Because the fingerprints on the plates are different.

Minnie – I got a fearful stitch in my side at the football match.
Toots – That's the worst of being hemmed in by the crowd.

Tam – What's green and red, striped with nine feet and one eye?
Sam – I don't know. What is green and red, striped with nine feet and one eye?
Tam – I don't know. I wouldn't have asked you if I knew!

When is a frog not a frog?
When it is being towed!

What is the most important thing to remember when you're learning chemistry?
Never lick the spoon!

Why did the orange have to go to the doctor?
Because it wasn't peeling well!

What did Dracula say when the dentist offered to pull out his teeth?
No fangs!

Which snake helps you see clearer in driving rain?
A windscreen viper.

What do you call an American drawing?
A Yankee Doodle!

Waiter – Did you have coffee or tea?
Diner – I'm not sure, but it tasted like soup.
Waiter – That would be coffee. The tea tastes like glue.

What's the height of stupidity?
Measure yourself and find out!

Brown – Have you spoken to your little boy about imitating me?
Jones – Yes, I told him not to act like a fool!

Mad scientist – With my new invention, train accidents will be impossible.
Assistant – How's that?
Mad scientist – Well, instead of moving the trains I move the stations.

Tourist – Why don't you buy a bicycle?
Farmer – I'd rather buy a cow.
Tourist – You'd look funny riding a cow.
Farmer – Not half as funny as I'd look trying to milk a bicycle.

Second – What did you think of his right?
Boxer – I was very much struck by it.

Millionaire – I didn't always have a limousine. When I started life I had to walk.
Young man – You were lucky! When I started life I couldn't even crawl.

Where do bees wait for transport?
At a buzz stop!

Where do fish wash?
In a river basin.

What's the best way to count cows?
On a cow-culator.

What does the American Indian ghost live in?
A creepy teepee!

What happens when you sleep under the car?
You wake up oily in the morning!

Publisher – Your story is quite well written, but this firm only publishes work by writers with well-known names.
Writer – Splendid! My name's Smith.

What is a Laplander?
A clumsy man on a bus!

Doctor – You should take a bath before you retire.
Patient – But, doctor, I don't expect to retire for another twenty years.

Judge – Describe what passed between you and the prison officer during your quarrel.
Prisoner – The plates were regular dinner size, your honour, and the teapot had a broken spout.

First angler – What's the bone for?
Second angler – I'm fishing for dog fish stupid!

Waiter in a new French restaurant – We are famous for our snails!
Bored diner – Yes, I know. I've been served by one already.

Why was Adam known as a good runner?
Because he was first in the human race!

Boy – Ouch! A crab just bit my toe.
Mother – Which one?
Boy – I don't know, all crabs look alike to me!

What's a monster's favourite soup?
Scream of tomato!

What is blue and yellow and has a wing span of 14 metres?
A 21/2 ton budgie!

What's the definition of a milk shake?
A nervous cow!

First snail – I'm exhausted.
Second snail – Yes, me too. We seem to have been walking for centimetres.

Little boy to golfer – You're lucky!
Golfer – Why?
Little boy – I just managed to stop your ball before it went down that little hole!

Why did the jester wear diamonds and rubies?
He thought they were the clown jewels!

Toots – Smiffy really is stupid!
Plug – What makes you say that?
Toots – He broke a washing-machine trying to wash the steps!

What would you see at a chicken show?
Hentertainment!

Why are people tired on 1st April?
Because they have just been on a 31-day March!

Worried brother – Doctor, doctor, my sister feels like a lift!
Doctor – Well, tell her to come in!
Worried brother – I can't. She doesn't stop at this floor!

What is the odd one out between a fork, a knife and a potato?
The fork is the odd one out. You can make chips with the other two.

Doctor – Your throat is in a bad way. Have you ever tried gargling with salt water?
Old sailor – Yes, I've been shipwrecked six times.

Doctor – You're looking a lot better.
Patient – Yes, I followed the instructions on the bottle you gave me.
Doctor – Let me see, what were they?
Patient – "Keep tightly corked."

Proud new father (holding his baby son) – He's the living image of me!
Mother-in-law – Why worry, so long as he's strong and healthy?

Grandson – Why do you have three pairs of specs, Grandpa?
Grandpa – One pair is for reading, one pair is for long distance and the third pair is for when I'm looking for the other two!

Helen – Mum, do you know what I'm going to give you for your birthday?
Mum – No, dear, what?
Helen – A nice tea pot.
Mum – But I've got a nice tea pot.
Helen – No you haven't. I've just dropped it!

PE teacher – I made twenty boys run, yet I didn't even have to ask them.
Maths teacher – How did you manage it?
PE teacher – Er . . . well, I ran and they ran after me!

Plug – If two's company and three's a crowd, what's four and five?
Smiffy – Nine.

What did the ivy plant say to the holly bush?
Stop being so spikeful!

What's the difference between an Indian elephant and an African elephant?
About 3,000 miles!

A man walked into a shop and stole a packet of salt and a packet of batteries. The police caught him and charged him for a salt and battery!

Jim – There's one thing I can never do without putting my foot in it.
Joe – What's that?
Jim – Put on my shoe.

Patient – Doctor, can you help me? My name is Bertha Higginbottom.
Doctor – I'm sorry, I can't do anything about that.

Office boy – Can I go to lunch now, sir?
Boss – Lunch? What do you want lunch for? You've been licking stamps all morning!

Mrs Green – Did you scold your little girl for mimicking me?
Mrs Brown – Yes, I told her not to act like a fool!

Shopkeeper – What made that customer walk out of the shop in such a temper?
Assistant – I don't know. He asked me for a hat to suit his head and I said, "Try this soft one!"

Kevin – Mum, may I go out to play with Bobby Brown?
Mum – No, you know I don't like Bobby.
Kevin – Then may I go out and fight with him?

Dentist (to patient) – Remember how you used to wallop me when we were at school, Bob . . . ?

What do you get when you cross a cockerel with a poodle?
A cock-a-poodle-doo!

Did you hear about the man who bought a sleeping bag?
He spent two months trying to wake it up!

What's as big as an elephant but weighs nothing?
It's shadow!

What do you call a deer with no eyes?
No-eye-deer!

Policeman – Stop! You were doing fifty miles an hour!
Speeding driver – Nonsense, I haven't been out for an hour yet!

How does a Zombie speak?
In a grave voice of corpse!

What do snakes do after a fight?
Hiss and make up!

What did the father ghost tell his son?
Spook only when you are spooken to.

What lives under the sea and carries a lot of people around?
An octobus!

What do you get if you cross the Atlantic with the Titantic?
Halfway!

Landlord – If you won't pay your rent, I want your room!
Tenant – Aw, you wouldn't like to live here!

Boarder – Look here, I haven't got a decent towel, sponge or piece of soap!
Landlady – Well, you have a tongue, haven't you?
Boarder – Yes, but I'm not a cat!

Customer – Well, what happens now that your opening sale has closed?
Shopkeeper – Our closing sale opens!

What do pixies eat at parties?
Fairy cakes!

What do young elves do after school?
Gnome work!

What has to be done by Friday?
Robinson Crusoe's washing!

What did the man say when he broke into the glue factory?
This is a stick-up!

Why are your hands shaking?
I suppose they must be glad to see each other!

Smiffy – What does the x-ray of my head show?
Doctor – Nothing.

What's yellow and holds up stage-coaches?
Dick Turnip!

Minnie – Dad, why are you going bald?
Dad – I am not bald! I just have a very tall forehead.

What goes cluck, cluck, click?
A hen in a seat-belt!

Weary diner – Are you the waiter who took my order?
Waiter – Yes, sir.
Diner – My, how you've grown!

Lady – How much are these chickens?
Butcher – Three pounds.
Lady – Did you raise them yourself?
Butcher – Yes, they were two pounds yesterday.

Dave – Why are you looking so puzzled?
Dan – Someone's stolen my car.
Dave – That's no reason to look puzzled.
Dan – Yes, it is. I wonder how he got it started.

Artist – I have been working like a horse all morning.
Farmer – What have you been doing?
Artist – Drawing a cart.

Customer – I'd like to see a really reliable second-hand car.
Salesman – So would I, sir!

Fred – Do insects cry, Sam?
Sam – Haven't you ever seen a moth bawl?

Peter – Are the people next door poor?
Mike – I don't think so.
Peter – Then why did they make a big fuss when their baby swallowed a penny?

What do you get if you cross a motorway with a wheelbarrow?
Knocked down!

What did the baby ghost say when he wanted his favourite food?
I scream!

Fatty – I feel as fit as a fiddle!
Plug – You look more like a bass drum to me!

Hiker – What a splendid sunset!
Villager – Yes, not bad for a little place like this, is it?

Johnson – I do spring cleaning in all seasons of the year.
Jackson – How's that?
Johnson – I'm a clock maker.

Jim – Look at these big oranges, John.
John – Yes, I'm sure you wouldn't get many of them for a dozen!

Aunt – Tommy, when will you come round to tea again?
Tommy (hungrily) – Now, if you like.

Tom – My father's got the softest job in town.
Bill – What is it?
Tom – He's a tester in the feather bed factory.

The miser's wife had a birthday coming up so he asked her what she wanted. "Something with lots of diamonds in it," came the reply.
He bought her a pack of cards!

Ringmaster – I will give five pounds to anyone who steps in the lion's cage.
Man – I'll do it, under one condition.
Ringmaster – Very well, what is your condition?
Man – You take the lions out first.

Girl – Did you hear about the telephone that fell in the river?
Boy – No, tell me.
Girl – It came out wringing!

How do you get a baby to sleep in space?
You rocket!

Do you need training to be a litter collector?
No, you just pick it up as you go along.

Mr Jackson – Are you using your mower this afternoon?
Mr Smith – Yes.
Mr Jackson – Fine. Then I can borrow your tennis racket as you won't be needing it!

First ghost – I see "The Phantom Killer" is on the telly tonight.
Second ghost – Yes, I saw it last week, and it nearly frightened the life into me!

Waiter – Did you say you wanted your eggs turned over, sir?
Diner – Yes, to the Museum of Natural History!

Chauffeur – Shall I pump up the tyres, sir?
Lord Toff – Wait until we get out into the country. My doctor tells me the air there is very good.

Caller – Who's the responsible man here?
Office boy – If you mean the chap who always gets the blame, it's me.

Librarian – I suppose you read Shakespeare?
Trainee librarian – Oh, yes, sir, I read all of his stuff, just as soon as it's published!

Teacher – Did your father punish you when you went home last night?
Tommy – Yes, sir.
Teacher – How did he do it?
Tommy – He made me stay in and help him with my homework.

Tom – I was so hungry, that the moment I got home, I began eating the tables.
Tim – Do you expect me to believe that?
Tom – Yes- they were vegetables!

Passenger (to captain of sinking ship) – How far are we from land?
Captain – About 200 metres.
Passenger – In which direction?
Captain – Straight down!

Which King of England was a milkman? Alfred the Crate!

Why did the boy take sugar and milk to the cinema?
Because they were showing a serial!

Adult ghost – What are you going to do when you're grown up?
Young ghost – I like the seaside, so I'm going to join as a ghost guard.

Owner – I'm very proud of my horse. He only lost one race the whole of last season.
Friend – My word, that's good! How many times was he entered?
Owner – Once.

Corporal – Hey! You're not paying the slightest attention. What is your head for?
Recruit – To prevent my collar slipping off?

Friend – Aren't you afraid sometimes when you look down at the road?
Steeplejack – Yes, I once felt sure that a man I saw was going to be run over.

American – I come from the greatest country in the world.
Scotsman – Oh, aye – I see you've lost your Scottish accent, then.

First boy – My father's got an upright piano.
Boy next door – And my father say it's a downright nuisance.

Fatty – Is dinner ready yet?
Mother – No, it'll be an hour yet.
Fatty – Huh! My tummy must be fast!

Policeman – It would be best if you could provide an alibi. Did anyone see you at the time of the crime?
Criminal – Fortunately, no!

Man – Could I have a dog for my son, please?
Pet shop owner – I'm sorry, sir. We don't do swops!

Teacher – Andy, I hope I didn't see you copying from Nicola's work.
Andy – I hope you didn't either!

Olive (the dinner lady) – Why is Cuthbert crying?
Fatty – He's crying because I'm eating my cake and I won't give him any.
Olive – Is his own cake all gone?
Fatty – Yes, and he cried all the time I was eating that as well!

Where do astronauts leave their space-ships?
On parking meteors!

Dad – Did your watch stop when it fell on the floor?
Roger – Of course, did you expect it to go right through?

Colonel – How is the new recruit getting on, sergeant?
Sergeant – Terrible, sir. I've taught him all I know and he still knows nothing.

Boarder – What's for breakfast? I hope it isn't bacon and eggs again.
Landlady – No, sir, not bacon and eggs again.
Boarder – Thank goodness. What is it?
Landlady – Bacon.

First hiker – Only six miles to home.
Second hiker – Good! That's three miles each!

Manager – Have you ever been on Government work?
Applicant – Nearly.
Manager – What do you mean?
Applicant – They hadn't enough evidence.

Mountain guide – Have you ever seen such a great sight as that volcano?
American tourist – Oh, your volcano's all right, but we've got a waterfall that could put it out in five minutes!

How do you know that carrots are good for your eyes?
Because you never see a rabbit with glasses!

Handyman – I would like a job as a handyman.
Employer – Can you mend a fuse, paint, do joinery work?
Handyman – No, I can't.
Employer – What's so handy about you, then?
Handyman – I live right next door!

Sue – Why is your dog wearing green wellingtons?
Jamie – Because his red ones are being repaired.

A cabbage, a tap and a tomato had a race.
The cabbage was head, the tap was running and the tomato tried to ketchup!

Patient – Doctor, doctor, I feel like a book.
Doctor – Well, sit down and tell me the story.

Cricketer – There's not much grass on this pitch, is there?
Umpire – Well, you haven't come here to graze, have you?

Did you hear about the plant in the maths class?
It grew square roots!

Why can't you depend on a parachute?
Because it always lets you down.

What do animals read in zoos?
Gnus-papers!

What do you call a Dutchman who gets "A"s in all of his exams?
Clever clogs.

What do you get if you cross a footballer with a smoked fish?
A goal-kipper.

Why did the girl keep her violin in the freezer?
Because she wanted to play it cool!

Teacher – Why did you kick Julie?
Jane – Because she failed her exams!
Teacher – That's no reason to kick her!
Jane – Yes, it is. I was copying her!

Gamekeeper – Oi! There's no fishing allowed here!
Johnny – I'm not fishing, I'm just washing my pet maggot!

Why did the farmer feed his cow on money?
To get rich milk!

Knock! Knock!
Who's there?
Cook
Cook who?
Oh, that's the first one I've heard this year.

What happened to the couple who met in a revolving door?
They're still going round together!

There was a man who sat up all night wondering where the sun had gone to. Next morning, it dawned on him!

Why did the witches call off the cricket match?
They couldn't find the bats.

Why don't bananas worry when people say bad things about them?
Bananas are noted for their thick skins!

Why don't centipedes play football?
The game's over by the time they get their boots on!

If you have ducks in cricket, birdies in golf, what do you have in bowls?
Soup!

Grant – What's yellow and good at sums?
Bruce – A plate of custard with a calculator in it!

Boss – What we prize most in this office is neatness.
New boy – Shall I straighten your tie, sir?

Playwright – In the third act there is an earthquake.
Manager – Ah, well, that should bring the house down.

Jim – Did you hear the thunder last night?
John – Eh? Why didn't you waken me? You know I can't sleep during a thunderstorm!

Diner – Waiter, what is your name?
Waiter – John Smith, but everyone calls me "billiard cue".
Diner – Why?
Waiter – Because I work much better with a tip.

First angler – Caught anything yet?
Second angler – Not yet. I don't think the silly worm is trying!

Teacher – What is your name, boy?
Boy – Tom, miss.
Teacher – Tom, is short for Thomas. In this class I want you to call everyone by their proper names. For example, what is Jack's proper name?
Boy – Er . . . Jackass?

Jones – I caught a pickpocket in the act of stealing my watch.
Smith – What did you say?
Jones – I told him I'd no time to spare.

Mrs Smith – Can I borrow your record player this weekend?
Neighbour – Having a party?
Mrs Smith – No, we just want some sleep.

Molly – Why is that squirrel tied to the back of your car?
Mandy – To gather up the nuts, of course!

Why does that man always shut his eyes when he sings?
Because he hates to see us suffer!

Clueless car owner – Have you got my car started?
Mechanic – No, sir, your battery's flat.
Clueless car owner – What shape should it be?

Mother owl – I'm worried about our son.
Father owl – Oh, why's that?
Mother owl – He just doesn't seem to give a hoot about anything.

What begins with T, ends with T and has T in it?
A teapot!

Teacher – When they take out an appendix, it's called an appendectomy; when they remove your tonsils, it's a tonsillectomy. What is it when they remove a growth from your head?
Danny – A haircut!

What is copper nitrate?
Police overtime.

Diner – Do you charge extra for bread in this restaurant?
Waiter – No, sir.
Diner – Then bring me a loaf.

Why can't you fool a snake?
Because he hasn't a leg to pull!

Timid clerk – Please, sir, my wife said I was to ask you for a rise.
Boss – Very well. I'll ask my wife if it's all right.

Mean father – What did I give you for your birthday last year?
Son – A balloon.
Father – Right, I'll blow it up for you this year!

Why did the teabag go into hospital?
Because he was under a strain!

First angler – How are the fish today?
Second angler – Dunno! I dropped a line but they haven't answered yet.

What is bigger when it is upside down?
The number 6.

Why is an elephant large, grey and wrinkled?
Because if he was small, round and white, he would be an aspirin!

Doctor – You need more exercise. You should try walking.
Patient – But, doctor, I'm a postman!

Accused (in court for speeding) – But, Judge, it's simply my nature to do everything fast!
Judge – Right! Let's see how quickly you can do thirty days!

Waiter – What did you think of the cottage pie?
Diner – Let's just say I could almost taste the thatched roof.

Boss – You've been with the firm for sixty years, but you'll have to leave.
Bob – Huh! If I'd known it wasn't to be a steady job I'd never have joined!

Office boy – The boss is beginning to take notice of me.
Clerk – How's that?
Office boy – This morning he asked me if I worked here.

Teacher – Aha! So I've caught you eating sweets, have I?
Tam – No, sir. They're so sticky that I keep them in my mouth instead of my pocket!

Why do witches fly on broomsticks?
Because a vacuum cleaner is too heavy!

First mum – What's your son going to be when he passes all his exams?
Second mum – A pensioner!

Boastful farmer – I can reap, plough and mow. Can anyone tell me something I can't do on a farm?
Friend – Can you lay an egg?

Tim – Think of those Spaniards going 2000 miles on a galleon.
Jack – Forget it! You can't believe all you hear about those foreign cars.

Waitress – But, sir, you asked me to bring you weak tea!
Diner – Weak, yes, but this stuff is helpless!

Angus – I've had to sell my Dachshund.
Geordie – Why?
Angus – It took him so long to get in and out of the door that we froze every winter.

Bill – You would believe anything a fool told you.
George – Not always, but you are most convincing!

Mum – I don't like the boy next door, so I want you to keep away from him as much as possible at school.
David – Oh, that's easy. He's usually at the top of the class.

Teacher – And what are you going to be if you can only count up to ten?
Jim – A boxing referee, miss!

Detective – Can you give me a description of your missing teller?
Bank manager – He's about five feet eight inches tall and £70,000 short.

Teacher – When was the Magna Carta signed, Toots?
Toots – At a quarter past twelve.
Teacher – At a quarter past twelve?
Toots – Yes, 12.15!

What are private detectives called in fairyland?
Sherlock Gnomes.

Billy – Mum, I came top in arithmetic today. Teacher asked what 5 x 12 was and I said 58.
Mum – But that's not right. 5 x 12 is 60.
Billy – I know, but I was closer than anyone else!

What happened to the schoolboy who did his homework with sticky hands?
He got stuck in the middle of a sum!

Why did Father Christmas get himself a garden?
So he could Ho, Ho, Ho!

Brown – Smith is an old miser.
Grant – Why?
Brown – He jumps over his gate to save wear and tear on the hinges!

Big Bill – Why are you so small?
Small Sam – I was raised on shortbread and condensed milk!

Prison governor – Any complaints?
Prisoner – Yes, there aren't enough exits!

Bore – And then the burglar threatened to blow my brains out!
Listener – And did he?

Dad – Did you get my boots soled?
Son – Yes! I got 20p for them!

Constable – You are accused of stealing a motorcar!
Prisoner – Well, search me!

Who invented spaghetti?
An Italian man who used his noodle!

What happened to the ship that crossed the Pacific with 25 tons of yo-yos on board?
It sank 42 times!

If horses wear horseshoes, what do camels wear?
Sandshoes

Tom – One of my ancestors fell at Waterloo.
Jim – Really!
Tom – Yes, he fell off platform five!

Why did the boy take his bicycle to bed?
He was too lazy to sleepwalk.

What did the mother worm say to her baby when he was late for breakfast?
"Where in earth have you been?"

What game do horses like best?
Stable tennis!

Football manager – I've found the very man for us: eyes like a hawk, strong as an ox, speed of a racehorse and a kick like a mule.
Director – It's a forward we want, not a farmyard!

Dud golfer – I suppose you get a good many weekenders on this course, caddie?
Caddie – Yes, also a few weak beginners.

Teacher – How many sexes are there?
Smiffy – Three.
Teacher -What are they?
Smiffy – The male sex, the female sex, and the insects.

Jim – What rent do you pay?
Bill – I don't pay it.
Jim – What would it be if you did pay it?
Bill – A miracle.

Boy – Are you offering ten pounds for finding your dog?
Lady – Yes. Have you found him?
Boy – No, but I'm going out to look, and I wondered if you'd like to advance me some of the money?

Old man – When do you go back to school, Tommy?
Tommy – When Dad finds out I'm playing truant.

Fat man – I've travelled all over the world and there's nothing I haven't seen in the past few years.
Voice from audience – What about your own feet?

Driver in racing car (to companion) – We are doing ninety miles an hour. Are you game for another ten?
Companion (swallowing another mouthful of dust) – Yes, I'm full of grit.

Teacher – Your essay is very good, Plug, but it is word for word the same as Cuthbert's. What shall I conclude from that?
Plug – That Cuthbert's is very good, too?

Eric – Can you tell me the weakest part of a steam engine?
Alec – That's easy. The tender!

Teacher – What is Australia bounded by, Peter?
Peter – Kangaroos, miss.

Suspicious PC – Hey, didn't I hear a window smash?
Dennis – Oh, no, sir. It was me breaking the glass of my watch.

Bus diver – You ought to be driving a pram.
Lorry driver – And you ought to be in it.

First prisoner – What are you in for?
Second prisoner – I just picked up a rope I found on the road.
First prisoner – What? Is that all?
Second prisoner -Well, there happened to be a cow on the end of it.

Bruiser – Hullo, Bill, you look annoyed. What's the matter?
Burglar – Matter! Do you see this bill in the police window? They're only offering a hundred pounds for my arrest, and it used to be two hundred pounds. Disgusting, that's what it is.

MONSTER JOKES

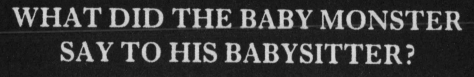

WHAT DID THE BABY MONSTER
SAY TO HIS BABYSITTER?

I WANT MY MUMMY!

WHY DID THE SEA MONSTER
EAT 5 SHIPS THAT WERE
CARRYING POTATOES?

NOBODY CAN EAT JUST ONE
POTATO SHIP!

Lady (to driver of steam roller) – Driver, did you see a packet of butter down the road? I think I must have dropped it.
Driver (scratching his head) – Come to think of it, miss, I did feel a bit of a bump.

Dodgy Dan – He called me a barefaced scoundrel.
Crafty Ken – Never mind, perhaps he didn't notice your moustache.

Teacher – I am going to send for your father, Sandy, and show him what a shocking composition you handed in today.
Sandy – All right, send for him. I don't care. He wrote it.

Dentist – I'll have to charge you fifty pounds for extracting that tooth.
Patient – But I thought you charged ten pounds?
Dentist – Yes, but you yelled so loudly you scared four other patients out of the place!

Teacher – Johnny, take your cap off in school.
Johnny – I haven't got my cap on, sir.
Teacher – Yes, you have.
Johnny – No, I haven't. This is my brother's.

Shopkeeper – Aren't you the boy who came last week and asked me to employ you?
Boy – Yes, sir.
Shopkeeper -But didn't I tell you I wanted an older boy?
Boy – Yes, sir, but I'm older now.

First golfer – Oh I meant to tell you where that bunker was.
Second golfer – It's quite all right, thanks. I found it for myself.

Sandy -Troubled with toothache, Jock?
Jock – You don't suppose I'm pleased with it, do you?

Farmer – Why did you not tell me there was a hare?
Pat – I never saw the hare till it was out of sight!

A quiet, patient little man had been hustled and jostled about in the crowd which boarded a train. For a long time he suffered in silence. At last he spoke to a young fellow standing in front of him. "Young man, I hope you don't think me rude, but may I ask your age?"
"Eighteen."
"Well, don't you think you're old enough to stand on your own feet?"

Medicine man – What's the matter, sire?
Cannibal king – I've got indigestion. I've just polished off a millionaire.
Medicine man – Well, I told you not to eat anything too rich.

Beginner at golf – How many have I taken to that hole? Is it fifteen or sixteen?
Caddie – Oh, I don't know. It's not a caddie you need, it's a cricket scorer.

Globetrotter – Yes, while we were in Egypt visiting the pyramids we found them literally covered with hieroglyphics.
Lady – Oh, and weren't you afraid some of them would bite you?

Know-all – I can answer any question you like to ask.
Bored friend – Well what did the Dead Sea die of?

Bertie – I took the piece of cake that was in the cupboard to give to a poor boy.
Mother – Oh, that was very good of you. And did he thank you for it?
Bertie – Well, I waited for a long time and no poor boy came, so I ate it myself.

Guide – Look at that half-ruined castle. It might be at least eight hundred years old. Believe me, folks, they don't build such ancient castles nowadays.

Gnock! Gnock!
Who's there?
Winner.
Winner who?
Winner you gonna get this door fixed?

Doctor – Have you been anywhere else?
Patient – I went to the chemist first.
Doctor – And what idiotic advice did he give you?
Patient – He told me to come and see you.

Teacher – Now, boys, it's quite common to speak of two things together. For instance, health and happiness, gold and silver. Tommy, give me another example.
Tommy – Liver and onions, miss.

First thief – You know that lantern I pinched?
Second thief – Yes.
First thief – Well, some dirty thief's been and gone and stole it.

Doctor – What's wrong with you?
Smiffy – Oh, I've got a splinter in my finger.
Doctor – You should have more sense than scratch your head.

Minnie – Where are you going?
Dennis – Nowhere.
Minnie – Wait a minute. I'll come, too.

Voice from the river – Help! Help! I've fallen in and cannot swim!
Voice from the bank – Now's your chance to learn, mister.

Father – Don't ask so many questions, child. Curiosity killed the cat.
Little boy – What did the cat want to know, Dad?

Smith (to man who is standing in front of him at football match) – Do you know how to play draughts?
Man – Yes.
Smith – Well, it's your move.

Housekeeper – There's no bread in the house, sir. What shall I do?
Absent-minded professor – Oh, don't bother about that. Just make some toast.

Servant – Sire, there is a messenger without.
King – Without what, fool?
Servant – Without the gate.
King – Then give it to him.

A cyclist was travelling along a lonely road on a dark night and came to a very tall signpost. The sign was so tall and the night was so dark that he could not make out what the sign said. With difficulty he struggled to the top and read "Wet Paint"!

Teacher (setting problem) – A train leaves Perth travelling at thirty miles an hour. Half an hour later another train leaves the same station, travelling at fifty miles an hour. Where will the second train run into the first?
Curly – At the back, miss.

Ship's engineer (to new assistant) – Say, I thought you said you knew something about engines?
Assistant – So I do, sir, but on a smaller scale.
Ship's engineer – What's your regular job?
Assistant – Watchmaker, sir.

Old lady (visiting prison) – Have you any plans for when you leave prison?
Prisoner – Yes, lady. A bank, two mansions, three jeweller shops, and a post office.

Counsel – How far from the door were you?
Witness – Four yards, two feet, three and a half inches.
Counsel – How can you be so sure?
Witness – Because I expected some fool would ask me, and so I measured it.

Moe – When the tourist arrived home he fell on his face and kissed the pavement of his native city.
Joe – Emotion?
Moe – No. Banana skin.

Freddie – Do you know what keeps the moon in place, Charlie?
Charlie – I think it must be the beams.

Mother – Your face is fairly clean, Wilfrid, but how did you get your hands so dirty.
Wilfrid – Washing my face, mother!

Customer (looking at socks) – Aren't they rather loud?
Shop assistant – Yes, sir. They are specially made for people whose feet are in the habit of going to sleep.

Policeman – You say you were held up by a robber with a revolver this morning. At what time?
Shop assistant – Five minutes to one.
Policeman – How can you fix the time as precisely?
Shop assistant – Because I could see the church clock, and I noticed the hands were in the same position as mine.

First footballer – I once took a penalty kick and broke the net.
Second footballer – That's nothing. Once I hit the crossbar with a penalty kick. The next day walking round the ground I noticed the bar was still shaking.

Diner -Waiter, this chicken has no wishbone.
Waiter – He was a happy and contented chicken, sir, and had nothing to wish for.

Conceited Colin is so used to getting his own way that he writes up his diary for a week ahead.

Thug – Can't you help a poor, lonely man who hasn't got anything in the world except his loaded revolver?

Angry producer – What do you mean by smiling in that death scene?
Actor – With the salary you pay, death seems a pleasant relief.

Passenger (on board ocean liner) – Doesn't the ship tip frightfully?
Dignified steward – The vessel, madam, is trying to set a good example to the passengers.

"Mind that step," said the young policeman to the very old offender as he led the way to the cells.
The hardened thug growled. "I knew that there step afore you was born."

Robbie – What does "knows no bounds" mean, Dad? Explain it.
Dad (buried in newspaper) – Kangaroo with rheumatism.

Land owner – Don't you see this notice, "No Fishing Allowed in these Grounds"?
Angler – But I'm not fishing in the grounds. I'm fishing in the river!

Lodger – This steak is like a cold day in June, Mrs Bordem – very rare.
Landlady – And your board bill is like March weather – always unsettled.

Sergeant – Now, then! Line up alphabetically. What's your name, my lad?
Private – Philips, sergeant.
Sergeant – Well, what are you doing up here? Get amongst the "F"s at once.

Private – The tallest chap in our company is six feet nine inches.
Corporal – That's nothing. In our barracks we have a sergeant who has to kneel when he wants to scratch his head.

Lady – Are you sure this salmon in fresh?
Salesman – Fresh! Why, madam, I've just had to cut him up to keep him from jumping at the flies!

Moe – I don't like that fellow Brown.
Joe – Why not?
Moe – He is the sort of man who pats you on the back to your face, and smacks you in the eye behind your back!

WHY DO THEY HAVE A FENCE
AROUND THE GRAVEYARD?
EVERYONE IS DYING TO
GET IN!

WHY DIDN'T THE SKELETON
GO TO THE DANCE?
HE HAD NO 'BODY' TO GO WITH!

Businessman – I am a self-made man, sir. I began life as a barefoot boy.
Shop assistant – Well, I wasn't born with shoes on either.

Footballer – I'm sorry, but you'll have to clear out.
Angler – Indeed I won't. I've permission to fish in this river.
Footballer – River? This is our football pitch!

Notice outside football ground – There are two kinds of kick-offs. One is seen, the other is felt. To see one and avoid the other, please pay at the gate.

Lady – Are you sure these field glasses are powerful?
Salesman – Powerful? Why, when you use these glasses, anything less than ten miles away looks as if it's behind you!

Sailor (shouting) – Man overboard!
Seasick passenger (with a groan) – Lucky dog!

Teacher – What is a cannibal?
Sandy – I don't know, miss.
Teacher – If you ate your father and mother what would you be?
Sandy – An orphan.

Teacher – Now if I subtract 29 from 87, what's the difference?
Smiffy – That's what I say. Who cares?

Diner (to waiter) – The man who killed this chicken must have had a very kind heart.
Waiter -What makes you think that, sir?
Diner – He must have hesitated six or seven years before doing it!

Mother (to music teacher) – Do you think my son will be able to do anything with his voice?
Teacher – Well, it might come in handy in the event of a fire!

Teacher – What is a volcano?
Danny – A mountain that keeps on interrupting.

Witness (entering box) – Good gracious! They've caught a pretty tough bunch, I must say!
Policeman – Those aren't the prisoners, sir. You're looking at the jury!

Manager of restaurant (haughtily) – I'm very sorry you don't like our cakes, sir, but I can assure you this business has been built up almost entirely on our cookery!
Diner – Yes, and with a few more buns like these you could build a fortress!

Teacher – How many bones have you in your body, Tommy?
Tommy – Thousands of them. We had kippers for breakfast.

Clerk – If the boss doesn't take back what he said, I'm leaving.
Office boy – What did he say?
Clerk – "You're sacked."

Old-fashioned lady (at concert) – Is that a popular song that man is singing?
Nephew – It was before he sang it.

Terry – Do you ever hear of the money you lent your neighbour?
Jerry – I should think I do! He bought a CD player with it.

Teacher – Why, when I was your age I could repeat the names of kings and Queens of England backwards and forwards.
Pupil – Yes, but when you were my age there weren't so many kings and queens.

Mother – Your teacher complains that you're always late for school. Why is that?
Tommy – It's not my fault, mother. They always ring the bell before I get there.

Tim – I've fallen into the bad habit of talking to myself lately.
Bob – I wondered why you were looking so bored.

Motorist – Robert is going mad over his new car.
Friend – Strange, the last time I saw him he was going mad underneath it.

Contractor – Does the foreman know that the trench has fallen in?
Labourer – Well, sir, we're digging him out to tell him.

Small boy (to fallen man) – You big bully. Look what you've done to Tommy's banana.

Contortionist – Too bad about the lion-tamer, isn't it?
Sword-swallower – What happened to him?
Contortionist – He's got such a swelled head through being praised so much that he can't get it into the lion's mouth.

Motorist (telephoning after he has had an accident) – Send assistance at once, I've turned turtle.
Voice from the other end of telephone – This is a garage, not a pet shop.

Visitor to circus – What's wrong?
Dejected circus hand – The elephant's dead.
Visitor – Were you very fond of it?
Circus hand – Well, yes . . . but, you see, I've been given the job of digging its grave.

Reporter – To what do you attribute your long life?
Oldest inhabitant of village – Well, you see, I was born long ago.

Foreman (to workman entwined in rope) – What do you think you're doing, snake charming?

Judge – After you saw the prisoner put his fist through the window, did you observe anything?
PC Sapp – Yes, I observed a hole in the glass.

Village shopkeeper – Well, that's three hot-water bottles, a dozen lemons, a jar of honey, a packet of paracetamol, a large bottle of cough medicine and three boxes of tissues. I'll send them right away. All well at home, sir?

Workman – Can you give me a job, mate?
Foreman – I've got a man here today who hasn't come, and if he doesn't turn up tomorrow I'll send him away and take you on.

Golf instructor – Swing the club, man. Swing it! Don't chop at the ball as if you were a butcher.
Beginner – Why, that's just what I am.

New resident – This village boasts a choral society, doesn't it?
Old resident – Well, we don't boast about it; we put up with it.

Boss – You're an idiot! Why my last office boy was worth twice as much as you.
Office boy – I bet he didn't get it.

Visitor – I don't know how you can work here. Your office is as hot as an oven.
Boss – Well, I make my daily bread here, you know.

Customer (buying a dog) – Is this dog fond of children?
Assistant – Oh, yes, but I would advise you to give him biscuits, they're better for his digestion.

Diner -Waiter, what kind of meat is this?
Waiter – It's spring lamb, sir.
Diner – Ah, then it must have been a spring that I've been chewing this last half-hour.

Old man – You're rather a young chap to be left in charge of a chemist's shop. Have you a diploma?
Assistant – Why . . . er . . . no, sir; but we have a preparation of our own that's just as good.

Judge – What passed between you?
Defendant – One turnip, seven rocks, and a lump of mud.

Gardener – What are you tying those onions down for?
Assistant – Well, they're spring onions, aren't they?

Teacher – Now, boys what do we get out of the earth besides coal and iron?
Pupil (after a long pause) – Please, sir, worms.

Magistrate (discharging prisoner) – Now, then, I would advise you to keep away from bad company.
Prisoner – Thank you, sir. You won't see me here again.

First scout – Are there any matches left?
Second scout – Yes, there's one.
First scout – Only one? What if it doesn't light?
Second scout – No fear, it won't do that. I've tried it already.

Professor (lecturing on the rhinoceros) – I must beg you to give me your undivided attention. It's absolutely impossible that you can form a true idea of this hideous animal unless you keep your eyes fixed on me.

Football captain – If we win you'll be richer by fifty quid.
Referee – And if you lose?
Captain – You leave on a stretcher.

Artist – I hope you don't mind if I sketch in your field?
Farmer – Oh, no. You'll help keep the birds off the peas.

Moe – What's the matter?
Joe – I've just lost a hundred pounds.
Moe – Oh cheer up, and take things as they come.
Joe – That's far easier than parting with things as they go.

First workman – That chap's really lazy. He's been sitting doing nothing for two hours.
Second workman – How do you know?
First workman -I've been sitting here watching him.

Terry – That's a bad cold you've got. You'll have to take care of it.
Jerry – Take care of it! Gracious, I want to lose it.

Peter – I say, Dad, when I had toothache you took me to the dentist to have my tooth filled.
Dad – Yes, what about it?
Pete – Well, I've got a stomach ache. What about going into that tuckshop?

Diner – I believe it is improper to speak disrespectfully of one's elders.
Waiter – Yes, sir, it is.
Diner – Well, then I shan't say anything about this chicken.

Boss (to boy applying for job) – This reference from your last employer seems pretty black.
Boy – Yes, sir. You see, he licked his pencil before writing it.

Boss – On the way to the bank you'll pass the football ground.
Office boy (expectantly) – Yes, sir?
Boss – Well, pass it.

Waiter – Tea or coffee, sir?
Diner – Don't tell me. Let me try to guess for myself.

Teacher – How is sawdust produced?
Pupil – Why . . . er-
Teacher – Come, come, use your head!

WHAT IS DRACULA'S FAVOURITE FRUIT?
NECKTARINES!

WHY DIDN'T DRACULA HAVE MANY FRIENDS?
HE WAS A PAIN IN THE NECK!

WHAT DID THE VAMPIRE SAY WHEN HE WAS DONE BITING SOMEONE?
ITS BEEN NICE GNAWING YOU!

WHAT IS A VAMPIRE'S FAVOURITE TYPE OF BOAT?
BLOOD VESSELS!

WHAT IS DRACULA'S FAVOURITE PLACE IN NEW YORK?
THE VAMPIRE STATE BUILDING!

Inspector – So this is the bloke who stole the barrow-load of turnips. Did you get the turnips?
Constable – No, sir.
Inspector – Well, search him!

Teacher – Why can't you repeat your history lesson, Sandy? Didn't you learn it?
Sandy – No, sir. You see, I thought history always repeated itself.

Diner (holding up fork with meat on it) – Do you call this pork, this stuff on the end of my fork?
Waiter – Which end, sir?

First golfer – That ass Green crossed my tee when I was driving.
Second golfer -Well, if he crossed your tee you should have dotted his eye.

Tourist – Is it healthy in this part of the country?
Local – Sure it is, guv'nor. Why, we had to shoot people to start a cemetery.

Officer – Right face!
New recruit – What?
Officer – Right face, I said.
New Recruit – Yes, this is my right face.

Clerk (making excuse) – But, sir, man isn't a machine. He can't go on forever.
Boss – Yes, he can. You're going forever at the end of this week.

Recruit – What's the password tonight?
Sentry – Metempsychosis.
Recruit – Thanks; but I think I'll stay in camp tonight.

Photographer (to foreman) – Can I take a photograph of your men at work?
Foreman – Yes, if you get a chance.

Castaway (as he sees a passing ship) – Just my luck. It would be going in the direction I don't want to go.

Visitor (at museum) -Where are those Oliver Cromwell relics that were here last week?
Attendant – I don't know, sir. I fancy they must have been returned to Mr Cromwell.

Young Bob was thrilled by a succession of wonders on his first train journey. The train rushed into a tunnel, then came out into the open.
"Gosh!" said young Bob. "It's tomorrow!"

Teacher – Today the school breaks up for the holidays. What could be more glorious than spending the following week's holiday in the country?
Pupil – Spending the following two weeks in the country, sir!

First footballer – Why do you call your manager "sulphur"?
Second footballer – Because he flares up at the end of every match!

Boarder (on arriving at lodgings to find them burnt down) – Oh, Mrs Cater, did you save anything that belonged to me?
Landlady – Yes, sir, your bill. Here it is.

Merchant (to salesman) – What's wrong with your nose? Somebody hit it?
Salesman – No. You said I wasn't to show it in here again, so I've tied it up!

Farmer – Let me tell you, my friend, that that horse knows as much as I do.
Friend – Well, don't tell anybody else; you might want to sell him some day.

Burglar Bill – My opinion is that you can't get too much of anything.
Housebreaking Horace – What about "time"?

Mr Jones – You've made a rotten job of painting this fence.
Handyman – Well, you said it wanted painting badly.

Stranger (as gun fires from castle) – What's that noise?

Local inhabitant – Why, don't you know? It's sunset.

Stranger – Well, I've been in a lot of towns, but this is the only one where the sun went down with a bang like that!

Mr Screecher (about to sing) – What's your favourite air?

Friend (making for door) – Fresh, and plenty of it!

Doctor – What's the matter this time?

Patient – I've got pains in my back, sir.

Doctor (handing him a bottle) – Take a dose of this a quarter of an hour before you feel the pains coming on.

Customer – I've brought back those shoes. I've changed my mind, and I don't like them.

Shopkeeper – Sorry, I can't take them back. You'll just have to change your mind again.

Actor – I must insist on real food in this banquet scene.

Manager – Yes, and I think you should have real poison in the death scene.

Dad – The last time I gave you £2 you said you wouldn't walk into the nearest shop and spend it.

Danny – Yes, Dad.

Dad – But I saw you do it.

Danny – Don't you know the difference between a walk and a sprint, Dad?

Boss (to office boy who is late, as usual) – Don't you know what time we start?

Office boy – No, sir. You're always started when I come in.

Visitor – Does Mr Murphy live here?

Neighbour – He used to, but he's dead.

Visitor – How long has he been dead?

Neighbour – Well, if he had lived till tomorrow, he'd have been dead a fortnight.

Judge – You still say you're innocent, though six witnesses saw you steal the hen?

Prisoner – Your Honour, I could produce six thousand people who didn't see me.

Diner – I want some meat without bone, gristle or fat.

Waiter – How would an egg do, madam?

Small boy (to pal pursued by bull) – Run round in circles, Sandy, and make him giddy.

Pickpocket (visiting pal in jail) – I hired a lawyer for you this morning, Slim, but I had to leave my watch with him as part payment.

Pal – And did he keep it?

Pickpocket – He thinks he did.

Pupil (at boxing class) – I want my money back. It says on the notice outside, "Boxing taught first floor," and I've been floored half a dozen times, and I don't know any more about it than I did when I first started.

Terry – I see they have stopped running the 7 a.m. train. Do you miss it?

Jerry – Not so often as I used to.

Nervous speaker (before large audience) – Ladies and g-gentlemen, when I c-c-came here tonight, only t-two people knew my speech: my father and myself. N-now only F-f-father knows it!

Mother (at table) – Will you have some bread, Tommy?

Tommy – No, I don't want bread.

Mother – Where are your manners, Tommy? No what?

Tommy – No fear. Not when there's cake on the table.

McTavish – I always do my hardest work before breakfast.

McHaggart – What's that?

McTavish – Getting up.

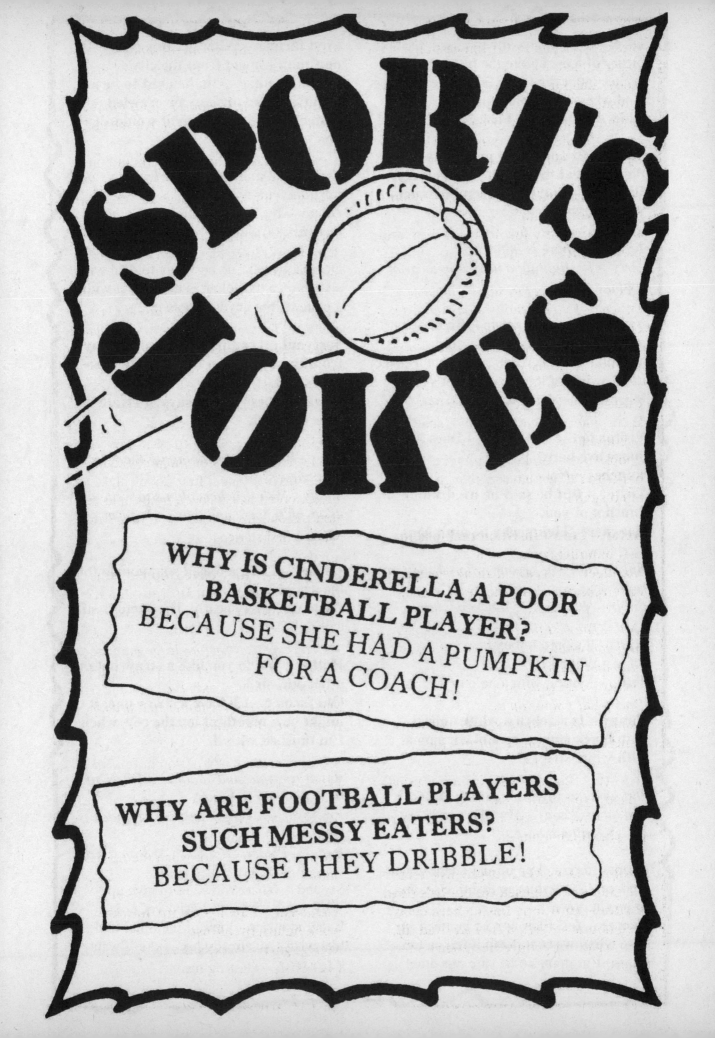

SPORTS JOKES

WHY IS CINDERELLA A POOR BASKETBALL PLAYER? BECAUSE SHE HAD A PUMPKIN FOR A COACH!

WHY ARE FOOTBALL PLAYERS SUCH MESSY EATERS? BECAUSE THEY DRIBBLE!

Diner – Quick, give me two eggs and six pieces of toast before the big fight starts.
Waiter (after diner has finished eating) – And where is the big fight, sir?
Diner – Right here! I haven't any money!

Judge – Prisoner, the jury finds you did not steal the watch. You may go.
Prisoner – And can I keep the watch, your worship?

Terry – Nothing is impossible.
Jerry – Try lighting a match on a bar of soap.

Youthful football captain – Bit of luck getting Bill Bashem to play for us.
Youthful club secretary – Yes, but it cost us £3-worth of toffees, and that's the biggest transfer fee we've paid yet.

Visitor to the Wild West – Does Mr Jones live here?
Rancher – No.
Visitor – But he said he lived within gunshot of you.
Rancher – That's why he ain't here.

Billy – How big is your roller-skating rink?
Bobby – It seats two thousand people.

Terry – It's hard to beat!
Jerry – What is?
Terry – A drum with a hole in it.

Danny – Is a zebra a white animal with black stripes or a black animal with white stripes?

Old lady (seeing boy carrying bale of hay on his head) – My goodness! That lad's needing a haircut!

Farmer (to yokel up tree) – Come down, George. Don't you see that tree's going to be cut down?
George – Yes, I know it is; but the last time a tree was cut down it fell on top of me, so I'm going to be safe this time!

First farmer – What became of the new man you got from the city?
Second farmer – Oh, he used to be a chauffeur and one day he crawled under a mule to see why it wouldn't go.

Teacher – Danny, don't you know it's bad for little boys to fight?
Danny – Yes, but I'm teaching Cuthbert; he doesn't know.

Domestic tips: The best way to deal with a stain on a tablecloth is to cover it with a plate before anyone spots it.

Sergeant (at camp) – Hey, come away from there; you can't go into the general's tent.
Private Jones – But it says "Private" over the door.

Plug – What are you doing up there on that horse?
Smiffy – Well, teacher told us to write an essay on a horse and that's what I'm doing.

Butcher – Did the roast I sold you do for the whole family?
Customer – Very nearly. The doctor's still calling!

Hatter – Would you like a straw hat or a felt one, sir?
Old farmer – I'll have a straw one; it might be a mouthful for the cow when I'm finished with it.

Butler (outside study door) – Please, sir, here's a letter for you.
Professor – All right. Just slip it under the door.
Butler – Please, sir, I can't. it's on a tray.

Second – What! You want to give up? Why, you're not half licked yet.
Battered boxer – Well, if the other half is like what I've already had, I don't want it.

Danny – Does ppnneeuummoonniiaa spells double pneumonia?

Father (to son picking himself up at bottom of stairs) – Did you miss a step?
Son -Well, I missed one, but I hit all the rest.

Prison warder – Ain't you asleep yet?
Burglar – No, it seems so funny to be lying in bed in the middle of the night.

Father – What are you grumbling about?
Tommy – Well, me and Sandy Brown were arguing about our favourite football teams, and teacher made us write them out 100 times after school.
Father – Well, that's fair enough.
Tommy – But his is Ayr, and mine is Inverness Caledonian Thistle!

Doctor – Well, you are certainly looking much better than I expected to find you.
Patient – I think that is because I followed the directions on your medicine bottle.
Doctor – Very likely. What were they?
Patient (grimly) – Keep the bottle tightly corked!

Small boy – Daddy, what do you call a man who drives a car?
Father – It all depends on how close he comes to me.

Reporter – Good morning, Mrs Brown. Is that prize-fighter husband of yours in?
Boxer's wife – He's in, but not up. Since he's been a boxer, he never gets up before the stroke of ten.

What would a football team be without a goalie?
A man short, of course.

Optician – Can you read the chart?
Jimmy – Yes, I can read it, but I'm wondering how to pronounce the word!

Teddy (at boat race, pointing to cox) – That man at the back of that boat doesn't seem to be doing much.
Eddy – Perhaps he's a stowaway.

Native – These tiger tracks lead north.
Nervous explorer -Then we go south?

Pupil – Please, sir, did you ever hear a rabbit bark?
Teacher – Rabbits do not bark.
Pupil – But my natural history book says that rabbits eat cabbage and bark.

Town boy (at country farm for first time) – What are the hens making such a noise for?
Farmer – I expect they want something to eat.
Town boy – Well, if they're hungry, they should lay themselves some eggs!

Mike – Get up, Sandy, the ship's on fire!
Sandy (dreamily) – That's all right, Mike; it's on water too.

First farmer – Did the gale damage your barn?
Second farmer – I don't know. I haven't found it yet.

Auntie – Would you like some bread and butter, Willie?
Willie – No.
Auntie – No what?
Willie – You shouldn't say "what" auntie; you should say "I beg your pardon".

Johnny – I wish father hadn't invented that new soap of his.
Mother – Why?
Johnny – Well, every time a customer comes in, I'm washed as a sample.

Old lady – Why has the ship stopped?
Sailor – Can't get along for the fog.
Old lady – But can't you go by the stars?
Sailor – We ain't going that way unless the boiler bursts.

Sidney – Dad, there's a black cat in the kitchen.

Father – That's good. Black cats are lucky.

Sidney – This one is . . . it's eating the fish you were going to have for dinner.

Officer – Kit all complete?
Private – Yes, sir.
Officer – Buttons on everything?
Private – No, sir.
Officer – What's without buttons?
Private – My socks sir.

Angry pedestrian (who has been knocked down by man carrying grandfather clock) – Why don't you wear a wristwatch?

Teacher – Read the first sentence, Harry.
Harry – See that horse runnin'.
Teacher – Don't forget the "g" Harry.
Harry – Gee! See that horse runnin'.

Seasick passenger – How far are we from land?
Captain – About a mile.
Passenger – Thank goodness! Which direction is it?
Captain – Straight down!

Butler – You should be proud to be in the service of such a famous General.
Page boy – General? Huh, I thought he was a gangster.

Customer – Hey! You're giving me a piece of bone.
Butcher – Oh, no, I'm not, you're paying for it!

Mother – A little bird told me that you've been stealing biscuits out of the pantry.
Johnny (under his breath) – I'll wring that blinking parrot's neck.

PC Dobbs – You'll have to accompany me, my man.
Street musician – Splendid! What'll you sing?

New lodger – And what's the food like here?
Old lodger – Oh, we get chicken every morning.
New lodger -That's great. Roasted?
Old lodger – No, in its shell!

Lady – Oh, so you've been in touch with royalty, have you?
Boy – Yes, lady. I was once stung by a queen bee!

Jimmy – If I had been offered the plate first I would have taken the smallest apple.
Tommy – Well, you've got it! What are you grumbling about?

Motorist (in court) – My speed was nothing like fifty miles an hour, sir, nor forty, nor thirty-
Magistrate – Careful now, young man, or you'll be backing into something!

Lord Posh – How did you puncture the tyre so badly?
Chauffeur – Ran over a bottle, sir.
Lord Posh – Didn't you see it in time?
Chauffeur – No, sir. You see, the man had it in his pocket.

Hostess – And where is your brother?
Bobby – Only one of us could come, so we tossed for it.
Hostess – And you won?
Bobby – No, I lost!

Tim – I say, old chap, will you be using your fishing line this afternoon?
Henry (who is rather mean) – Er . . . y-yes, I think so.
Tim – Righto! Then you can lend me your football boots.

City chap (pointing to haystack) – What kind of a house is that?
Country chap – That's not a house, that's hay.
City chap – Go on, you can't fool me. Hay doesn't grow in a lump like that.

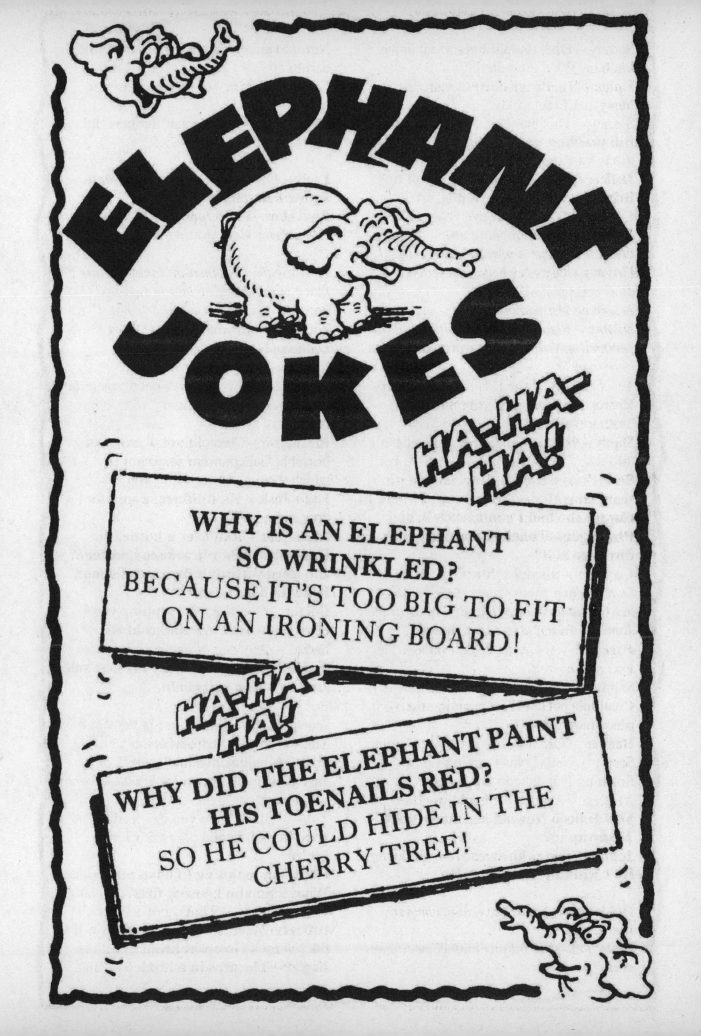

Scout – Father, I shall have to lie down.
Father – Why, are you ill?
Scout – No; I have done so many good turns that I feel giddy.

**Bill (holding up two fingers) – My old uncle can't use these two fingers.
Jack – That's strange. Why can't he?
Bill – Because they're mine.**

*Teacher (without looking up) – Tommy, did you do your homework?
(Tommy shakes his head, but teacher does not see him.)
Teacher – Answer me!
Tommy – Please sir, I shook my head.
Teacher – Well, I can't hear it rattle from here, can I?*

Visitor – And what is your new little brother's name?
Sandy – He can't speak yet, so he hasn't told us.

Very fat golfer – When I stand where I can see the ball I can't reach it, and when I stand where I can reach it I can't see it.

*Dad – When I was young, I thought nothing of walking thirty miles.
Jimmy – Well, I don't think much of it myself.*

Sandy – Is it right, mother, that you shouldn't put off till tomorrow what you can do today?
Mother – Yes. Why?
Sandy – Well, I was thinking I'd better finish up that cake in the cupboard.

**Mrs Jinks – Now, then Johnny, what's Teddy up to?
Johnny – Up to the ears, Mrs Jinks. He's just fallen into the river.**

*Old man (to little boy) – Are you lost, sonny?
Little boy – No, but my mother and father are.*

Airman (to only passenger, after doing a daring dive) – I bet half of the people down there thought we were going to crash.
Passenger – And I bet half up here did, too!

**Producer – Now, I want you to walk across that narrow log.
Film star – But supposing it breaks?
Producer – Gee, that's an idea.**

*First traveller – London is the foggiest place in the world.
Second traveller – Oh, no, it's not. I've been in a place much foggier than London.
First traveller – Where was that?
Second traveller – I don't know where it was, it was so foggy.*

Art teacher – Suppose you were in the National Gallery when it caught fire, which three pictures would you save?
Phil – Please, sir, the three nearest the door.

**Dr Dobbs – Did you take my advice and sleep with all the windows open?
Patient – I did, doctor.
Doctor – Good! And I suppose you have pretty well lost that cold you had?
Patient – No, doctor. Only my best suit and my watch and chain.**

*Teacher – Well, Billy, what is the difference between mouse and mice?
Billy (after thinking hard) – Well, one mice is a mouse, and a lot of mouses are mice.*

Tom – Can I go and play with Jim Brown?
Mum – He isn't a nice boy to play with.
Tom – Then can I go and fight with him?

**Officer – What call would you blow if the barracks were on fire?
Bugler – The cease fire, sir!**

Gnock! Gnock!

Who's there?
Toodle.
Toodle who?
Toodle-oo to you, too.

Mother – Harry, who broke this window?
Harry – Joe! He ducked when I threw a stone at him.

Diner – **Is it customary to tip the waiter in this restaurant?**
Waiter – **Why, yes, sir.**
Diner – **Then hand me the tip. I've waited three-quarters of an hour for the steak I ordered.**

Diner – This is a very small portion of ice cream.
Waiter – Well, do you expect to be able to ski on it for two pounds?

Lady Posh – Are you the plumber?
Plumber – Yes, madam.
Lady Posh – Well, be very careful while you are doing your work. All my floors are highly polished.
Plumber – Oh, don't worry, about me madam, I won't slip. I've got nails in my boots.

Tim – **Snakes are wise creatures.**
Tom – **Why?**
Tim – **Ever heard of a snake getting its leg pulled?**

Shopkeeper – Has anyone given any orders while I've been away?
Assistant – Yes, sir. A man came and ordered me to put up my hands while he emptied the till.

Teacher – Now, Sandy, can you tell me why swans have long necks?
Sandy – To keep them from drowning at high tide, miss!

Tom – **There's one thing, Jack, that everyone shuts his eyes to.**
Jack – **What's that, Tom?**
Tom – **Soap.**

Lady – Do you know that jam I bought was full of twigs?
Shopkeeper – I know. It said on the jar, "Branches Everywhere".

Bob – You know that old vase you said had been handed down from generation to generation?
Mother – Yes.
Bob -Well, this generation has dropped it!

A large crowd had gathered round an overturned car.
"Hello, Bill!" came the voice of a new arrival. "Car turned turtle?"
"Oh, no, old chap," said Bill sarcastically. "These kids wanted to see how the car worked, so I turned it over for them."

Traveller (to old villager) – Have you lived in this village all your life?
Old villager – Oh, no, not yet.

Infuriated motorist (in car up to the mudguards in water after being informed by a local that it was not deep) – Idiot! You said this wasn't very deep!
Local – I can't understand it, mister; the water only comes halfway up our ducks!

Mother – Every time you are naughty I get another grey hair.
Bobby – You must have been a terror. Look at grandpa!

Diner – Waiter, my bill comes to thirteen pounds, and you have made it fourteen.
Waiter – Sorry, sir, but I heard you tell your friend you were superstitious.

Father – An apple a day keeps the doctor away.
Sandy – Well, I must have kept eleven doctors away from the Hallowe'en party, but there's a feeling in my tummy that tells me one will be coming soon.

Joiner – Have you measured the length of that piece of wood?
Apprentice – Yes, it was the length of my foot and two thumbs over with this piece of brick, the length of my arm from here to there, bar two fingers!

Diner – Have you any wild duck?
Waiter – No, sir, but we can get a tame one and irritate it for you!

Sandy – Gosh! I've cut down the tree and here's Dad coming. Now, what am I going to climb up to get out of his reach?

Teacher – I heard that you stayed off school yesterday to play at football.
Tommy – That's not true, and I've got a string of fish to prove it!

Charlie -What's the time, old chap? I've an invitation to a party at six, and my watch isn't going.
Sammy – Why? Wasn't your watch invited, too?

Lady – You naughty boy. You should give and take.
Boy – Well, lady, I gave him a black eye and took his sweets.

Professor – Give me the names of the bones that form the human skull.
Student – I've got them all in my head, but I can't remember them.

First workman – Where's Joe gone for his dinner?
Second workman – Having it in his steam roller. He says with so many car thieves about he's not taking any chances.

Soldier (indicating his heart) – I was shot round about here.
Old lady visitor – Oh no, that's impossible; you would have been killed outright.
Soldier – But my heart was in my mouth at the time!

Explorer – The lion was nearly on me. I could feel its breath on my neck. What do you think I did?
Bored listener – Turned up your coat collar?

Jock – If you can guess how many nuts I have in my hand, I'll give you them.
Jack – Don't be silly. How can you give me your hands?

First traveller (watching train steam out of station) – If you hadn't wasted so much time at home we shouldn't have missed the train.
Second traveller – Yes, and if you hadn't made me run so quickly, we shouldn't have had so long to wait for the next one.

Jones – I don't need a speedometer on my car. I can easily tell the speed.
Brown – How do you do it?
Jones – When I go twenty miles an hour my headlights rattle, at thirty miles an hour my mudguards rattle, and at forty miles an hour my teeth rattle!

Prison visitor – Don't any of your relatives come to see you, my poor man?
Prisoner – They don't have to; they're all in here.

The speaker was getting tired of being interrupted.
"We seem to have a great many fools here tonight," he said. "Wouldn't it be advisable to hear one at a time?"
"Yes," said a voice. "Get on with your speech."

Toots – What's that bump on your forehead?
Smiffy – Oh, that's where a thought struck me!

Airman (explaining crash) – I just happened to get into an air pocket.
Sympathetic old lady – Oh dear, and I suppose there was a hole in it?

Asylum doctor – This room is for motor maniacs.
Visitor – I don't see any.
Asylum doctor – They are all under their beds making repairs.

WHY DON'T ELEPHANTS LIKE TO GO SWIMMING?

BECAUSE IT'S HARD TO KEEP THEIR TRUNKS UP!

Landowner (angrily) – What's the idea of fishing in my pond?
Angler – That's what I'm beginning to wonder. I can't get a bite.

George (to his pal, Bill, who is about to fight a man three times his size) – Don't get windy, Bill. Keep on saying you will beat him.
Bill (gloomily) – That's no good, George; you know what a liar I am.

"My teacher has never seen a horse, Dad," said Bobby.
"Oh, and what makes you think that?" said his father.
"Well, I did a drawing of a horse at school today and my teacher asked me what it was."

General – A brave soldier is always found where the bullets are thickest. Where would you be, Smith?
Smith – In the ammunition waggon, sir.

Doctor – I'm afraid your stomach is out of order. You must diet.
Patient – What colour?

Absent-minded professor – I believe my wallet has been stolen.
Wife – Didn't you feel a hand in your pocket?
Absent-minded Professor – Yes, but I thought it was my own.

Baker – I want a lad who is not afraid of early hours.
Boy – That's me, sir. I don't mind how early you close.

McTavish – Hey, that cold remedy you sold me turned out to be a laxative.
Chemist – Gosh! I ought to have charged you another pound.

Old lady (regarding perspiring football player) – You seem hot, my good man. Why don't you use one of those football fans I've heard so much about?

Friend – What did the editor think of your drawings?
Artist – When he looked at them he clapped his hands.
Friend – Splendid!
Artist – Er . . . over his eyes!

Doctor – Well, and how are your broken ribs this morning?
Patient – Quite well, but I've had a stitch in my side all day.
Doctor – Excellent! That shows that the bones are knitting.

Policeman – You can't go down that street. It's one-way traffic along there.
Motorist – Well, I'm not going two ways, am I?

Tourist – That church clock is all wrong.
Old inhabitant – Well, you see, when the little hand points to five and the big hand points to nine, and it strikes six, all the folks in these parts know it's two o'clock!

Ticket collector – Tickets, please!
Old man (first time on train) – No fear. You go and buy one for yourself like I had to.

Patient – How can I cure myself of sleep-walking?
Doctor – Sprinkle tacks on the floor!

Teacher – What was Lord Nelson famous for?
Toots – His memory.
Teacher – What makes you think that?
Toots – Why, they erected a monument to it!

Resident – The young student upstairs has a lot of correspondence, postman. You always have something for him.
Postman – Yes. I quarrelled with him once, and ever since he has sent himself a postcard every day because I have to climb five flights of stairs to deliver it.

A teacher set his class to write a composition of one hundred words.
One boy wrote:
"My uncle went for a trip in his car. After a few miles it broke down, and he had to walk home. The other eighty words are what he said on the way home."

Passenger – This train is very slow, guard.
Guard – Yes, madam, it's those sleeping carriages behind.

Judge – Have you any concrete evidence to show that you were attacked?
Prisoner – No, your worship. I was hit by a brick.

Motorist – Constable, my car has been stolen.
Constable – You're lucky! I was going to summon you for parking here without permission.

Wife (to absent-minded professor) – Have you seen this? There's a report in the paper about your death.
Professor – Is that so? We must send a wreath.

Busker – I say, sir, you've given me a fake pound coin.
Gent – Keep it for your honesty.

Tenant (paying bill) – Well, I'm square now.
Landlord – Yes, sir and I hope you'll soon be round again.

First neighbour – Do you know that your hens are always coming into my garden?
Second neighbour – Yes.
First neighbour – How did you know?
Second neighbour – Because they never come back!

Schoolmaster – What can a canary do that I can't do?
Scholar – Take a bath in a saucer.

Sidney (who has been trying to get to the chocolate biscuit tin hidden on the top shelf of the larder, deliberately out of his reach) – It's no use, Tom, mother's hidden it too well.
Tommy – Well, then, all we can do now is to wait until mother comes home and ask her for something for being good boys.

Golfer – Where's the caddie I went round with yesterday, boy?
Caddie – Gone fishing with the worms you dug up, sir!

A teacher was reading a story to his class.
"'The weary soldier leaned upon his rifle, and stole a few minutes' sleep.' Where did he steal it from?"
"Please, sir, I know," said Tommy. "From someone's knap-sack."

White – My car has wonderful brakes. No matter how fast I'm going I always stop dead. Would you like to try them?
Brown – No, I'd much rather stop alive.

Landlord (to stoney-broke tenant) – Look here, I'll meet you halfway. I'm ready to forget half of what you owe.
Tenant – Right! I'll meet you. I'll forget the other half.

Master – Before I start the next lesson, has anyone a question to ask about thermometers?
Wullie – If I swallowed a thermometer, would I die by degrees?

Master – What is an engineer?
Sandy – A man who works an engine.
Master – Correct. Now tell me what a pioneer is?
Sandy – A man who works a piano.

Uncle – Yes, my boy, for fifty years I had my nose to the grindstone.
Nephew – Gosh uncle, it must have been a big one to start with.

Man (in ironmonger's) – I'm going to a fancy-dress ball as Father Time. Could you sell me a scythe?
Ironmonger – We've no scythes, sir. Would a lawnmower do?

Domestic tips: When driving a nail into wood you can avoid hitting your thumb by getting a friend to hold the nail.

Dad – Now, children, don't quarrel. What's the matter?
Jimmy – We're playing shipwreck, and Peter won't get in the bath and drown himself.

Villager – Yes, sir, I always go to church when you preach.
Parson – But why not go every Sunday?
Villager – Because I get a good seat when you're preaching.

The professor had a very bad memory. One day he was at a dinner party when he suddenly exclaimed: "Dash it, I didn't want to come tonight. I meant to forget to come, but I forgot to forget."

Seasick passenger – Captain, is it true that Britannia rules the waves?
Captain – Yes sir.
Passenger – Well, I wish she would rule them straight.

Pat recently received the following letter from his friend Tim:
Dear Pat,
I am sending you my old coat by parcel post. I have cut off the buttons, because it will make it lighter. You will find them in the breast pocket.
Yours,
Tim

Boastful farmer – I can reap, sow, plough and mow. Can anyone tell me anything I can't do about the farm?
Small voice – Can you lay an egg?

Irish farmer (to friend) – My neighbours are a bad lot.
Friend – Why do you think that about them?
Farmer – Well, every night some of my sheep come home missing.

Mean man (to bald-headed barber) – Have you any hair restorer?
Barber – Yes, we have some that makes hair grow in twenty-four hours.
Mean man – Well, put some on your head, and I'll come back in twenty-four hours to see if you're telling the truth.

Professor's wife – Septimus, baby has swallowed the ink. Whatever shall I do?
Absent-minded professor – Oh, write with a pencil!

Smart guy (to angler who has just landed a two-pounder) – Is that fish for sale?
Angler – I'm a sportsman, not a saleman. I fish for the pleasure of catching them.
Smart guy (kicking fish back into water) – Well, you can have the pleasure of catching that one again.

Captain (to newly-recruited sailor) – I suppose it's the same old story: the fool of the family sent to sea?
Newly-recruited sailor – Oh, no, sir. That's all changed since your day.

Rick – Uncle, how is it that no hair grows on your head?
Uncle – What a silly question. Why doesn't grass grow on a busy street?
Rick – Oh, you mean it can't get up through the concrete?

Little boy – Say, mister, can I help you?
Porter (struggling with crate) – You help me! What could you do?
Little boy – Why, I could grunt while you lift.

Prison governor – Any complaint?
Prisoner – Yes, there ain't enough exits.

WHAT DO YOU GET WHEN YOU CROSS A SPIDER AND AN ELEPHANT?
I DON'T KNOW, BUT IF IT CRAWLS ON THE CEILING YOUR ROOF WILL COLLAPSE!

WHAT IS GREY AND HAS A TRUNK?
AN ELEPHANT ON HOLIDAY!

"Here, boy," said the wealthy motorist, "I want some petrol, and get a move on. You will never do anything in this world unless you push. Push is essential. When I was young, I pushed and that has got me where I am now."

"Well," said the boy, "you can push again, for we haven't got a drop of petrol in the place."

Lady – What kind of ships are those out there?
Old sailor – They're men-o'-war, madam.
Lady – And the small ones round about them?
Old sailor – They're tugs, madam.
Lady – Oh, yes, they will be the tugs-of-war I've heard about.

Boy – I've been sent to buy a small mirror.
Shop assistant – A hand mirror?
Boy – No, one that you can see your face in.

First shipwrecked sailor – Why does that big cannibal look at us so strangely?
Second shipwrecked sailor – Perhaps he's the food inspector!

An explorer was wandering round an island with a cannibal chief. They came upon a spot strewn with bones. "Ah," said the explorer, "a cemetery, I suppose?" "No," replied the chief, smacking his lips, "a restaurant."

Mrs Brown – Tommy, go over and ask how old Mrs Moore is.
Tommy (returning) – Mrs Moore says it's none business of yours how old she is.

Two mean men were held up by a robber. Realising that they were both going to be robbed, one of the victims turned to the other and said:
"Here, Jock, take this. It's the ten pounds I owe you."

Binks – What do you mean by telling me that I should never send my son to the country?
Jinks – Well, he's so green that the cows might eat him.

Smiffy – Dad, are flies flies because they fly?
Dad – I think so.
Smiffy – And fleas fleas because they flee?
Dad – Er . . . maybe.
Smiffy – Well, I told teacher bees were bees because they be.
Dad – Er . . . well done.

Foreman (as bricklayer lets brick fall on his head) – Now, then, you clumsy fool!
Bricklayer – What are you grumbling at? It didn't stop on your head for more than half a second.

Man (after 20 minutes' hard work trying to deliver trunk) – We'll never get this trunk in through the doorway!
Helper – In? I thought you were trying to get it out!

Mother – That was very greedy of you, Tommy, to eat your little sister's share of the pie.
Tommy – But you told me, mother, I was always to take her part.

Sergeant (to sentry) – If anything moves, you shoot.
Sentry – Yes, sir, and if anything shoots, I move.

Jimmy – Do fish grow very fast?
Sammy – I should think so? Father caught one, and it grows ten centimetres every time he mentions it!

Old lady (to boy writing on a wall) – What would your mother say if she knew you were vandalising a wall?
Small boy – What would your husband say if he knew you were talking to a strange man in the street?

Gnock!
Gnock!
Who's there?
Shamp.
Shamp who?
Why, do I have lice?

Angry man (whose car is in the garage for repairs, to manager) – Do you hear? Everything I say goes.
Youthful mechanic – Then ask him to say "Engine".

A weary-looking fellow who had been looking for a job for months happened to see a police poster headed "Theif Wanted".
"Well," he said, "it's better than nothing, anyway. I'm going to ask for the job."

A great woman singer was singing a solo.
Tommy – Why is that man hitting at the lady with his stick?
Father – He's not hitting at her. He's the conductor.
Tommy – Then what's she yelling for?

Old lady – Did you fall?
Sarcastic man – Oh, no! I'm trying to break a bar of chocolate in my back pocket.

Father – I hope you aren't at the foot of the class.
Johnny – No, father; I'm about at the ankle!

Golfer – This can't be our ball. It's a very old one.
Caddie – Still, it is a long time since we started.

"Isn't it hard," said the kind-hearted landlady, "to think this poor lamb was cut down in its youth to satisfy our appetites?"
"Yes," admitted the sour-faced lodger, struggling with his portion, "it is tough."

"Is my son getting well grounded in languages?" asked the millionaire.
"I would put it even stronger than that," replied the private tutor. "I could say that he is actually stranded on them."

Teacher – If your father and your uncle separately could do the same piece of work in six days, how long would your father and uncle take together?
Tommy – They'd never get it done. They'd sit down and talk about golf.

Teacher – What are the four words most used by schoolboys?
Smiffy – I do not know.
Teacher – Quite correct.

Boastful person – My hens lay double-yolked eggs twice the size of yours.
Smart – That's nothing. Last week my uncle laid a foundation stone.

Minnie – I say, mother, you remember you said the dentist was painless?
Mother – Yes, what about it?
Minnie – He isn't, because when I bit his finger he yelled like mad.

New maid – Was it at seven or eight you wanted your breakfast, madam?
Lady Posh – Er . . . what time is it now?
New maid – Twenty to nine, madam.

"Come out here and I'll lick the lot of you," said the bold little boy to the big sticks of candy in the shop window.

Moe – Why do you call your car "Fishy"?
Joe – Because I've got to kipper look out that it doesn't bloater pieces!

Dad – You know that unbreakable toy you gave Danny for this Christmas?
Mum – Yes, he hasn't broken it, has he?
Dad – No, but he's broken nearly everything else in the house with it!

Scout – Dad, I've done my good deed for today.
Father – Well, what was it?
Scout – I saw Mr Smart running for the train this morning, and he was almost sure to have missed it, so I set the bulldog after him.

Jimmy – Scientists have discovered that our feet are growing bigger.
Johnnie – Never mind. Just think how much more our Christmas stockings will hold!

Janey – We had chicken-pox at Christmas!
Minnie – That's nothing. We had turkey.

Postmaster – This Christmas parcel's so heavy you'll need another stamp on it.
Irishman – Gosh, if I put another stamp on it, that'll make it heavier still!

McHaggis – Look at the snowflakes dancing!
McTaggart – Yes, they're practising for the snow-ball!

First clown – Have you ever seen an apple turn over?
Second clown – No, but I've seen a Christmas pudding look round.

Johnny – Do your glasses make things smaller, Auntie?
Auntie – Yes.
Johnny – Well, take them off while you give me my Christmas pudding.

Teacher (practising Christmas carols) – You must sing louder than that.
Johnny – But I'm singing as loud as I can.
Teacher – Well, let yourself go. Open your mouth and throw yourself into it.

Diner – I can tell a turkey's age by the teeth.
Waiter – Turkeys have not teeth.
Diner – No, but I have!

A cabbage head, a hose and a bottle of ketchup had a race.
How did it go?
The cabbage was ahead, the hose was still running, and the bottle of sauce was trying to ketchup!

Patient -What is your favourite winter sport, doctor?
Doctor – Sleighing.
Patient – No, I mean apart from business.

Country man (in London for Christmas) – Is this Piccadilly Circus?
Policeman – Yes.
Country man – What time does it start?

Andy – Why does Santa come down the chimney?
Sandy – Because it "soots" him.

Billy – I wish you had the toothache instead of me.
Granny – Oh Billy, that's most unkind!
Billy – Well, you can take your teeth out, I can't.

Uncle – It was nice of you to lend your little brother your skates, Sandy.
Sandy – Oh, I only wanted to see if the ice was thick enough!

Doctor – You should take a walk every morning on an empty stomach.
Patient – Whose?

Tommy entered a shop and said that he wanted a Christmas present for his grandfather.
"A tie?" suggested the assistant.
"No, he has a long beard."
"Well, a fancy waistcoat?"
"No, it's a very long beard."
"Well, how would carpet slippers do?"

PC 99 – Now, then, where are going with that sack?
Christmas burglar – Ssh! Don't tell anyone. I'm Santa Claus.

Why is a coach trip like a tree?
They both branch off in different directions!

What did the sea say to the sand?
Nothing, it just waved!

HA-HA-HA!
WHAT'S A BIRD'S FAVOURITE PROGRAMME? THE FEATHER FORECAST.
HEE-HEE!

"Daddy," said young Eddy, "I dreamed last night that you gave me a hundred pounds for Christmas."
"Well, as you've been a good boy lately, you may keep it."

Bertie – Will this Christmas card reach London if I post it now?
Postman – Certainly.
Bertie – Well, that's funny. It's addressed to Glasgow.

What did the policeman say to the three-headed monster?
Hello, hello, hello!

How does an Eskimo dress?
As quickly as possible!

What did the polite vampire say?
Fang you very much!

Diner – Waiter, waiter, there's a bug in my soup. I want the manager here at once!
Waiter – Sorry, sir, he's scared of them as well!

What's brown and sneaks around the kitchen?
Mince spies!

What do you get if you cross two banana skins and a bottle of tomato sauce?
A pair of red slippers!

Tommy (to his big sister) – Does it hurt when you stand on the scales?
Big sister – No, why?
Tommy – Oh, because when you stand on them you always cry!

Which floats best, tin or stainless steel?
Tin, because you always find stainless steel sinks!

How do you stop a dog from barking in the back seat of a car?
Make him sit in the front!

Knock, knock!
Who's there?
A little boy who can't reach the doorbell!

Why did the rooster cross the road?
To prove he wasn't chicken!

Did you hear about the man who listened to the match?
Yes, he burnt his ear!

What's yellow and goes click, click?
A ball-point banana!

Sidney – What did the sand say when the tide came in?
Toots – Long time no sea!

Bob – I went fishing yesterday, and caught a fish, but it hit me in the face!
Bert – Oh, that's a load of codswallop!

How do you make a Mexican chilli?
Take him to the North Pole!

Why is a fish so easy to weigh?
Because it has its own scales!

What gunfighter lives at the bottom of the sea?
Billy the Squid!

Teacher – Name five things that contain milk.
Toots – Butter, cheese, cream and two cows!

Nurse – I bet your wife misses you a lot.
Patient – No, her aim's very good. That's why I'm here.

Why do we dress baby girls in pink, and baby boys in blue?
Because they can't dress themselves!

What's the difference between a cat and a comma?
A cat has claws at the end of its paws, and a comma has a pause at the end of its clause!

Teacher – Now, Danny, tell us what you know about the Iron Age.
Danny – Er . . . I'm afraid I'm a bit rusty on that subject, sir.

Diner – I say, waiter, why is my food all mashed up?
Waiter – Well, you did ask me to step on it, sir!

Why are so many people fishermen?
Because it's an easy sport to get hooked on!

What did one ghost say to the other?
"Do you believe in people?"

Did you hear about the demons who went on a protest march?
They were having a demon-stration!

Why are potatoes good detectives?
Because they keep their eyes peeled!

What goes put-putt-putt?
A bad golfer!

Plug – (waving left hand) Why doesn't the Queen wave with this hand?
Danny – I don't know, why doesn't the Queen wave that hand
Plug – Because it's mine!

Why is the letter "E" lazy?
Because it is always in bed!

When vampires go to jail, where are they kept?
In blood cells!

What do snowmen use for money?
Ice lolly!

Patient – Doctor, doctor, I feel like the moon!
Doctor – I can't see you now, come back tonight!

Why is the moon like a hole in the roof?
Because it is a skylight!

Why do hairdressers always get home early?
They know the short cuts!

What did the dentist say when his wife baked a cake?
"Can I do the filling?"

Old woman – Come out of that puddle at once, young man!
Boy – No way. I saw it first!

Did you hear about the frog who became a secret agent?
He wanted to be a croak and dagger man!

Why did the magician include a football boot in the spell?
To give it a little kick!

What did the trampoline champion say?
Life has its ups and downs, but I keep bouncing back!

Bobby – Why did Slim Tim eat a brick?
Tommy – Because he wanted to build himself up!

Diner – Waiter, waiter, what's that fly doing in my ice-cream?
Waiter – Learning to ski, sir!

Why don't bananas snore?
They don't want to waken the rest of the bunch!

What is the difference between a nail and a bad boxer?
One gets knocked in and the other gets knocked out!

Pupil – Would you like to buy a pocket calculator, sir?
Teacher – No, thanks. I already know how many pockets I have!

Where do ghosts do their shopping?
In a spooker market!

How did Vikings keep in touch with each other?
They used Norse Code!

Boy – How do ghosts get through locked doors?
Pal – They use skeleton keys!

What's worse than an elephant in a china shop?
A hedgehog in a balloon factory!

Moe – Every time the door bell rings my dog goes in a corner.
Joe – Why is that?
Moe – Because he's a boxer!

Why do tall people sleep better?
Because they're longer in bed!

What do you get if you cross a stereo with a fridge?
Cool music!

Girl to her mum – If teachers are so clever, why do they always ask us questions?

What happened to the man who crossed an electric blanket with a toaster?
He kept popping out of bed all night!

What happens to a man who doesn't know toothpaste from putty?
All his windows fall out!

What does an octopus wear on a cold day?
A coat of arms!

What's a monster's game?
Snap!

What do you get if you cross a pig and a flea?
Pork scratchings!

What's round, white, and laughs a lot?
A tickled onion!

What do you get if you cross a parrot and a caterpillar?
A walkie-talkie!

What do you call a short vampire?
A pain in the knee!

How do you start an onion race?
"Onion marks! Get set! Go!"

What do horses like to watch on television?
Neighbours!

Why do astronauts wear bullet-proof vests?
To protect themselves from shooting stars!

Did you hear about the Arab who bought a herd of cows?
He became a milk sheikh!

Why did the chicken cross the road and come back again quickly?
Because his braces got caught in the lamppost!

What do you get if you cross a crocodile and a camera?
A snap shot!

What do you call a cat who ate a duck?
A duck-filled-fatty-puss!

What kind of cat has eight legs, and can stay underwater?
An octo-puss!

What do you call a sneezing sweet?
A chew!

Which month of the year has twenty-eight days?
All of them!

Jimmy – Would it hurt your feelings if I called you a fathead?
Johnny – No, but it would hurt my knuckles!

Did you hear about the boy who put sugar under his pillow?
He wanted to have sweet dreams!

What did the duck say to the waiter?
"Why have you put this lunch on my bill?"

What have 18th-century scientists got in common?
They're all dead!

When is a river like a bird cage?
When there is a perch in it!

What is made of chocolate and lies on the seabed?
An oyster egg!

What's yellow, brown and hairy?
Cheese on toast that's fallen on the carpet!

Shall I tell you a story about a brick wall? No, perhaps not – you might never get over it!

Knock, knock!
Who's there?
Toby.
Toby who?
Toby or not Toby, that is the question!

Why is an astronaut like an American footballer? They both want to make safe touch-downs!

Moe – Why do you have a bag of manure in your garden?
Joe – To put on our rhubarb, silly!
Moe – What a daft idea. We put custard on ours!

Why did the astronomer hit himself on the head?
Because he wanted to see stars!

What is 18 feet tall, and sings Scotland the Brave?
The Loch Ness Songster!

How does a broom act?
With sweeping gestures!

In which month do people sleep the least?
February. It's the shortest month!

What do you call a cow that eats grass?
A lawn mooer!

Did you hear about the stupid ghost?
He's learning to climb walls!

What kind of motorbike can cook eggs?
A scrambler!

What's the speed limit in Egypt?
60 Niles an hour!

Did you hear about the shark who swallowed a bunch of keys!
He got lockjaw!

What do you call a dog that is on a lead and likes managing footballers?
Kenny Dogleash!

What did the wool say to the trampoline?
"I would make a good jumper!"

What has four legs, a back, and a body?
A chair!

What vitamins do fish take?
Vitamin sea!

Why did the liquorice sweet go swimming and play football and tennis?
Because it was a liquorice all-sport!

Two Martians landed beside a flashing traffic light.
"I saw her first," said one.
"So what?" the other said. "I'm the one she winked at!"

What kind of cat do you always find in a library?
A catalogue!

What trees are deck chairs made from?
Beech trees!

Sign in shop – "For sale – Space ship. One owner, only 6,750,000 miles!"

What do pandas play on in the park?
Bamboo shoots!

What's worse than raining cats and dogs?
Hailing taxis!

Where do cows dance?
A disc-cow-theque!

First angler – Did you get many bites today?
Second angler – Yes, forty-four.
First angler – That's amazing. What were they?
Second angler – Four fish and forty mosquitoes!

What did the buffalo say to his son when he left on a long journey?
"Bison!"

What do you get if you cross a radiator and six sheep?
Central bleating!

What is a lobster's attorney called?
His clawyer!

What jewels do ghosts wear?
Tomb stones!

What do people say when there's a terrible orchestra on board a boat?
"A-band-on ship!"

What animals need oiling all the time?
Mice, because they squeak!

What did the fishmonger say to the rotten fish?
Long time no sea!

Why can snowmen see very well?
Because they have good ice sight!

First rabbit – I bought a new gold watch yesterday.
Second rabbit – Was it very expensive?
First rabbit – Oh, yes! 24 carrots!

Knock, knock!
Who's there?
Ivor.
Ivor who?
Ivor sore hand from knocking on your door.

What kind of driver never gets a parking ticket?
A screwdriver!

Did you hear about the witch who was top of the class?
She was the best speller!

What do they call robberies in china?
Chinese takeaways!

Teacher – What family does the rhinoceros belong to?
Boy – I don't know, miss, nobody in our street has one!

Why do giraffes have long necks?
Because they can't stand the smell of their feet!

Did you hear about the duck that lost its voice?
He had to visit the quack!

First monster – Arg!
Second monster – Arg, Urg!
First monster – Don't change the subject!

What did one tree say to another tree that was annoying it?
"Please leaf me alone!"

A man went to the doctor and asked how he could prevent himself from ever dying.
"Make sure you never leave the living room!" said the doctor.

Did you hear about the lady who was knocked down by horses?
She's in a stable condition!

Producer – Have you ever been in a play before?
Actor – Well, my leg has been in a cast!

Why did the man wear two pairs of glasses?
Someone told him that he had second sight!

What is a millionaire's favourite soup?
Moneystronie!

Man (in plumbers) – Can I have a sink, please?
Plumber – Certainly, sir. Do you want a plug with it?
Man – Gosh, I didn't realise they were electric!

What has eleven heads and runs around screaming?
A school hockey team!

What is the smallest ant in the world?
An infant!

What do you get if you cross a TV with a TV?
A television repeat!

Why should you never tell peacocks any secrets?
Because they always spread their tales!

What do you call a farmer who used to like farm machinery?
An ex-tractor fan!

How do you get freckles?
Sunbathe under a collander!

A man whose car had broken down asked a motorist to help.
"I'm not a mechanic, I'm a chiropodist,"
said the man.

What do you call the overweight ghost who haunts the theatre?
The Fat Tum of the Opera!

Waiter – What's the new chef like?
Manager – Oh, he's really violent. You should see how he whips the cream!

What does Frankenstein do if he can't get to sleep?
Count Dracula!

Loudspeaker – Will passengers who took the train from platform six to Dundee, please put it back!

What kind of time did the two walnuts have on holiday?
A cracking good time!

Where do farmers leave their pigs when they go to market?
At porking meters!

What do you get if you cross a snowman with a shark?
Frostbite!

"Well," said the other man, "you can give me a tow!"

What is a beetroot?
A potato with high blood pressure!

What do you get if you cross a frog with a chair?
A toadstool!

How do Martians drink tea?
Out of flying saucers!

What has six legs, four ears and a tail?
A man on a horse!

What can a whole orange do that half an orange can't?
Look round!

Why is a rifle like a worker?
Because they can both be fired!

Why is the sky so high?
So the birds don't bump their heads.

Boy (at dentist) – Oh, I wish we were born without teeth!
Dentist – We usually are!

Man – My doctor has told me to give up golf.
Friend – Why? Because of your health?
Man – No. He looked at my score card!

What vegetable do plumbers fix?
Leeks!

What is a ghost's favourite biscuit?
A custard scream!

What do you call a motor-bike with a sense of humour?
A yamaha-ha-ha!

When things go wrong, what can you always count on?
Your fingers!

Diner – Excuse me please, waiter, may I have a pie?
Waiter – Anything with it, sir?
Diner – If it's anything like last time, I'd better have a hammer and chisel!

How far can a pirate ship go?
Fifteen miles to the galleon!

When is a green book not a green book?
When it is read!

What happened to the jellyfish?
It set!

What do you call a four-foot disc jockey?
A compact disc player!

What's a boxer's favourite drink?
Punch!

Terry – Why did your brother give up his job in the biscuit factory?
Jerry – He went crackers!

Do you know who invented spaghetti?
Someone who used his noodle!

Did you hear about the cat who ate a pound of cheese?
It waited for a mouse with baited breath!

Don – I've just had my appendix removed.
Ron – Do you have a scar?
Don – No, I don't smoke.

Jimmy – Why did the boy call his dog "Sandwich"?
Ned – Because it was half-bred!

First explorer – Take my advice – never play cards in the jungle!
Second explorer – Why?
First explorer – It's full of cheetahs!

Snake charmer – Be careful with that trunk, porter, there's a ten-foot snake in there.
Porter – You can't kid me. Snakes don't have any feet!

Which part of your body tells lies?
Your fibula!

What's yellow and stupid?
Thick custard!

What makes a boxer laugh?
A punchline!

First audience member – Why does that man always shut his eyes when he sings?
Second audience member – Because he hates to see us suffer!

Passer-by – Training for a race?
Athlete – No, racing for a train.

Instructor (to pupil) – Tomorrow you will fly solo.
Pupil – How low?

Why did the elephants leave the circus?
They were tired of working for peanuts.

Where do bees come from?
Stingapore!

Where do you take injured wasps?
To the waspital.

Why did the pear go out with the plum?
Because he couldn't find a date.

What's a wasp's favourite ice cream?
A hornetto.

What's the difference between a hippo with measles and a dead bee?
One's a seedy beast and the other's a bee deceased.

Teacher – Did you write, "Teacher is a fool" on the blackboard?
Danny – Yes, sir.
Teacher – Well, I'm glad you told the truth.

Lord Posh – You might get my bath ready for me.
Butler – I'm sorry, sir, it's being used by the goldfish. Lady Posh said it was to have a treat on its birthday.

Curly – See that picture over there? It's hand painted!
Walter – That's nothing! So is our hen-house!

Uncle – And how do you like going to school, Alfie?
Alfie – Oh, I don't mind going, but I don't like having to stay!

Smart Alec – Dad, I can do something you can't do.
Dad – What's that?
Smart Alec – Grow!

Mum – Now remember, Davie, there's a ghost in that cupboard where I keep the cake.
Davie – It's a funny thing, but you never blame the ghost when there's any cake missing.

Businessman – You should never worry. I pay a man two hundred pounds a week to worry for me.
Employee – Where do you get the two hundred pounds to pay him?
Businessman – That's his first worry.

Battered motorist (regaining consciousness) – Where am I?
Nurse – This is number seven.
Motorist – Ward or cell?

MacDuff – I hear your son is getting a to be big chap.
McDonald – Yes! Two years ago he wore my old coat – now I wear his.

Guest – There's something wrong with that clock in my room.
Landlady – Oh, you have to get used to it. When it strikes seven and shows a quarter to eleven, it's about ten past two.

Optician – Now, which line of the chart can you read.
'Erbert – What chart?

Boxing instructor – You say you've been here before? I don't remember your face.
Pupil – No, it's healed up now.

Why should you never shave a man with an umbrella?
It's much better to use a razor!

Moe – My sister is getting married to an Irishman.
Joe – Oh, really?
Moe – No. O'Brien.

What did the fireman's wife get for Christmas?
A ladder in her stocking.

Street artist (to lady) – Excuse me, but will you keep your cat in the house? Every time I draw a fish, the cat licks it away.

Teacher – If you had £10 and multiplied it by 20, what would you get?
Danny – A bicycle.

McTavish (rescued from drowning) – You've saved my life. I must give you a reward.
Rescuer (modestly) – Oh, no, I don't want any reward.
McTavish – Oh, you must take something! Have you change of a pound?

Customer – You know those chickens you sent me? Well, they escaped, and after searching the district I only found ten.
Farmer – Well, you should be satisfied. I only sent you six!

Old lady – That was very kind of you to take the small apple to yourself and give your little brother the big one.
Garry – Oh, it wasn't that. The big one is rotten.

Customer – Is your gorgonzola good?
Grocer – Good? It's unapproachable.

Mother – So you had dates to eat in the cinema? I hope you didn't throw the stones on the floor?
Jimmy – Of course not. I put them in the pocket of the gentleman beside me.

Teacher – You will always find birds where there are trees, and worms where there is earth. What would you expect to find where there are fish?
Bob – Chips, miss

Dad – No, Jimmy, you can't have the hammer to play with. You'll hurt your fingers.
Jimmy – No, I won't. Andy is going to hold the nails.

Teacher (to lazy Danny) – If you answer me one question, I won't ask you another today.
Danny – Very good, sir.
Teacher – How many hairs have you got on your head?
Danny – 107,005,679.
Teacher – How do you know?
Danny – Aha, that's another question.

Customer (in big store) – Why do you have the complaints department on the sixth floor?
Manager – Well, by the time the customers have climbed six flights of stairs they're too breathless to complain!

Plumber – Did you want a plumber, lady?
Lady – Yes, I phoned you in January.
Plumber (to mate) – Wrong house, Harry. The lady we're looking for phoned last December!

Teacher – How do you know when winter is approaching?
Davie – It begins to get late earlier.

Boaster – There's nothing I can't do if I set my mind to it.
Friend – Oh, no? Have you ever tried to slam a revolving door?

Judge – You are sentenced to fifteen years in prison.
Prisoner – But, Your Honour, I will never live to serve it all.
Judge – Never mind. Just you do as much of it as you can.

Customer – A pound of your strongest cheese, please.
Grocer – Willie, unchain No. 21!

Guest – This room is just like a prison cell.
Hotel manager – Well, it's all a matter of what one is used to, sir!

Archie – Dad . . .
Dad – What is it, Archie?
Archie – Where does a snake begin when it wags its tail?

What's the difference between a lion with a toothache and a rainy day?
One roars with pain and the other pours with rain!

Jim – Angus hasn't had a haircut for ten years.
Bob – He must be daft.
Jim – He isn't. He's bald.

Actor – It's not fair. I've got to die in the first act.
Producer – You should think yourself lucky! If I let you into the second act the audience would murder you.

Lady Posh – If you want eggs to keep fresh, they must be laid in a cool place.
Maid – All right, ma'am, I'll go and tell the hens straight away.